American Women's History

American Women's History

A New Narrative History

MELISSA E. BLAIR
Auburn University, Auburn, AL, USA

VANESSA M. HOLDEN
University of Kentucky, Lexington, KY, USA

MAEVE KANE
University at Albany, Albany, NY, USA

WILEY Blackwell

Registered Office

John Wiley & Sons, Inc., 111 River Street, Hoboken, NJ 07030, USA

For details of our global editorial offices, customer services, and more information about Wiley products visit us at **www.wiley.com**.

Wiley also publishes its books in a variety of electronic formats and by print-on-demand. Some content that appears in standard print versions of this book may not be available in other formats.

Library of Congress Cataloging-in-Publication Data applied for:

Paperback ISBN: 9781119683827

ePDF ISBN: 9781119683865

epub ISBN: 9781119683858

Cover Design: Wiley

Cover Image: © ArtHead/Shutterstock

Set in 10/12pt STIXTwoText by Straive, Pondicherry, India

SKY10054240_082923

Contents

Part II

Vanessa M. Holden

Part III

Brief Introduction

Our goal in writing this book is to highlight the multiplicity of American women's experiences, from the years before Europeans came to North America through the beginning of the twenty-first century. The experiences of women of color, working-class women, and LGBTQ women all figure centrally in these pages. Women from across the political spectrum, from radical leftists to white supremacists, are present. We hope that, by writing a new textbook that starts from the belief that American women's experiences must be rendered in all their diversity and contradictions, we help new generations of students to recognize the importance of women's history in understanding the history of our nation.

Part of understanding women's roles in the history of the nation is understanding the limitations of sources available for studying women's history. Throughout the text, we have attempted to highlight the way the limitations of historical sources shape what historians can know and discuss the way that gender shapes how we know what we know. Many women were unable to create records about themselves due to illiteracy, colonialism, or enslavement. Some remained silent about facets of their experience such as sexuality, gender identity, or simply everyday life, and what was thought to be important enough to record was shaped by ideas about gender. Historical records created about, rather than by, women were also shaped by intersecting hierarchies of power, race, class, colonialism, and gender. The historian's task is to understand these limitations as products of history. Throughout the text, we invite readers to explore both how women's experiences were excluded from records and what we can know about women's lives despite them.

While the three authors share equal credit, we were also each responsible for distinct sections, rather than writing pieces in collaboration. Part I was written by Dr. Maeve Kane, Associate Professor of History at the University at Albany, State University of New York. Part II was written by Dr. Vanessa H. Holden, Associate Professor of History at the University of Kentucky. Part III was written by Dr. Melissa Estes Blair, Associate Professor of History at Auburn University. Any errors in each section, therefore, are solely the responsibility of each author. The bibliography at the conclusion of each chapter lists the sources we used to write that chapter, and all three of us are deeply grateful to the historians listed there for their work. Without their research and writing, this book would not exist.

PART I

Maeve Kane

CHAPTER 1

Sky Woman, Dawnland, Turtle Island

Gender is foundational to how people, communities, and nations understand themselves and others. In studying the past, our own ideas about gender roles and gender differences shape what questions we ask and what answers we see. This is true for all historical periods, but it is especially true for the distant past and groups who did not leave direct oral or written records about themselves. In ancient North America, what we know about the past is that Indigenous women were important political, social, and economic actors in their nations and that their labor literally reshaped the landscapes of their nations. What we can know about this period comes from a variety of sources including oral histories, archeology, and DNA research, but the way these sources have been understood has been shaped by changing the understanding of gender and women's work.

In many Indigenous North American cultures, including the Haida, Haudenosaunee, and Diné, women are important actors in stories of creation and continue to be important political actors in the lives of their communities. These creation stories, and their continued importance in the twenty-first century, help us understand the diverse history of the peopling of the Americas and women's roles in shaping their nations. Differences in women's labor and trade in the Northwest, Northeast, Southwest, and Mississippian areas of what is now the United States illustrate the vast diversity of Indigenous women's experience in areas of ancient North America. These examples have been chosen to illustrate the way that gender roles changed in response to and parallel with economic changes, environmental conditions, territorial politics, and national histories. What the history of many Indigenous nations share is an emphasis on gender balance, sovereignty as part of an original and gendered connection to land, and cultural constructions of women as central to the economic, cultural, and spiritual lives of their nations. Gender, gender roles, and the way they are defined are important organizing features of all societies, and the way gender is defined and changes depend on complex and culturally specific histories. In the ancient Americas as in the rest of the world, gender and gender roles changed for a wide variety of reasons well before contact with Europeans and set the stage for contact in important ways.

American Women's History: A New Narrative History, First Edition. Melissa E. Blair, Vanessa M. Holden, and Maeve Kane.
© 2024 John Wiley & Sons, Inc. Published 2024 by John Wiley & Sons, Inc.

Studying the Past

The study of women in the past has been central to the historical profession for more than 70 years, and gender has always been part of how humans understand the world around us. The study of women and the study of gender are related but different. Who is or is not considered a woman has changed over time. In this book, we include trans women in our consideration of women, and we also examine the experiences of people who were assumed female at birth who may not have considered themselves women in order to analyze who was and was not considered part of the category of "woman" at different points in time, and why. The inclusion or exclusion of certain groups from the category of woman is part of the way gender has been used to enforce hierarchies of power.

Gender is the changing, unstable, and culturally specific system of meanings that communities attach to human bodies. *Sex* is a spectrum of physical traits such as chromosomes, genitals, and the presence or absence of breasts and facial hair, and these physical traits can change or have ambiguous expression. Humans have a wide range of natural variations in the expression of physical sexual characteristics that do not relate to their gender identity. *Gender* is the categorization of bodies based on a set of associated ideas that change over time and may differ between communities – the gender category of woman defined as someone who is sexually and financially independent in twenty-first century America is different than how the gender category of woman was defined as sexually chaste and financially dependent in early nineteenth-century America, for example. To say that something is *gendered* means that an idea is arbitrarily associated with a particular gender, like the color pink is commonly gendered feminine. Gender is therefore a *social construct*, meaning that a gender category is specific to the time, place, and community where it is used, and changes over time even within the same community.

The category of woman is a gender category, but it is not the only gender category. In many societies, gender is considered *binary*, or mutually exclusive between two separate categories such as men and women in which an individual person cannot occupy one category and have traits from the other. A *gendered binary* is the association of a set of traits that are understood as mutually exclusive such as black/white, active/passive, scientific/natural, and civilized/savage with gender categories. Not all cultures have two genders, and not all cultures understand gender categories as binary and mutually exclusive. Different understandings of gender are often a major part of the conflict between cultural groups because people often view their own gender system as natural.

As the historian Joan Wallach Scott argued in an article foundational to the scholarly study of gender, "gender is a primary way of signifying power" for many cultures. Gender has often been used by human societies in both literal and metaphorical ways to structure hierarchies of power. Defining another group's gender roles and categories as wrong or unnatural has often been used as a tool of colonization and domination because it dehumanizes the group defined as unnatural. Gender is therefore foundational to defining other systems of hierarchy like race.

Scholars debate when exactly the system of race we have become familiar with began. Like gender, race is a social construct and the arbitrary association of ideas with physical traits. A person's physical traits like hair color and texture, eye color and shape, skin color, and facial features are their *phenotype*, while *race* is the association of culturally specific ideas like perceived intelligence and personality with those physical traits. Although race is a social construct with no biological reality, it has often been perceived as inherited from parent to child as an inherent difference, and racial categories have been perceived as mutually exclusive. As a social construct, systems of race and racial categories have varied over time and space and had to be created and defined by people. Gender has been central to the way race and racial categories are defined. As the legal scholar Kimberlé Crenshaw has argued, the way race, gender, class, sexuality, and other hierarchies are experienced together are best understood as *intersectional*. Overlapping hierarchies create systems in which not all women have the same experience of gender or womanhood because of their race, class, sexuality, gender identity, physical embodiment, or religion. Understanding these intersectional experiences and how they have changed over time is a central focus of this book.

Creation

The histories of many Indigenous nations begin with women and their relationships to land. Gender is central to the way all cultures understand the world and human relationships, but in many Indigenous cultures women are central actors in both creation stories and everyday life. Indigenous creation stories are frameworks for understanding the world, not myths or legends. One of the main functions of Indigenous creation stories is understanding women's economic, cultural, and spiritual value within their societies. Unlike the Christian European cultures that eventually dominated North American societies, in many Indigenous cultures, women's economic, cultural, and spiritual work was valued as much or more than men's, which would become a major point of conflict between Europeans and Indigenous groups after contact. Just like Indigenous nations and cultures, Indigenous creation stories vary widely. The three creation stories shared here were selected to give examples of the way Indigenous nations relate to land in different geographic areas and the way women's roles in creation stories shaped women's spiritual and social roles in their communities.

In the Haudenosaunee (Iroquois) story of creation as told by elders Jacob Thomas Jadajigerenhtah and Jacob Swamp Tekaronieneken to Brian Rice in 1992, Sky Woman was cast out of the world above this one by her husband, who believed she had been unfaithful to him because she was pregnant. When she fell through the sky, she brought with her seeds of corn, beans, squash, tobacco, and strawberries, the most important crops for Haudenosaunee people. Sky Woman was rescued by birds, who created a place for her by placing soil from the bottom of the world on the back of a turtle where she later gave birth to a daughter. As soil built up on the back of this turtle, it became Turtle Island and the continent of North America. When Sky Woman's daughter later became pregnant, she gave birth to two boys, Sapling and Flint, who balanced the good and evil in the world, but the birth of Flint killed their mother. After Sky Woman buried her daughter, her grave grew the corn, beans, squash, tobacco, and strawberries that Sky Woman had brought into the world, and the good twin Sapling created *onkwe:honwe*, or Indigenous people, from the red clay covering his mother's body. Based in this creation narrative, Haudenosaunee women are responsible for the land and its crops and appoint male leaders who are of a good mind like Sapling.

In the Diné Bahane' (Navajo creation story) as told by Martin Vigil, Roseann Sandoval Willink, Arthur Sandoval, Mescalito, and Harry Bilagody to Paul Zolbrod in 1985, First Man and First Woman formed from the air of the First World at the creation of the universe. As they journeyed up through the Second and Third worlds, they met the animals and were given plants until they emerged into the Fourth, current world, where their daughter Changing Woman was born. Changing Woman gave birth to twin boys who were fathered by the sun. These twins hunted and destroyed the monsters who devoured the people descended from First Man and First Woman. The twins did not kill Cold Woman, without whom the seasons could not change; or Old Age Woman, without whom the people could not have children and a reason to pass on their knowledge; or Poverty Woman, without whom the people would not invent new things; or Hunger Man, without whom the people would not plant and grow crops. After the monsters were killed, Changing Woman and the twins left the people to live in a house in the west, where Changing Woman keeps the changing earth balanced with the hot disc of her husband the sun. The Diné Bahane' emphasizes a balance between male and female and the importance of caring for the constantly changing female-gendered world.

In the Haida story of creation as told by Bill Reid to Dell Hymes in 1990, humans were created when Raven was cast out of the Cloud Kingdom into this world, and beat his wings so hard that the ocean receded and created the land. When Raven grew bored of being all alone, he broke open clams and mollusks to bring the first human men and women into the world. Later, Eagle Woman joined the first humans and had daughters with them, and these daughters stayed with their mother and founded the Eagle clans, while the other humans formed the Raven clans. Clan membership was thus passed down from mothers to children, who share a connection to both land and sea.

Creation stories vary between nations and cultures. There is no one single "Native American creation story." There are some common threads among Indigenous North American creation stories, but not all nations and cultures share all of these common features. Creation stories often explain gendered spiritual and social responsibilities, relationships between humans and the natural and spiritual world, and ongoing duties of care toward tribal lands and sacred sites. Gender parallels between spiritual beings like Sky Woman, Changing Woman, or Eagle Woman and human women help explain women and men's roles and obligations to one another, their communities, and nonhuman beings like animals and rivers. Many Indigenous creation stories compare the emergence of humans from the soil or a hole in the ground to birth from a womb, explicitly connecting the Earth to sacred powers of female reproduction. For many modern Indigenous people, knowing one's identity and place in the world is impossible to separate from sacred stories of creation and traditional gender roles laid out in those stories.

Today, there are more than 560 federally recognized Indigenous nations in the United States and more than 600 First Nations in Canada, and the Indigenous peoples of North America speak more than 300 different languages. This is a small fraction of the number of languages and cultures that were present in North America before contact with Europeans, and the handful of creation stories related here are just a few of the wide diversity of Indigenous histories. The names of the elders who shared these creation stories in the twentieth century are included here because creation stories continue to live in the present and continue to guide Indigenous people and nations in the present. Indigenous people are the keepers of their own communities' knowledge, and elders in those communities continue to keep and share that knowledge. Creation stories shape how people understand the world, the relationship between men and women, gendered responsibilities, and the relationship between humans and nonhuman people such as animals, plants, and spirits. Creation stories are frameworks for understanding, not myths or legends, and specific understanding of gendered roles and obligations are a foundational part of these frameworks.

Peopling of the Americas

Many of these Indigenous histories are compatible with archeological, linguistic, and genetic evidence of how humans arrived in North and South America. Arikara creation stories tell of a long journey through darkness, the timing and direction of which align with archeological and genetic evidence of human migration across the Bering Land Bridge. Haudenosaunee narratives of the founding of the Haudenosaunee Confederacy describe a historical solar eclipse that can be dated precisely. Indigenous ways of knowing the past, which are often connected to Indigenous ways of knowing the land and defining gender, have often been dismissed as myths or legends by non-Indigenous writers. However, these Indigenous epistemologies (or systems of knowing) are often compatible with European and American traditions of scientific epistemologies.

Current academic understanding of the distant past is filtered through the gendered politics of the present. For much of the nineteenth and twentieth centuries, academic and popular understanding of the peopling of the Americas focused on stories of the male hunter following herds of big game across the Bering Land Bridge because this fit American and European ideals of gender roles at the time. Women very rarely appeared in these migration narratives because they were seen as passive followers by earlier academic researchers. This reflected then-current ideas of women and women's work as unimportant economically and socially.

New evidence suggests that early groups that migrated into North America – and indeed, many hunter-gatherer groups across the globe throughout time – relied on plants and small animals gathered and trapped by women and men for the majority of their daily calories. Large game hunting accounted for only a small amount of any group's calories. Men's and women's labor was often seasonal, with hunting providing more calories in winter and early spring and foraging and trapping providing more calories in summer and fall. In many hunter-gatherer societies, gathering and foraging activities directed by women determine how often and where the group moves, suggesting that early migrations into North America were also driven by women's foraging and gathering activities. The importance of women's labor in acquiring food for their communities suggests that these early foraging societies likely valued women's work much more than previous stories of male big-game hunters would suggest.

Ideas about gender continue to affect the way the past is studied. As research techniques evolve, we must continue to evaluate how our own ideas about gender have been shaped by the past and how our own ideas about gender affect what we think we know about the past. DNA research on the peopling of the Americas has the potential to vastly increase what we know about the past, but these research techniques are shaped by modern interpretations of gender in the same way Bering Land Bridge narratives were in the past.

Mitochondrial DNA (mtDNA) and Y-chromosome markers have been used in recent years to research these ancient population movements. mtDNA is passed down from mother to both male and female children, often with very little mutation. Y-chromosome markers are passed from father to son with little variation. This makes both mtDNA and Y-chromosome markers useful to trace back the relationships within large populations to ancestral women in a founding population. Genetic research in the Americas suggests that Indigenous people in North and South America descend from a relatively small population of women and men who originated in East Asia and Siberia via several waves of migration. Coast Salish creation stories describe a long journey across an ocean, while Blackfeet, Cherokee, and other creation stories describe emerging from a long, dark tunnel or a hole in the ground, possibly describing ancestral journeys to North America. These stories align with new archeological and genetic evidence that small groups of women and men crossed the Bering Land Bridge, migrated down the coast in small kayaks or canoes, or crossed the ocean.

Genetic research on the peopling of the Americas has some ethical issues. Many of these issues are gendered by the politics of the present. First, not all Indigenous people carry mtDNA, Y-chromosome markers, or other genetic markers commonly found among Indigenous people, and some people who have mtDNA or other genetic markers common among Indigenous people are not Indigenous. There are many reasons for this. Children do not inherit all genetic markers from their parents: an Indigenous child whose mother is not Indigenous might not have mtDNA markers common to Indigenous people. Inheritance of some genetic markers like the Y-chromosome is sex-dependent, and populations move and change over time. A person living right now could have two Indigenous grandparents – a maternal grandfather and a paternal grandfather – without inheriting mtDNA or a Y-chromosome with markers commonly found in Indigenous populations because the inheritance of these markers is sex-dependent.

There is no single Indigenous genetic marker. Indigenity in North America is a political identity of belonging to a specific Indigenous nation, and there is no genetic test for national belonging. The idea that an Indigenous person can be "full blood" or less than "full blood" is an invention of nineteenth-century colonial governments that had a vested interest in denying Indigenous nations' claims to sovereignty. As will be discussed in later chapters, American and European colonial governments attempted to impose gendered rules for Indigenous citizenship that excluded many women and their descendants from Indigenous status, further complicating the genetic politics of Indigenous identity in the present.

With the commercialization of genetic testing, there have been some cases in which researchers obtained blood and other genetic material from Indigenous people under false pretenses. Colonial possession of Indigenous bodies and settler attempts to prevent Indigenous women's reproduction have been closely tied to settler claims to land from the earliest settlement of European colonies in North America. *Settler* is a term used by modern scholars to describe non-Indigenous people in North America and elsewhere who occupy lands formerly held by Indigenous people as part of the process of settler colonialism. *Settler colonialism* is the attempt to establish permanent colonies with populations that replace the original, or Indigenous, inhabitants of an area. Settler colonialism is distinct from extractive colonialism, in which colonial powers seek to extract resources and wealth from an area without displacing the original inhabitants. The presence of women among colonizers is often a defining feature of settler colonialism in contrast to extractive colonialism because the presence of women and the birth of children in the colony helps legitimize settler claims to territory and replace the Indigenous population. Preventing the reproduction of

Indigenous groups by abducting Indigenous children, sexual assault of Indigenous women, or denial of Indigenous families' right to have children is another major feature of settler colonialism that furthers the replacement of Indigenous populations with settler populations.

Direct-to-consumer genetic testing that promises to identify an individual's racial heritage reinforces the idea of heritable, biological racial differences and emphasizes heritable race over political belonging to a specific Indigenous nation. This idea first emerged in the seventeenth century, as will be discussed in the next chapter, and began as a justification for enslaving children born to enslaved mothers. Genetic and archeological research are important parts of understanding the shared human history of North America, but the practice of that research in the present must be understood within the historical context of colonialism.

The Spread of Maize

As humans migrated and spread throughout North and South America, they adapted to a vast array of ecosystems and seasonal patterns. By about 14,500 years ago, human communities spread as far south as modern Chile at the far southern tip of South America and the Florida panhandle in what is now the eastern United States. Archeological evidence suggests that between nine thousand and five thousand years ago, communities across North and South America began to practice agriculture with many different types of plants suited to their local environments. This rise of agriculture across the Americas occurred at roughly the same time – and completely separate from – the advent of agriculture in what is now Turkey, Syria, Iraq, and Iran in Southwest Asia, China in East Asia, and the Ethiopian highlands and Sahel in Africa.

The spread of maize agriculture radically changed settlement and gendered labor patterns for many Indigenous groups in the Americas. In many areas of North America, archeological evidence suggests that a strong division of labor by gender only emerged with the adoption of maize agriculture as some tasks like hunting and house construction became solely men's responsibilities and agriculture, ceramics, and textile production became women's work. When Europeans first encountered Indigenous groups, they were often shocked that women were equal partners with men in agriculture or even the primary farmers and landowners in their communities. For many Indigenous nations, this was because of the spiritual association between women, land, and its crops that feature in many Indigenous creation stories. For most Indigenous groups who cultivated maize, its planting, care, harvest, and distribution were the domain of women, giving women an effective veto over warfare by denying warriors the supplies necessary to travel. Many Indigenous creation stories emphasize the need for balance between men and women, and balance between men's work and women's work, reflected in the division of labor in everyday life.

Maize is one of the most calorie-dense crops in the world, and its spread from what is now southern Mexico through the rest of North America radically changed gendered labor from hunting, trapping, and gathering to gendered agriculture. Maize was originally domesticated from wild teosinte, an inedible grass, meaning that Indigenous farmers around 4300 BCE bred a long-lasting, calorie-dense food from an inedible plant (BCE stands for "Before Common Era" and is used as a neutral alternative to BC or "Before Christ).

Unlike many wild foods, maize can be stored for long periods, and its calorie density means that small groups can grow large amounts to support others or store as surplus. This surplus maize production likely helped develop the complex gendered labor system of the Maya, in which both male and female farmers grew maize and other crops, while women were responsible for processing, cooking, and storing food. Maya women's social and religious labor came to include brewing and serving the diplomatically and religiously important *chicha*, a maize-based beer that continues to be made in Mexico. The spread of calorie-dense maize allowed a small number of farmers to produce surplus food to support a growing number of artisans, scholars, and religious leaders in many groups.

The study of maize's history and spread is another case of nineteenth- and twentieth-century researchers sometimes projecting their own gender roles backward into the past. Until recently, most accounts of Mayan and other Indigenous groups' early history asserted that only men farmed. This was in part because American and European researchers believed that male farming and female housekeeping was a "natural" arrangement of European gendered labor norms, and in part because many Indigenous groups in Mexico in the twentieth century did follow the practice of male farming and female housekeeping. Many twentieth-century researchers believed that these groups had not changed their labor patterns for thousands of years. However, Maya and other groups' labor arrangements not only changed before contact with Europeans with the spread of maize but also changed because Spanish and other colonizers enforced what they believed to be the more "natural" or "proper" gendered division of labor on Indigenous communities, which will be discussed further in the next chapter. In studying history, it is always important to acknowledge that our own ideas of gender roles and gendered differences can color our understanding of the past.

Around 2000 BCE, maize cultivation spread north of the Rio Grande into what is now the United States, and by about 900 CE reached the Atlantic coast (CE or "Common Era" is used here as a neutral alternative to AD or "Anno Domini"/"Year of our Lord"). Throughout most of North America, maize cultivation was the responsibility of women, and as maize cultivation spread, Indigenous women bred many subspecies adapted to their particular environment. Maize cultivation coexisted alongside other forms of food gathering including foraging, fishing, and hunting, and women were often responsible for trading and distributing these foodstuffs. Early Dutch settlers in the seventeenth century described encounters with Haudenosaunee and Mahican women who traveled long distances carrying maple sugar, dried fish, and maize to trade with other Indigenous groups. Women often combined these trading trips with seasonal foraging rounds that included visits to family fishing and trapping camps and visits to family in other communities. Maize cultivation likely spread through these Indigenous women's trade and familial networks.

For many North American groups, maize cultivation was a collaborative activity that needed both men's and women's labor. Not all North American Indigenous groups cultivated maize, but among those that did, men typically cleared new fields by carefully controlling burns of underbrush and by girdling trees to kill them. Women were responsible for planting fields, but both men and women as well as children and the elderly often took turns guarding the fields from birds and other animals. During the summers as the maize grew, small mixed-gender family groups traveled for fishing and seasonal plant gathering and came back to the maize fields in the late summer so both men and women could harvest. Fields were often intercropped with beans and squash, which return important nutrients to the soil that maize needs to grow.

This practice kept fields productive for longer than monocropping and increased the calories it was possible to grow in a smaller, denser area. To maintain the productivity of the soil, many Indigenous groups allowed maize fields to lay fallow (or unplanted) after several harvests and managed these fallow fields and the surrounding landscape with occasional controlled burns. These managed burns created landscapes rich in new growth that attracted animals for hunting and trapping and created ideal conditions for fruiting bushes and other foraged plants to grow. This reduced the distance both men and women had to travel to hunt, trap, and forage, and early European settlers marveled at the rich, park-like landscapes that surrounded many Indigenous communities. Indigenous women's agricultural practices and landscape management literally remade the lands surrounding their communities.

The first harvest of green maize in late summer or fall is a significant event for many Indigenous nations in eastern North America and is often associated with gendered celebrations. Among the Haudenosaunee, the Green Corn Ceremony days are when clan mothers appoint chiefs and spiritual leaders and bestow clan names on children who become adults. Among the Mvscogee, the Green Corn Ceremony is a time of renewal and repair. Men fast and undergo ritual purification, while women sweep out the old year's fire and rekindle their home fires with coals from a central fire. The Seminole separate into women's and men's camps for part of the Green Corn Ceremony and come back together for the spiritually significant Stomp Dance. Many Indigenous nations and individuals continue to observe green corn ceremonies and other rituals in the twenty-first century.

Interpreting Cahokia

The fertile floodplains of what is now the American Midwest were ideal for maize agriculture, and it was here that one of the largest cities in North America and the world developed thanks to the surplus food storage of maize agriculture. Women's agricultural production and botanical knowledge created a vast surplus of food that allowed for the rise of Cahokia as a political power and the creation of an elaborate spiritual and cultural system. Women's cultivation of calorie-dense maize made it possible for a relatively small portion of the female population to supply food, freeing other women and men to focus on increasingly specialized artistic, political, and spiritual roles. Sometime between 750 CE and 1000 CE, several smaller nations coalesced into one larger regional power supported by women's maize agriculture. The large food surplus supported a growing population of specialized artisans, and by 1150 CE there were nearly 20,000 people living in the large central city of Cahokia. Small towns and family farms surrounded this central metropolis, and Cahokia remained the largest urban area in North America until 1780.

The large population and abundance of food at Cahokia allowed for the development of complex social roles and specialized professions. However, much of what we know about the religious, political, and social systems at Cahokia have been filtered through the interpretation of later American gender roles. Almost everything that is now known about Cahokia is from archeological excavations, because sometime around 1400 CE, the population of the large central city moved elsewhere and abandoned the city. The rise of Cahokia coincided with the Medieval Warm Period, a phase of globally warmer than average temperatures from about 950 CE to about 1250 CE. This period is also known as the Medieval Climate Optimum because in many parts of the world it provided ideal growing conditions, and it may have encouraged the spread of maize agriculture in North America.

As Cahokia and its surrounding towns grew in the period between 1150 CE and 1400 CE, its towns, buildings, and homes grew more specialized, with designated areas for specific religious and cultural tasks. Researchers' own ideas about gender color what they are even aware to look for when trying to find patterns in these spaces. As Cahokia and the surrounding towns grew more complex, people began building circular communal buildings in neighborhoods of rectangular homes. The question of what these circular buildings were used for is a gendered one.

There are at least three possibilities that scholars currently debate. Because these circular buildings are so unusual in their neighborhoods of rectangular buildings, researchers believe they have some ritual or ceremonial use. Early written accounts of the area several hundred years later describe sweatlodges as circular buildings that only men were permitted to enter for ritual use, and for much of the twentieth century, researchers believed the circular buildings at Cahokia to be male-only sweatlodges. A second theory is that circular ritual spaces are also used by other descendant groups in the area for religious ceremonies that include both men and women. In the third theory, there are a handful of early written records that describe women in descendant groups using circular menstrual huts. There are very few of these early written descriptions because of European taboos around discussing menstruation. Women around the world at different times have practiced menstrual seclusion, which is the practice of withdrawing to a shared, female-only space for the duration of menstruation for prayer, purification, or rest. Indigenous women in the nations that succeeded Cahokia practiced menstrual seclusion, but until recently there was very little academic interest in determining whether this was practiced at Cahokia or what it might look like archeologically. Our own gendered frameworks can define what kinds of questions we are – or are not – even able to ask.

Cahokia seems to have had a strongly gendered political and religious system that influenced many of the nations around it in what is called the Mississippian culture sphere or the Southeastern ceremonial complex. As Cahokia grew in power in the region, the role of women in their creation story seems to have changed. Many Indigenous nations in the region have creation stories of male sky beings who impregnated the feminine earth or night to create humans. Many of these creation narratives also included an element of female sacrifice, in which a mother figure's body brought forth corn, as in the Haudenosaunee creation story at the opening of this chapter. As Cahokia grew more powerful and waged war on nations around it for control of fertile land, male religious or political figures began to be buried with objects symbolizing a birdman or skybeing. These men were also sometimes buried with women who had been ritually killed as a sacrifice. This suggests that as land became more valuable after 1200 CE, the sacrifice of women's bodies in the creation story shifted from being viewed as metaphorical to literal. This may have affected women's status in everyday life as well. Without direct oral history, however, it is hard to say how the people of Cahokia understood these changes that we see now only in the archeological record.

Cahokia's cultural influence in the Mississippian culture sphere extended throughout much of what is now the eastern United States, but the many cultures and nations within this culture sphere retained their own experiences of gender. Cultures often change as a result of contact, trade, and war with other groups, but that change is not one-directional or complete. Cahokia's smaller neighbors chose to adopt pieces and facets of Cahokian culture while preserving aspects of their own culture, showing that changes in gender systems are complex and in a constant state of change. After contact with Europeans, colonialism changed many aspects of many Indigenous cultures including gender roles, but not all cultural or gender change happened due to colonialism or due to contact with Europeans, and not all cultural change is complete or wholly adopted.

Many Indigenous nations in the Mississippian culture sphere had similar agricultural and town building patterns to Cahokia, with large ceremonial mounds surrounding a central plaza, but only Cahokia seems to have sacrificed women when burying male leaders. Cahokian male and female artists created statuettes of both male and female spiritual figures of corn or earth mothers and male warrior figures, but only male warrior statuettes are found exported outside of Cahokia and only female statuettes are found at Cahokia itself. Researchers know that these male and female statuettes were produced in Cahokia because they all use a specific, distinctive type of stone only found near Cahokia, but it is unclear why these gendered figures were distributed so differently, or what the political or religious significance of their gender was. What they do show is that Cahokia's political, military, and social influence over the nations surrounding it did not always change the gendered social and religious life of those surrounding nations.

Gender is central to how people understand themselves and how researchers understand the past. Women's agricultural labor made the rise of Cahokia as a political and military power possible, and Cahokia's evolving political and spiritual power changed ideas about gender both within Cahokia and in neighboring communities. It is impossible to understand the full story of how Cahokia and other cultures change without fully understanding women's experiences and the way gender shapes and is shaped by culture.

Jigonsaseh and the Founding

The political and social history of Cahokia is mainly known through archeology, but other Indigenous North American groups' history before contact is maintained through oral histories. These oral histories are an important source for understanding long-term historical change and cultural understandings of gender and gendered political and social roles. Among the Haudenosaunee, the story of creation, the founding of the Confederacy, and the Great Law of Peace is still recited in the twenty-first century, and a full telling can take several days to complete. The history is typically told and passed down by male Faithkeepers and emphasizes the long history of Haudenosaunee nationhood, the importance of women to the creation and ongoing maintenance of the Confederacy, and the balance between men's and women's gendered and political roles.

According to oral histories of the founding of the Confederacy, the five original nations of the Haudenosaunee, the Mohawk, Oneida, Onondaga, Cayuga, and Seneca, were at war with one another after Sapling made the first *onkwe:honwe* from the body of his mother. These wars were so terrible that there was no trade or movement between nations, and some people resorted to cannibalism of their enemies or their own families during times of famine. This period of warfare is also visible in the archeological record, in which towns withdrew from fertile but hard to defend river bottom farmlands and became fortified with large walls on hilltops far from women's fields.

According to oral history, a prophet was born in the early fifteenth century CE to a virgin mother at what is now Tyendinaga Mohawk Territory. (According to modern Haudenosaunee practice, it is considered disrespectful to use the name of the prophet outside of a formal telling of the story, so he is called the Prophet here.) As an adult, the Prophet traveled to the Haudenosaunee territories in what is now New York and was met with skepticism and hostility as he tried to spread the Creator's message of peace. After wandering for many years, the Prophet was taken in by Jigonsaseh, a woman who lived along a road that warriors traveled on to make war against other nations. Jigonsaseh supplied these warriors with food from her fields for their travels, so she took in and fed the Prophet as well. While he rested, he told her about his message of peace from the Creator and his concept of the Longhouse in which all nations would live together peacefully as a family ruled by the Creator's Great Law and not make war against one another.

When she accepted the Prophet's message, Jigonsaseh became the first person to help spread the Creator's message of peace. From then on, she refused to give food and supplies to war parties, and she allowed the Prophet to use her home to host meetings of the chiefs of all the nations, where they were brought together in peace for the first time. For this reason, Jigonsaseh was named the Queen of Peace and Mother of Nations, a hereditary title that is still passed down in the twenty-first century. When the Prophet brought the chiefs of all nations together, the evil sorcerer Tadodaho killed the daughters of Hiawatha, one of the Onondaga chiefs, in an attempt to destroy the new Confederacy. Jigonsaseh calmed Hiawatha's grief and gave the Prophet and Hiawatha a holy medicine to heal Tadodaho's evil, and she helped heal Tadodaho's mind and body to bring him into the Confederacy with a good mind. For this reason, Haudenosaunee clan mothers name and depose chiefs, because of Jigonsaseh's role in restoring Tadodaho and Hiawatha to a good mind.

The historical creation of the Haudenosaunee Confederacy around 1451 CE is corroborated by the occurrence of a solar eclipse reported in the founding narrative, as well as archeological evidence for the spread of peace between the Five Nations of the Haudenosaunee. In the late fifteenth century, Haudenosaunee towns moved down from fortified hilltops closer to farmland, became less fortified, and showed less evidence of warfare. Archeologically, there is also evidence that women began moving between towns and nations more frequently as well. Prior to 1400, ceramic pots made by women had designs that were distinct to each nation, suggesting that there was very little mixing between women from different nations. After 1500, these ceramic pot designs show a mixture and blending of designs from many Haudenosaunee nations, suggesting that the women who made the pots traveled or met women who made other designs. Archeological and oral evidence can be used together to expand what we know about women's history in different places and times.

Chaco and Pueblo

Women and women's social, political, and religious power are significant for all human societies, but the place of that power is not always without conflict in North American history or elsewhere. At Chaco Canyon in what is now the American Southwest, significant religious conflict revolved around women's social and religious power beginning around 900 CE. Between 900 CE and 1150 CE, 16 pueblo "Great

Houses" were built in Chaco Canyon with enormous ceremonial spaces, thousands of rooms, sophisticated astronomical observatories, and surrounding villages that provided food and tribute. Diné (Navajo) oral histories record that a male gambler from a foreign nation arrived and used rigged gambling games to trick and coerce people around Chaco Canyon into building these Great Houses for the gambler and his followers. In the centuries that follow, Chaco exerted social and religious influence as far away as what is now Utah, Colorado, and Chihuahua, Mexico in colonies that emulated Chaco architecture and hierarchy.

Archeological and oral history evidence suggests that the rise of the Great House phenomenon at Chaco represented a conflict between the new male-dominated elite hierarchy resident in the Great Houses and a more gender egalitarian social structure among the common people of the villages. Very few women were buried in Great Houses, and those that were had very few burial goods, while male elites buried in Great Houses were interred with many high-status goods. Among the common people of the villages, women's burials had more and higher status goods than did men's burials, suggesting that the elites of the Great Houses and the common people in the surrounding villages thought of women's roles in society in very different ways.

Architecture of ceremonial spaces in Chaco Canyon likewise shows major shifts from female to male religious power with the rise of the Great House elite. Kivas are circular, partially underground rooms used as sacred spaces by many Indigenous groups in the Southwest. Early kivas were also domestic spaces, and archeological evidence shows that they were often used by women for activities like grinding corn and making pottery. As the Great House elite rose to power, these blended domestic and religious kiva spaces became purely a male space as women's food preparation activities were pushed to the literal edges of the settlements and pushed out of the kivas. Kivas became ceremonial spaces where male priests called on rain in formerly female spaces.

Chaco Canyon and the power of the Great Houses declined suddenly around 1250 CE when long-term droughts undermined the power of the male priesthood that relied on control of rain and agricultural production. When the Great Houses and their supporting villages dispersed, fortified towns grew up in their place to protect inhabitants from increasing wars over scarce farmland. Environmental change caused massive upheaval as people migrated in search of stable farming, and the combination of long-term drought and overcrowding in fortified towns caused increasing rates of infant and maternal mortality. This period of famine, drought, and political chaos caused what may have been gendered, religiously driven warfare. At almost all towns that were destroyed by war after 1250 CE, the majority of victims were women and children, with the towns completely burned or razed to the ground with the aim of total destruction. The specific targeting of women and children in these attacks may have been intended to destroy enemy groups' ability to reproduce and compete for scarce resources.

The Katsina religion, which is now practiced widely among Puebloan Indigenous groups, arrived as an evangelical movement during this time of upheaval and violence. Katsina religious practice promised to bring rain and stability, and once more brought gendered changes to ceremonial spaces. Even at the height of the Great House elites' power, kivas in common peoples' villages were used by women as well as men, and after the fall of Chacoan Great Houses, many more kivas resumed use by women. The arrival of the Katsina religion in the region changed this. In many early oral narratives of the arrival of Katsina spirits, male spiritual and political leaders called on the power of Katsina spirits to violently drive corruption from the people.

Often the corruption in these narratives was in the form of women who sought entry into kivas for sex, women who seduced men into evil deeds, sorceresses who used magic to seduce, or women who caused jealousy between men that led to war.

In modern Katsina religious practice for some Indigenous groups, women are prohibited from most ritual spaces and knowledge, and archeological evidence after 1300 CE suggests that women were excluded from kivas similar to the process in which women were excluded from the kivas of the Great Houses. At the same time, women maintained and developed separate and parallel religious societies that taught their own sacred rain prayers and passed this knowledge down. The historical changes in Puebloan religious practice after Chaco Canyon show that women's roles in Indigenous societies were not static and changed as a result of political and social upheaval.

Near the Rocks and Seagulls

Not all Indigenous nations practiced agriculture. The qʷi·qʷi·diččaq (Makah) of the northwest coast, whose name for themselves translates as "the people near the rocks and seagulls," subsisted mainly on salmon, whale, and other ocean harvest before contact. The richness of this area resulted in the development of distinct gendered labor patterns.

Both women and men fished, but whale hunting has spiritual, gendered significance for the Makah into the present. Before a whale hunt, men fast, pray, and bathe away from their wives, and only men participate in the whale hunt itself. Women are prohibited from touching whaling equipment, and during the hunt a whaler's wife is thought to have a spiritual connection to the whale; she is to lie still so that the whale will be docile during the hunt. After the hunters bring the whale ashore, women gather on the beach to butcher the whale and collect oil, and both men and women smoke the meat and blubber.

The wealth of resources that whale hunting provided helped stratify Makah society. Elite, patrilineal, and patrilocal lineages controlled the right to whale hunt and distributed the harvested meat, oil, and bone to the community. Lineages controlled both material and immaterial sources of wealth, including specific locations such as cranberry bogs, stands of trees, the right to hunt whales or collect abalone, as well as stories, dances, and knowledge. The male head of an elite lineage sometimes had multiple wives and descent was usually patrilineal, with clan belonging passed from father to children. Children could inherit rights and knowledge from both mother and father and could move between any longhouse they were related to, even distantly. Male children typically inherited houses, goods, rights to hunting and fishing, and sacred knowledge while their fathers were still living, while female children typically inherited only movable property such as names, stories, and dances when they married and moved to the home of their husband's family.

Elite lineages maintained their status not by controlling wealth, but by giving it away. Large, highly decorated cedar longhouses housed heads of elite families and their children, siblings, and cousins, as well as other nonelite families who were persuaded to join the longhouse of an elite family by their generosity. The large labor pool provided by housing many nonelite families further enabled elite lineages to produce clothing and surplus food to produce more gifts. This gift-giving status system is known as potlatching and continues today despite being outlawed in the nineteenth century in both the United States and Canada.

Conclusion

Women are important historical actors in all Indigenous societies, but there is no single story of Indigenous women's history in North America before contact. Women's social, political, and religious roles varied widely between cultures and nations, and the histories of their nations shaped gender roles. In many Indigenous communities before contact, women held important agricultural, economic, and spiritual roles that were reflected in and shaped by creation stories. Indigenous women's agricultural and other labor created an important foundation on which many diverse cultures were built. The complex history of North America before contact with Europeans influenced Indigenous gender roles that differed significantly from European expectations, and these differences would significantly affect the experience of contact. Our own modern concepts of gender can shape how we understand the past, and as current understandings of gender change, our understanding of gender in the past changes as well. Cultural conceptions of gender and women's roles are socially and culturally constructed and change over time; this cultural construction of gender also shaped early interactions between Indigenous people and European settlers.

Bibliography

Alt, Susan M, and Timothy R Pauketat. "Sex and the southern cult." In *Southeastern Ceremonial Complex: Chronology Content Contest*, 232–250, edited by King, Adam. The University of Alabama Press, 2007.

Barr, Juliana. "There's No Such Thing As 'Prehistory': What the Longue Durée of Caddo and Pueblo history Tells Us About Colonial America." *The William and Mary Quarterly* 74, no. 2 (2017): 203–240.

Brooks, James F. "Women, Men, and Cycles of Evangelism in the Southwest Borderlands, A.D. 750 to 1750." *American Historical Review* 118, no. 3 (2013): 738–764 **http://www.jstor.org/stable/23426242**.

Claassen, Cheryl, and Rosemary A Joyce. *Women in Prehistory: North America and Mesoamerica*. University of Pennsylvania Press, 1997.

Cote, Charlotte. *Spirits of Our Whaling Ancestors: Revitalizing Makah and Nuu-Chah-Nulth Traditions*. University of Washington Press, 2017.

Crenshaw, Kimberlé W. *On Intersectionality*. The New Press, 2017.

Echo-Hawk, Roger C. "Ancient History in the New World: Integrating Oral Traditions and the Archaeological Record in Deep Time." *American Antiquity* 65, no. 2 (2000): 267–290.

Hymes, Dell. "Mythology." In *Handbook of North American Indians*, Volume 7, 593–601, edited by Sturtevant, William. Northwest Coast: Smithsonian Institution, 1990.

Mt. Pleasant, Jane, and Robert F Burt. "Estimating Productivity of Traditional Iroquoian Cropping Systems From Field Experiments and Historical Literature." *Journal of Ethnobiology* 30, no. 1 (2010): 52–79.

Rice, Brian. *The Rotinonshonni: A Traditional Iroquoian History through the Eyes of Teharonhia: Wako and Sawiskera*. Syracuse University Press, 2013.

Robin, Cynthia. "Gender, Farming, and Long-Term Change: Maya Historical and Archaeological Perspectives." *Current Anthropology* 47, no. 3 (June 2006): 409–433.

Scott, Joan Wallach. "Gender as a Useful Category of Historical Analysis." *American Historical Review* 91, no. 5 (1986): 1053–1075.

TallBear, Kim. *Native American DNA: Tribal Belonging and the False Promise of Genetic Science*. University of Minnesota Press, 2013.

Zolbrod, Paul G. *Diné Bahane': The Navajo Creation Story*. University of New Mexico Press, 1987.

CHAPTER 2

Settling and Unsettling, 1492–1600

Indigenous, settler, and enslaved women and their reproductive labor were an essential part of the creation of colonies in North America from the very beginning. Contact, colonialism, and the creation of colonial societies were all gendered. The conflict between very different cultural definitions of gender, sexuality, and power was central to how Indigenous, European, and African people experienced contact, colonialism, and enslavement. Gender is a primary way of signifying power, and vast global changes in politics, economics, and social structures were primarily shaped by conflicts over gender and gender roles. Europeans attempted to exert control of Indigenous peoples' land and enslaved African peoples' labor by imposing European gendered labor roles, gendered relations to land, and definitions of sexuality, but these attempts were not always complete or successful.

Early direct encounters between Indigenous people and Europeans were directed by Indigenous women as diplomats and leaders and shaped by Indigenous and European concepts of gender and sexuality. Gender was one way people attempted to understand one another, and Europeans used images of Indigenous and Black women to characterize intercultural contact, settlement, and the North American landscape. To justify the appropriation of Indigenous land and sexual violence against Indigenous women, Europeans deployed narratives about Indigenous women as virginal and welcoming and Indigenous men as unnatural. At the same time, Europeans deployed images of African women and men as animalistic and hypersexualized in order to justify the sexual assault of African women, the brutal dehumanization of the slave trade, and exploitation of enslaved peoples' labor. Together, these constructions of Indigenous and African gender and sexuality laid the foundation for a system of racial hierarchy, land seizures, and labor exploitation that continued for centuries.

Early Encounters

Indigenous women directed the "first contacts" between their communities and Europeans, even if Europeans did not always recognize this. The first direct contact (after a short-lived tenth-century Viking settlement in what is now Canada) between

American Women's History: A New Narrative History, First Edition. Melissa E. Blair, Vanessa M. Holden, and Maeve Kane.
© 2024 John Wiley & Sons, Inc. Published 2024 by John Wiley & Sons, Inc.

Indigenous people in North America and Europeans may have been between Indigenous communities and all-male Basque fishing crews off the coast of what is now Canada and New England. From these encounters, small trade goods like pieces of metal and word of Europeans filtered through Indigenous trade networks along with maize and fish carried by Indigenous women. For more than a century in much of eastern North America, many Indigenous peoples' experience of "first contact" with Europeans was via trade with other Indigenous people as European goods were assimilated into Indigenous communities. In Haudenosaunee communities, European goods such as metal pot fragments and glass beads were incorporated into women's and men's decorative and spiritual possessions alongside spiritually charged objects acquired from other Indigenous nations like parrot feathers, shells, and copper.

Indigenous women also directed some of the earliest recorded encounters with Europeans. When the matrilineal Taino of what is now the island of Hispaniola (location of modern Haiti and the Dominican Republic) encountered Christopher Columbus, Columbus and his crew believed that the predominence of women in Taino agricultural work would make them easy to conquer and enslave. European gender roles that emphasized male agriculture led Columbus and his crew to believe that Taino men were lazy. In Columbus' description of his first encounters with the Taino, he wrote that because women did "all the work" and men "concern themselves only with fishing and eating," the Taino were "fit to be ordered about and made to work, plant, and do everything else that may be needed, and build towns and be taught our customs, and to go about clothed."

This was a pattern that would repeat in many encounters between Europeans and Indigenous people. European explorers and colonizers frequently characterized Indigenous and later African men as lazy, barbaric, homosexual, effeminate, or otherwise incorrectly performing masculine gender roles. Indigenous and African women were often characterized as virginal, sexually available, sexually insatiable, overburdened with work by lazy men, and physically suited to both frequent childbirth and hard physical labor in direct contrast with the delicate, chaste ideal expected of European women. These seemingly contradictory European characterizations of Indigenous and African gender roles were used to justify colonization, slavery, and brutality because these tropes portrayed Indigenous and African people as outside of civilized norms and therefore not fully human.

Informed by these gendered assumptions, Columbus and his administration attempted to enslave and coerce labor from the Taino in gendered patterns. When Columbus and his crew abducted Taino men to work, they also enslaved Taino women in the belief that men would behave better with the company of women, with the implication that the women were being provided for sex work while the men were expected to labor. The Taino *caciques*, or male and female leaders, allied together against the Spanish for nearly five years of open warfare until Taino population decline due to introduced diseases forced Taino subjugation to paying tribute to the Spanish and the reorganization of their labor.

The introduction of European diseases in North and South America had wide ranging and devastating effects on Indigenous communities not only because of deaths but also because of the way contagious disease disrupts the reproductive labor of a community. Indigenous people were not genetically more susceptible to European diseases. They suffered the same mortality rates from smallpox, influenza, tuberculosis, and other European diseases that Europeans, Africans, and Asians who had never contracted those diseases suffered. The major difference in Indigenous experience of introduced diseases was that no one in Indigenous communities had ever been exposed to European diseases before, so there were no survivors of previous epidemics who could care for the sick or grow or forage food without becoming sick themselves. Maternal and infant mortality goes up during periods of epidemic disease and food shortage, making it more difficult for affected communities to recover. Deaths from epidemic diseases also disrupted the passage of knowledge from elders. Successive waves of introduced diseases disrupted Indigenous communities' abilities to feed themselves, pass on spiritual and cultural knowledge, and protect themselves from attack.

For the Taino, their losses suffered from disease were exacerbated by attacks by the Spanish and later Spanish demands for tribute paid in labor. By 1503, Taino population losses made open warfare difficult for the weakened communities and the Spanish instituted an *encomienda* system. In the *encomienda* system, Spanish individuals were granted a monopoly on the labor of entire Indigenous towns in exchange for converting Indigenous people in Christianity and "civilization," including the enforcement of European gender roles. Taino men were required to pay tribute by spending four to six months per year laboring for the Spanish *encomenderos*, while Taino women remained in their towns. Resistance was punished brutally with beatings and murder. Bartolome de Las Casas, one of the earliest Spanish anti-slavery writers, wrote that the Spanish in Hispaniola subjected "all males to the harshest and most iniquitous and brutal slavery that man has ever devised for oppressing his fellow-men, treating them, in fact, worse than animals." Far from safe in their towns, Taino women were sexually assaulted by the Spanish and required to provide tribute in the form of cotton, bread, corn, and fish, and sometimes chose or were coerced into domestic servitude or marriage with Spanish men.

Like their experiences of enslavement, Taino experiences of resistance were also gendered. Taino men drafted to work in Spanish mines, agriculture, and fortification building by breaking tools, destroying food stores, and running away. Taino village life was disrupted by the prolonged absence and deaths of men subjected to the harsh Spanish labor regime. Archeological evidence suggests that Taino women took on many trades like stone tool making, hunting, and fishing that had previously been performed mostly by men, and they may have taken on male roles in religious rites as well. In Spanish towns, *encomenderos* attempted to force Taino conversion to Christianity and European gender roles through the enforcement of European-style clothing, tool use, buildings, and other material objects. Spaces occupied by enslaved Taino men in Spanish towns show a mixture of Taino and Spanish material objects in archeological excavations. Away from direct Spanish enforcement, however, Taino women and men very explicitly rejected Spanish objects and Spanish attempts to enforce Christianity and cultural change. Archeological excavations of Taino town sites occupied after the institution of the *encomienda* system show next to no Spanish material culture.

Taino people continued to resist Spanish colonization and enslavement despite the *encomienda* system. In 1503, a woman named Anacaona became *cacica*, or female chief, of one of the five kingdoms of the Taino and she drew together the other Taino kingdoms in a planned insurrection against the Spanish. When these plans were discovered by the Spanish, the governor Nicolás de Ovando requested a meeting with Anacaona and the other caciques and then burned the meeting hall where they had convened. Anacaona herself was hanged in Santo Domingo by the Spanish. Her nephew Enriquillo and her granddaughter Mencía later mounted a successful rebellion against the Spanish in the 1520s. They secured a small autonomous region and reforms to the encomienda system within their region. Anacaona is still remembered as an important cultural figure in Haiti in the twenty-first century.

Indigenous women like Anacaona were influential in many early encounters with Europeans, often in ways that conflicted with European gender expectations. In 1540, Hernando de Soto followed rumors of a large kingdom rich in gold in what is now the southeastern United States. When de Soto and his party arrived in Hymahi, the first town subject to this rumored kingdom, the Indigenous residents refused to direct the Spanish further and attempted to direct them back out into uninhabited areas of swamps. In Indigenous diplomacy, an all-male group was a warning of hostile intentions; groups were expected to travel with women if they had peaceful intentions. Without any women in the army of six hundred Spanish and enslaved Africans that accompanied him, de Soto could not feign that he had peaceful intentions. After de Soto and his men took hostages and began to burn them to death one by one to coerce information from the residents of Hymahi, the ruler of Cofitachequi, the principle town of the area, agreed to meet with de Soto.

The Lady of Cofitachequi, as the Spanish called her, arrived carried on a litter dressed in fine white cloth and protected from the sun by an awning of white cloth. As a powerful ruler in her own right, the Lady of Cofitachequi emphasized her own diplomatic and economic power to the Spanish with the number of people who accompanied her, her clothing, and her gifts to the Spanish of pearls, hides, blankets, and food. These gifts demonstrated her control over neighboring towns and her ability to exact tribute from them. In the Timucuan diplomacy of the region, these gifts obliged de Soto and his men to act peacefully and reciprocate with their own gifts because they had been received with hospitality. In their early interactions, the Lady of Cofitachequi allowed de Soto and his more than six hundred Spanish troops to take pearls and eat from her subjects' food stores, perhaps waiting to assess his strength and potential as an ally.

However, the Lady of Cofitachequi correctly assessed that de Soto and the army with him were only as strong as their ability to steal Indigenous resources, and that without his own supplies, his army would weaken and be both less useful to her and less of a threat. After a few days of hosting the hungry Spaniards, the Lady of Cofitachequi abandoned the Spanish. De Soto and his men stole and pillaged from towns subject to Cofitachequi as they searched for her and the rumored riches of her kingdom. When the Spanish found the Lady's primary town of Talimeco, the majority of the population including the Lady had withdrawn.

This deception enraged de Soto and completely altered the way he described her. At their first encounter, de Soto had written favorably of the Lady and complimented her as graceful and modest in terms similar to those used to describe European women. In her absence at Talimeco, de Soto's assessment shifted. De Soto's men pillaged her town looking for gold and pearls, ate the reserved food stores, and de Soto ordered his men to find and capture the Lady in order to use her as a hostage. When de Soto perceived her as a useful ally, he described the Lady in complimentary feminine terms. Once the Lady acted in her own nation's interest, as a threat to de Soto's ability to supply his invading army, he described her in derogatory, masculine terms. The way De Soto and other Europeans described Indigenous women often tells us more about how Europeans perceived the women than the women themselves. De Soto used descriptions of the Lady's gendered behavior to justify his treatment of her as either a welcoming hostess when she seemed to aid him, or justify brutality toward her and her subjects when she defied him.

De Soto was able to briefly capture the Lady of Cofitachequi and use her as a hostage to coerce food from her subjects. The Lady may have used this to her advantage by leading the Spanish away from her own major towns and toward her enemies. Once at the border between her territory and a neighboring hostile kingdom, she escaped with the aid of her own subjects and African men who had been enslaved by the Spanish expedition. Enraged and without supply lines, de Soto was once again out maneuvered by the Lady, who returned to Talimeco. De Soto's expectations of feminine compliance and subservience were confounded by the Lady of Cofitachequi's diplomatic and political savvy.

"Virgin" Landscapes

De Soto and other Europeans' early expectations of Indigenous women were shaped by a binary understanding of gender and gender roles. In an early engraving depicting the metaphorical meeting of America and Europe titled "Allegory of America," Dutch artist Jan van der Straet depicted a nude Indigenous woman reclining on a hammock and welcoming the Florentine explorer Amerigo Vespucci (Met Museum 1974.205, **https://www.metmuseum.org/art/collection/search/343845**). Vespucci is shown naming the woman "America," in a parallel to the Christian story of Genesis (3:20) in which Adam named Eve and all the animals because he was given dominion over them by God.

The standing figure of Vespucci and the reclining woman are contrasted in several ways. First, the male Vespucci is shown as clothed and wearing armor in contrast to the nude woman who wears only a feathered headdress and skirt. Her outstretched hand, reclining pose, and nudity imply laziness, welcome, and sexual availability. Vespucci carries a cross, flag, sword, and astrolabe with a ship behind to highlight European technologies of navigation, war, and religion, while the woman is shown in a supposed wilderness with only animals behind her, a club beside her, and no sign of agriculture or towns. Between Vespucci and the woman, other Indigenous figures in the background roast a human leg over a fire. Together, the contrast between the metaphorical woman and Vespucci helped communicate the European understanding of binary differences between themselves and Indigenous people. Where Indigenous people were seen as feminized, unproductive, barbaric, and simultaneously unthreatening and welcoming, Europeans constructed a vision of themselves as masculine, technologically superior, civilized, and in control of the encounter. This binary was often false, oversimplified, and led Europeans into difficulty, as de Soto found out, but they nonetheless shaped European interactions with Indigenous people.

This gendered binary also shaped how Europeans saw the very land of North America as well. Echoing the images of "Allegory of America," English writer Thomas Morton described New England as "a faire virgin, longing to be sped,/And meete her lover in a Nuptiall bed." Samuel Purchas, promoting English settlement in Virginia, wrote that "her lovely lookes (howsoever like a modest Virgin she is now veiled with wild Coverts shady Woods, expecting rather ravishment then Marriage from her Native Savages)" had "riches [that] might be attractive for Christian suitors." These descriptions of virgin lands were often accompanied by descriptions of the North American landscape as open, park-like, ready for planting, and empty of people.

This empty, supposedly "virgin" landscape was the product of Indigenous women's work. As noted in the previous chapter, many Indigenous communities cleared vast fields for women's agriculture. Many of these communities were affected by introduced epidemic diseases before they directly encountered Europeans, with new diseases often carried along Indigenous trade routes with European goods. Some communities, like those of Cofitachequi, practiced quarantine of affected towns and were able to escape some waves of epidemic disease. In many other areas, entire Indigenous communities were devastated before or immediately after contact with Europeans. At the failed English colony of Roanoke in what is now North Carolina, Thomas Hariot observed that at every town the English visited, vast numbers of Indigenous people died very quickly. Hariot called these deaths a "marvelous accident" that God had sent to clear Indigenous towns and fields for use by the English. Further north in New England, when the Mayflower landed in December 1620, they found woods and meadows that had recently been burned, cornfields that had been recently harvested, and nearby villages empty of people. The Mayflower Pilgrims interpreted this as God's providential intervention to make way for their own settlement in the "wilderness." Early European colonies did not settle a virgin wilderness. They reoccupied towns and fields that had been settled by Indigenous women's agricultural work and that was only recently unsettled by epidemic disease.

These European views of the virginal and welcoming North American landscape provided to aid European settlement also filtered back into European accounts about actual Indigenous women. The story of Pocahontas, who was called Matoaka by her own people, saving John Smith in 1607 is perhaps the most famous of these stories. In Smith's account, he was taken captive by the Powhatan Confederacy while scouting the area around the newly founded Jamestown. Matoaka's father Wahunsonacock, the leader of the Powhatan Confederacy, had Smith brought before him and threatened with execution. In Smith's account this execution was interrupted by the 11-year-old Matoaka covering his body and begging for his life.

There are two ways to interpret this story. The first interpretation is that an event like this did happen, and the Powhatan staged an adoption ceremony in which Smith's English identity was "killed" and he was reborn as Wahunsonacock's son. Like the Lady of Cofitachequi, Wahunsonacock may have sought to incorporate the English in norms of Indigenous diplomacy and establish an alliance with useful foreigners. The Powhatan Confederacy and English at Jamestown did establish tentative trade relations after the 1607 encounter, though they were rocky before deteriorating a few years later. As she grew to adulthood, Matoaka acted as a translator and mediator between her people and the English even after the English took her hostage in 1613.

Another interpretation of Smith's account is that he related some event that may have happened, but he retrospectively embellished Matoaka's role. Smith's first account of the event was not published until 10 years after it supposedly happened, by which point Matoaka had been a hostage of the English for several years, married to the English plantation owner John Rolfe, and visited the court of the English Queen Anne. Smith's account of his encounter with Pocahontas has several parallels with the earlier account of Juan Ortiz, a Spanish sailor who was taken captive in the Timucua town of Uzita in what is now Florida in 1528. During Ortiz's captivity, he was repeatedly spared torture or execution by the wife and daughters of the Uzita cacique. After Ortiz's rescue by the de Soto expedition in 1539, his account of his captivity was eventually published and translated into English several years before Smith's first account of his encounter with Matoaka. John Rolfe and Matoaka's 1616 trip to England was sponsored by the burgeoning Virginia Company in hopes of attracting more settlers and support from the English crown. Smith's embellished account published in 1624 may have been part of an attempt to rehabilitate his own image as the colony foundered and promoted the widely circulating image of the welcoming Indian maiden. Thomas Hariot's description of virginal landscapes, Allegory of America's reclining maiden with an outstretched hand, and Smith's portrayal of Matoaka as Pocahontas created this image of a welcoming Indian maiden as a symbol for North American colonization separate from actual Indigenous women.

The story of Matoaka as Pocahontas and the welcoming Indian maiden has had a long life in legitimizing colonization. Into the nineteenth and twentieth centuries, many prominent white Virginia families claimed descent from Pocahontas as an "Indian Princess" via her son with John Rolfe, as a way of legitimizing their own claims to Indigenous lands. Smith's account took on new life as a love story in later centuries to justify the forced assimilation and Christianization of Indigenous people by providing a story of a fictional Indigenous woman who welcomed conversion.

The Pamunkey Indian Tribe, the tribe within the Powhatan Confederacy that Matoaka belonged to, still exists today. For much of the nineteenth and twentieth centuries, Virginia law only recognized the racial categories of "White" and "Colored," with intermarriage between people of different races forbidden. This created the legal fiction that Indigenous people no longer resided in Virginia. This legislation of reproduction and lines of descent erased the existence of Indigenous people and further justified the claims of wealthy white families who claimed to be the rightful inheritors of Pocahontas and her peoples' land. However, the Pamunkey and 11 other Indigenous nations continue to exist within the borders of what is now Virginia. In 2016, the Pamunkey won an important US federal case that recognized their government's continued existence.

Gender, Slavery, and the Creation of Race

Slavery was a foundational part of all European colonies in North America, but the concept of race only emerged slowly over time. Race as it is understood in the twenty-first century did not exist in the sixteenth, seventeenth, or eighteenth centuries. Indigenous people, Europeans, Africans, and others understood differences between themselves and others primarily along lines of nation and religion. The categories of "Indigenous," "European," and "African," only emerged slowly as gendered hierarchies of difference began to harden in law.

European concepts of difference and "otherness" had a long history predating contact with the Americas that was based on descriptions of deviant sexuality and gender dating all the way back to Greek and Roman writers. English, French, Spanish, and other Europeans thought of themselves by national identity rather than European or "white," a concept that would not solidify until much later. When encountering people in Africa or the Americas, Europeans in the sixteenth century were more likely to differentiate between themselves as civilized Christians and those they encountered as uncivilized or non-Christian. The gendered overtones of the way these differences were articulated to help create the concept of race as a set of physical and cultural characteristics that are inherent and can be inherited.

The idea of inherited, race-based slavery in the Americas has its roots before Columbus. As part of Spanish and Portuguese attempts to bypass Islamic Ottoman control of overland trade with China and India in the fifteenth century, Portugal and the Spanish kingdom of Castile sponsored sea voyages down the western coast of Africa. To support these voyages, Portugal settled the uninhabited islands of the Azores, Cape Verde, and Madeira archipelagos and Spain conquered and enslaved the indigenous population of the Canary Islands off the coast of what is now the nation of Morocco. Slavery was well known and practiced in Spain and Portugal, as well as the rest of Europe and Africa, before contact with the Americas. As much of 10% of the population of some regions of Spain and Portugal were enslaved, but slavery was not race-based or inherited. Papal doctrine prohibited the enslavement of fellow Christians. Many enslaved people in Europe were born in sub-Saharan Africa, but some of these enslaved people were phenotypically "white." Their enslavement was legal because they practiced Islam or traditional African religions, but their enslavement was not inherited by their children. As the Azores, Madeiras, and Canaries grew as shipping resupply points, Spanish and Portuguese merchants bought growing numbers of enslaved people from the large, wealthy ports of West Africa as a steady source of non-Christian enslaved people. For the powerful African kingdoms of Mali, Kongo, Benin, Wolof, Dahomey, Great Fulo, and Songhai that controlled these ports, the trade of enslaved people to Europeans was a useful way to send away prisoners who had been taken in war from other African nations. Like Europeans, the people of these African nations thought of themselves primarily by their ethnic or national identity, and not by a phenotype-based racial identity that would later grow out of the transatlantic slave trade.

Slavery in the Americas grew from this foundation. Many European colonies in the Americas first attempted to enslave Indigenous people in the Americas, but declining Indigenous populations due to disease and the lingering military and diplomatic power of some Indigenous groups to resist European encroachment made the existing African slave trade more profitable. The earliest European colonies in the Americas included enslaved Africans, but these enslaved people also resisted enslavement: a 1526 Spanish colony in what is now South Carolina was destroyed by a slave rebellion. By 1540, about 1200 enslaved people were brought each year from sub-Saharan Africa to Spanish and Portuguese colonies in South America, Mexico, and the West Indies to work in mines, in building projects, and domestic labor. As sugar and other plantation crops grew in profitability this trade in people grew astronomically and with it the need for a legal and moral justification for enslavement.

As the slave trade grew, it reshaped African communities. As many as one-quarter of captives sold into slavery were children, which disrupted the generational transfer of knowledge in many communities. The slave trade also unbalanced gender ratios both among enslaved Africans who were taken to the Americas, and in communities left behind in Africa. In many west African nations, women were the primary farmers and textile workers, both important sources of wealth creation. Some west African nations used the trans-Atlantic slave trade to dispose of male captives who were taken in war, in order to prevent military rivals from raising armies in the future. European slave traders, who sought enslaved workers for mines and plantations, paid higher prices for enslaved men than women and also raided villages to take captives. Together, this combined to create vast political instability in western Africa.

The combination of changed gender ratios and political destabilization changed everyday life and gender roles in large parts of west Africa. In areas most severely affected by depopulation from the slave trade, polygyny, or the marriage of multiple women to one man, developed. In some areas where agriculture had previously been men's work, women took on field labor as the number of young, working-age men declined due to war and slavery. In the west African kingdom of Ndongo, in what is now modern Angola, Portuguese attacks, wars to capture slaves, and depopulation from the slave trade destabilized the country to such an extent that it began to fracture. At the height of the slave trade in Ndongo, there were two women to every one man, when a normal population is close to one woman to one man. Although women were political and religious leaders in other African nations, Ndongo was patrilineal and traditionally led by male kings. In the political chaos created by the slave trade, however, a woman named Njinga Mbandi was left as her brother's last heir after her brother seized power from their half-brother and killed their male relatives during a long conflict with the Portuguese and surrounding African nations. Although militarily outnumbered by the Portuguese, Queen Njinga created a series of alliances with other European and African powers to eventually stabilize her country and reduce the number of people who were kidnapped as slaves from her nation. During her almost four decades of rule, Njinga used the slave trade as a weapon against her enemies to protect her own nation. The destabilization caused by the slave trade changed traditional gender roles in many areas of Africa, but there was not yet a sense of solidarity between Africans against Europeans.

The categories of "European" and "African," white and Black, did not solidify until much later. Early European descriptions of Africans distinguished between those Europeans considered civilized and uncivilized, often in gendered terms. In 1622, English traveler Richard Jobson described the Fulani and Mandinka women he encountered near the Gambia River in Africa as "cleanely meaning" and possessing "a shamefast modestie" similar to English women. However, other African women were described in dehumanizing terms that laid the groundwork for the dehumanization of enslavement. In 1602, Dutch traveler Pieter de Marees described the women he encountered in what is now the African nation of Ghana as beastial and similar to animals, in a work that was published widely throughout Europe in English, German, French, and Dutch. De Marees and other European writers contrasted African women's womanhood with European women's, writing that African women gave birth in a "most shamelesse manner," surrounded by men, women, and children, suffered no pain in childbirth, had no nurses attend them in childbirth, and returned to work immediately after birth rather than waiting a lying-in period after birth like European women of the time did.

These descriptions of African women's birth practices served to dehumanize them in the eyes of European readers and would be used as a justification for the enslavement of Africans for several centuries as "proof" that people of African descent were less human than people of European descent. Many early European writers including de Marees discussed African women in animalistic terms, describing their breasts as touching the ground when they stooped down to work in the fields and long enough to cast over their shoulders to nurse a child carried on their backs. De Marees argued that this showed that African women were "of a cruder nature and stronger posture than the Females in our Lands in Europe." These dehumanizing, sexualized descriptions of African women's bodies linked their supposed lack of pain in childbirth to a capacity for manual labor and created an image of Black women as both animalistic and inherently different from European women that underlay the development of race and justifications for slavery throughout the seventeenth, eighteenth, and nineteenth centuries.

Through these sexualized descriptions, African women became hypersexualized in the European imagination. This served to justify sexual violence against them throughout enslavement and into the twenty-first century, by constructing women of African descent as outside of the protections of white womanhood, inherently sexually available, and therefore unable to be raped. This false and damaging stereotype has lingered well into the twentieth and twenty-first century and continues to prevent Black women who have been sexually assaulted from receiving justice. The construction of African women as hypersexual and animalistic, Indigenous women as virginal but welcoming, and white settler women as chaste mothers and wives were all foundational to the European colonization of the Americas. The sexual construction of Indigenous women justified settler seizure of their nations' lands, while the sexual construction of African women justified their dehumanization and the exploitation of their labor. Although settler women were constrained to a narrow range of socially acceptable behaviors and roles and had few legal rights, elite women benefited from the wealth generated by exploiting enslaved African labor on Indigenous lands, while poor and indentured white women had access to the respectability of presumed sexual chastity not available to African and Indigenous women. There was no one experience of womanhood in early America, but a faceted construction of gender that was shaped by the intersection of race, labor, and class.

Sex, Gender, and Sexuality

The ways Indigenous people, Europeans, Africans, and others made sense of one another and their differences were filtered through their expectations of gender. When the Lady of Cofitachequi expected hostility from de Soto's all-male army and de Soto expected submission and deference from the Lady, they understood one another through their own society's construction of gender. Categories like race and gender may have social and legal reality, but they are not tied to inherent physical traits. A person's phenotype – or the color of their hair, skin, and eyes, or the shape of their facial features – is separate from the cultural values attributed to those features. Similarly, the kind of work a person does, the personality traits expected of them, and the type of clothing they wear are not physically determined by their genitals, their physical sex characteristics, or their chromosomes. Gender and race are social constructs, and the intersections between the two are often used to reinforce one another.

The idea of female and male as two separate, binary and mutually exclusive genders is itself socially constructed, and not shared by all cultures. Some Indigenous North American groups recognized three or more genders, including female, male, and "two-spirit." The term two-spirit emerged in the 1990s as a Pan-Indian umbrella term that was at times used as an umbrella term for gay, lesbian, bisexual, nonbinary, genderfluid, intersex, and transgender. It is now most often used to mean a third gender identity that is separate and distinct from male and female but shares aspects of both. Two-spirit is distinct from nonbinary, genderqueer, or genderfluid. Many Indigenous groups have terms and concepts in their own languages for a third gender, including *winkte* in Lakȟótiyapi (Lakota) or *nadleeh* in Diné (Navajo). Some, but not all, North American Indigenous cultures have historically recognized some version of two-spirit or third gender identity; some others differentiate four genders between people who were assumed male at birth and took on a female role, people who were assumed female at birth and took on a male role, and people who take on the gender roles they were assumed at birth. In current usage, two-spirit is a more neutral replacement for the older term *berdache*, which was used in academic scholarship for much of the twentieth century but has fallen out of favor because of its pejorative connotations.

Europeans who encountered Indigenous groups with gender categories different than their own binary male/female categories often struggled to interpret these Indigenous gender categories and gender roles. As part of the French colonization of Canada, the Catholic Jesuit order sent missionaries to live among French allies the Huron beginning in 1634. The copious documentation the Jesuits wrote about their mission efforts are among the best ethnographic sources scholars have describing Huron life because the Jesuits were particularly concerned with changing Huron family life and gender roles. However, this also shaped Jesuit descriptions of Huron life because Jesuits documented what they saw through the lens of gendered morality and immorality. Jesuits and other European writers described what they saw as Indigenous sexual immorality or "unnatural" gender roles as one way of differentiating between themselves and Indigenous people at a time in which racial categories had not fully coalesced.

Writing for a European audience, Jesuit missionaries praised Huron women's modesty and both men and women's faithfulness in marriage, but also called the Huron lascivious and immodest because they allowed divorce, sex before marriage, and what the Jesuits perceived as immoral homosexuality. Jesuits called Huron people who were assumed male at birth and took on women's gender roles *berdache*, from a Persian word meaning "kept boy" or "male prostitute." The Jesuits believed *berdache* acceptance of a passive or receptive role in penetrative sex with men was a sign of Huron immorality, and French traders and colonists looked down on people they believed took on a lesser, feminine role. The Jesuits for their part confounded Huron gender expectations for men by refusing to marry Huron women. Huron and other Indigenous women sometimes extended offers of marriage to European men to establish diplomatic, matrilineal kinship ties. The celibate Jesuits interpreted these overtures of marriage as offers of prostitution, while the Huron interpreted missionary celibacy as unnatural or unmanly. Both groups struggled to understand the other's categories of gender and interpreted their interactions within their own culture's gender framework.

European expectations about sex, sexuality, and gender roles were often used to justify colonization and enslavement of Indigenous people. In what is now the American Southwest, the Spanish linked Pueblo sexual mores and sexuality to Catholic disgust for what the Spanish perceived as devil worship in Pueblo spiritual practice. In 1598, Spanish conquistador Juan de Oñate led an army from Spanish Mexico into what is now the state of New Mexico, following rumors of large, wealthy cities. Starving and running out of food and water, Oñate's army approached Acoma Pueblo for supplies. The Acoma Pueblo had encountered previous Spanish expeditions and were reluctant to supply Oñate's army out of their own limited stores ahead of the coming winter. Oñate rejected Acoma invitations to negotiate in the pueblo's kiva, which Oñate feared as a space of devil worship and possible site of an ambush by the Acoma. Spanish soldiers ranging across Acoma territory attacked and possibly sexually assaulted Acoma women at work in their fields. This led to a confrontation in which some of the Spanish soldiers were killed by Acoma warriors and Oñate retaliated with a three-day massacre that killed more than 20% of the four thousand residents of Acoma Pueblo as a warning to surrounding Indigenous communities. Of the surviving Acoma, all captured women and girls over the age of 12 were enslaved by the Spanish, while captured boys and young men between 12 and 25 were enslaved. Men over 25 had their right foot amputated, to prevent further resistance.

Over the next several decades, survivors of Acoma Pueblo and other Indigenous communities in the area were forced by the Spanish into reorganized pueblo communities that were required to pay tribute to the Spanish in food, cotton, and labor. These communities were required to adopt Spanish-style clothing and gender roles which the Spanish justified as being for the good of the Indigenous people they brutalized. In response to the brutalities committed by Columbus in Hispaniola, in 1501 Spanish Queen Isabella I had declared Indigenous people in North America subjects of the Spanish Crown, making it illegal to enslave them. She believed this was necessary to ensure their conversion to Catholicism, "since this is the greatest benefit We can desire for them, for which it is necessary that they be taught the things of Our faith in order to come into the knowledge of it." The Spanish law of preaching required Spanish colonizers to attempt to convert Indigenous subjects, but if Indigenous people rejected conversion efforts, this justified Spanish war against them and appropriation of their land. Indigenous subjects who accepted Spanish rule were also made legal minors under Spanish law. This paternalist system, in which Spanish authority limited Indigenous autonomy, was justified as morally and spiritually necessary to save Indigenous peoples' souls by requiring them to convert to Catholicism.

In the case of the Pueblo, this paternalist approach was justified in part by Spanish views of Indigenous gender roles and sexuality. In 1606, Juan de Oñate was recalled by Spanish officials to Mexico City after a decade of rule in New Mexico. There, he was put on trial and convicted for cruelty against both Spanish colonists and Indigenous people and banished from the colony. Oñate's officer Gaspar Pérez de Villagrá justified the cruelty of the Oñate government by describing what the Spanish believed was sexual depravity. Villagrá and other Spanish writers described Indigenous peoples' religious practice as idolatrous, superstitious, and instigated by the devil. Villagrá argued that the Pueblo and other Indigenous people who made overtures of peace offended Spanish modesty when Indigenous men "brought a great number of beautiful many blankets, which they gathered together, hoping to entice with them the Castilian [Spanish] women whom they liked and coveted." Worse, Villagrá argued that "these people are addicted to the bestial wicked sin [of sodomy]." Penetrative sex between men carried the death penalty in Spain and much of early modern Europe because it was believed to disrupt the supposedly natural gender binary of active, penetrating male bodies, and passive, receptive or penetrated female bodies. Villagrá and other Spaniards who observed berdache or two-spirit presence in the otherwise all-male religious space of the kiva believed that Pueblo religious practice, sex between women and men outside of marriage, and sex between men or the presence of two-spirit people were all immoral and in need of change.

Conclusion

Early experiences of contact and colonization were gendered. Gender is socially constructed and differs across all societies, and these differences were a major part of how Indigenous and European people attempted to understand one another, establish diplomatic relations, or rationalize colonization. Images and narratives about Indigenous women, both fictional and real, helped Europeans justify colonization tactics and appropriation of Indigenous land, while images and narratives about African women helped Europeans justify the brutal dehumanization of slavery.

Bibliography

Candido, Mariana. *An African Slaving Port and the Atlantic World: Benguela and its Hinterland*. Cambridge University Press, 2015.

Deagan, Kathleen. "Reconsidering Taíno Social Dynamics after Spanish Conquest: Gender and Class in Culture Contact Studies." *American Antiquity* 69, no. 4 (2004): 597–626. **https://doi.org/10.2307/4128440**.

Driskill, Qwo-Li. *Asegi Stories: Cherokee Queer and Two-Spirit Memory*. University of Arizona Press, 2016.

Hagler, Anderson. "Archival Epistemology: Honor, Sodomy, and Indians in Eighteenth-Century New Mexico." *Ethnohistory* 66, no. 3 (July 1, 2019): 515–35. **https://doi.org/10.1215/00141801-7517922**

Heywood, Linda. *Njinga of Angola: Africa's Warrior Queen*. Harvard University Press, 2017.

Kolodny, Annette. *The Land Before Her: Fantasy and Experience of the American Frontiers, 1630–1860*. The University of North Carolina Press, 1984.

Martel, Heather. *Deadly Virtue: Fort Caroline and the Early Protestant Roots of American Whiteness*. University Press of Florida, 2019.

Montrose, Louis. "The Work of Gender in the Discourse of Discovery." *Representations*, 33 (1991): 1–41. **https://doi.org/10.2307/2928756**.

Perrault, Melanie. "American Wilderness and First Contact." In *American Wilderness: A New History*, edited by Lewis, Michael. Oxford University Press, 2007: 15–33.

Snyder, Christina. "The Lady of Cofitachequi." In *South Carolina Women: Their Lives and Times*, Volume 2, edited by Spruill, Marjorie Julian, Valinda W Littlefield, and Joan Marie Johnson. University of Georgia Press, 2009: 11–25.

Thornton, John K. *Africa and Africans in the Making of the Atlantic World, 1400–1680*. Cambridge University Press, 1999.

CHAPTER 3

Growth and Disruption, 1600–1690

The idea of race as a physical, inherent reality that is passed from mother to child is an idea that emerged slowly over time. As a social construct rather than a biological reality, boundaries between racial categories differed across European colonies in North America. One thing these emerging concepts of race shared was their intersection with European conceptualizations of gender and gender roles. Gender was used to define race socially and legally, and enslaved women used ambiguous racial boundaries and legal definitions to advocate for themselves and their families. Free women of European descent likewise used the demographic differences between Europe and North American colonies to navigate social and legal roles not available in Europe. All settler women shared constraints on their legal and social rights due to their gender, but those restrictions also differed greatly between colonies.

Intersecting hierarchies of gender, race, sexuality, and class created some spaces for individual women to advocate for themselves or exercise a measure of control over their lives, but one of the few experiences many women shared in this period was restricted agency. In many ways, dependency and lack of control defined womanhood within colonial societies and differed only in degree across hierarchies of race and class. Coverture, or the legal merging of a wife's person and property with her husband's after marriage, defined the legal personhood of the majority of settler women with few exceptions. Vulnerability to sexual assault was assumed to be a matter of degree as well. Settlers routinely used sexual violence as a tool of terror against Indigenous women and enslaved African women, while marriage required wives to be sexually available to husbands and indentured and enslaved women's bodies were presumed to be as available to their employers as their labor. Gender was central to defining racial social order, and women's reproductive bodies were central to defining race and creating colonial societies, but individual women's lives were exceptionally restricted within this system as a result.

American Women's History: A New Narrative History, First Edition. Melissa E. Blair, Vanessa M. Holden, and Maeve Kane.
© 2024 John Wiley & Sons, Inc. Published 2024 by John Wiley & Sons, Inc.

Creating Race

The Middle Passage and subsequent enslavement of millions of Africans in the Americas shaped and was shaped by experiences of gender. Over the course of the seventeenth, eighteenth, and nineteenth centuries, more than 12 million Africans were kidnapped and sold as slaves in the Americas; more than two million of these died during the trans-Atlantic voyage, known as the Middle Passage. During the same period, a little over two million Europeans immigrated to the Americas, about the same number of enslaved Africans who died during the Middle Passage. By some estimates, about 80% of all women who arrived in the Americas were African. Human captives were literally commoditized during transport, as slave ships attempted to pack so many people so tightly for the most profit. Chained captives were packed so tightly that they had no room to stand, lie fully extended, or roll over. One English ship's surgeon who was tasked with separating the dying from the living said that the floor on which captives were made to lay was so covered with blood, feces, and vomit that it was worse than a slaughterhouse. Women and children, who were transported in fewer numbers because they were seen as less profitable, were sometimes transported separately from men and allowed to walk on the deck of the ship. This exposed them to a different kind of danger, as greater contact with the ship's male crew increased the likelihood of sexual assault.

More than two-thirds of those transported in slavery were men. After arrival in the Americas, this created a wildly skewed gender ratio in early enslaved communities. The first one to two years after arrival were known as "seasoning," in which newly arrived Africans were sold and forced to become accustomed to brutal new work and living conditions. By some estimates, as many as 10–50% of all enslaved people died during this period of seasoning, whether from overwork, disease, or suicide to escape the brutal conditions. Enslavers forced enslaved people to learn a new language, often breaking up family groups and separating people who spoke the same African languages in order to force them to learn European languages and severe all community bonds. In these conditions, new family bonds were difficult to impossible to form for enslaved people. European enslavers who created these conditions used the lack of family formation among enslaved people as yet more justification that enslaved people were animalistic.

Slavery was integral to all the economies of early America. Because slavery was so widespread and enslaved people worked in many different environments and economies, the experience of slavery varied greatly. At the Spanish colony of San Miguel de Gualdape in what is now South Carolina, in 1526 dozens of enslaved Africans were tasked with growing food and tending livestock until the colony failed due to disease and slave rebellion. The earliest English plantation colony of Bermuda imported enslaved Africans to cultivate tobacco to make the colony profitable. The enslaved Africans who were brought to New Amsterdam, later New York City, in 1626 were owned by the West India Company, a private corporation that used them to build roads, canals, and sewage systems to create the vital infrastructure necessary for the colony to grow. Africans were vital to both the profitability and survival of early European colonies.

The 2019 400th anniversary of the 1619 arrival of the first enslaved Africans at Jamestown, Virginia, was deeply politicized because historical narratives explain who we are as a nation in the present. By 1619, slavery had been deeply entrenched throughout European colonies in the Americas, but the arrival of enslaved Africans at Jamestown marked the beginning of what would become the plantation slave economy that fueled the American economy for more than two centuries to follow. By 1690, slavery was widespread across the colonies that would become the United

States. In Boston, one in every 10 white families owned at least one enslaved person; in New York City, 4 in 10 white families owned at least one enslaved person. In some areas of the Caribbean and what became the American South, enslaved Africans outnumbered whites 8 or 10 to one.

Tobacco, the crop that made Virginia profitable and laid the foundation for later cotton, rice, indigo, and sugar plantations in what would become the United States, was an extremely labor-intensive crop. To provide labor for the strict schedule demanded by tobacco plants, enslaved people's labor was controlled in a regimented "gang" system. Enslaved women and men worked together with few breaks from early in the morning to late at night under the supervision of an overseer who used whipping to enforce the schedule. In early Virginia, enslaved women sometimes outnumbered men in tobacco fields because men were more likely to be employed in skilled trades like barrel making. Women workers were not taxed the way men were, because women's labor was presumed to be within the household and not for profit. This incentivized plantation owners to employ and buy women fieldworkers, but the laws would soon change to tax Black women but not white women, defining race through the kinds of labor women were presumed to perform.

Enslaved people who worked within a gang system were provided with some food rations, but it was often inadequate for their needs. Enslaved people were sometimes required and sometimes sought to cultivate their own vegetable gardens to supplement their meager rations. Together with the work of repairing clothing, caring for children, the sick, and the elderly, and simply preparing food, much of this work fell to enslaved women. Women enslaved in the nineteenth century would call this care work their "sundown" or "sunset shift," the work they performed after a long day in the fields to simply sustain themselves and their families that often stretched long into the night. Although they performed much of the same agricultural labor in the gang system, enslaved women's experience often differed greatly from enslaved men's because of their gender.

In other areas such as South Carolina and later Georgia where rice cultivation was more common, enslaved people worked under a "task" system. Under this system, plantation owners placed most of the responsibility of feeding themselves on enslaved people, who were required to raise their own food as well as complete tasks set for them by the plantation owner. Although this form of slavery was no less brutal than other forms, it did allow enslaved people to make some decisions about their labor. This allowed some enslaved women to raise West African strains of rice to feed their families. Women's rice growing provided familiar food and continued West African traditions of gendered labor and allowed some women to grow surplus crops to sell at markets. In many West African nations, women were primarily responsible for selling produce at public markets, and women's market culture became an important way enslaved women created and maintained communities.

As plantation owners noticed the success of rice crops enslaved people grew for themselves, rice cultivation became an industrial-scale export to other plantation colonies that produced crops like tobacco and sugar, further fueling the slave economy. South Carolina planters specifically sought out Mande-speaking enslaved women from regions in Africa that produced rice. These women were sought out for their specialized agricultural knowledge because rice required specific planting, growing, and harvesting techniques to flourish. Unlike other plantation colonies, South Carolina imported more enslaved women than men, and enslaved women were valued equally with men for their specialized agricultural knowledge. The spread and profitability of rice cultivation thus had a dual legacy of preserving some elements of West African culture in food and gendered patterns of work, but also created ever harsher demands on enslaved peoples to produce more rice for export.

Slavery was not limited to what became the American South or to fields. Vast areas of Long Island in New York were worked by 60 or more enslaved people on a single farm, and in both northern and southern colonies, enslaved women and men worked in domestic spaces alongside enslavers and in urban areas. Enslaved women's domestic work was not safer or gentler than fieldwork. Tasks like laundry and nursing required backbreaking labor, and some enslaved seamstresses were kept sewing so late into the night they fell asleep where they stood. Enslaved women who worked in domestic spaces alongside their enslavers were often exposed to sexual violence from both white men who sexually assaulted them and white women who punished them for being exploited because white wives could not protest their husbands' actions. Over the course of the seventeenth century, white women's womanhood was increasingly defined as the right to be only sexually available to one man within marriage and the ideal of work within domestic spaces, while Black womanhood was increasingly defined as presumed sexual availability and the presumption of field labor.

Race and Reproduction

The legal and social hierarchy of race grew up alongside slavery in order to justify it, and gender was essential to the way race was defined. The solidification of early concepts of sexual, cultural, and religious difference into what became the concept of inherited race took place slowly over time. Like gender, race is a social construct and developed differently in different areas. In areas governed by Spanish law, the pre-contact concept of *limpieza de sangre* or "cleanliness of blood" influenced the development of racial thinking in the Americas. In Spain in the early 1400s, *limpieza de sangre* referred to the idea that families descended from Jews and Muslims who had converted to Christianity after the Spanish Reconquista of the Iberian Peninsula from Muslim rule were in fact false converts. These families with converso (converted Jew) or Morisco (converted Muslim) ancestry were barred from some professions, offices, and immigration to the Americas. In New Spain, this influenced the creation of the *castas* system in which fractional Spanish, Indigenous, and African ancestry through both the mother's and father's line were used to divide people into a hierarchy of as many as 16 separate groupings. Men with only Spanish parents or one Spanish parent and one Indigenous or mixed Indigenous-Spanish parent could hold appointed political offices, study at universities, or be ordained as priests and were exempt from paying tribute to the Spanish crown, while men with African ancestry or only Indigenous ancestry were barred from universities and seminaries and required to pay tribute.

Women's ancestry and "cleanliness of blood" therefore had a major impact on the future fortunes of their male children. In 1789, Christobal Ramon Bivian petitioned the courts that the race of his wife, Margarita Casteñada, had been recorded incorrectly. At baptism, Casteñada had been registered in the libro de castas, or register of people of mixed Spanish, Indigenous, and African ancestry, rather than the libro de españoles, or register of people of only Spanish ancestry. Bivian submitted affidavits from several priests that testified to the good character of his wife and her family. None of these affidavits referred to their physical appearance or skin color, and Casteñada herself did not appear in court at all. Bivian successfully obtained the court's legal judgment that his wife Casteñada was only of Spanish ancestry, and not of mixed castas ancestry. Casteñada and Bivian's case was not unusual in Spanish courts and illustrates the fluidity of castas categories, their legal rather than physical basis, and the role of women in shaping their families' and childrens' racial identities.

In areas governed by Dutch law like Dutch New Netherland (what is now the state of New York), enslavement was first defined by religion before becoming defined by descent. Beginning in 1625 enslaved African women and men were purchased by the West India Company (WIC), which controlled the colony, to work fields and build roads for the WIC. In 1644, many of these enslaved men petitioned the WIC for their freedom. The men made their argument on three grounds: that they had worked for the company for nearly 20 years and the WIC had promised them their freedom; they and their families had been baptized as Christians; and the men needed freedom to support their wives and children. The WIC granted a conditional freedom, which historians call "half-freedom." The men had to pay yearly dues of food, militia service, and labor to the WIC; if they did not pay this tribute they could be re-enslaved; the men had to pay for the half-freedom of their wives; and any children born to these families, including those not yet born, remained enslaved to the WIC.

This was one of the first codifications of enslavement as an inherited trait passed from parents to children. However, African parents continued to use the Dutch legal system to secure their children's' full freedom. Parents used baptism to create family networks to protect their children. In 1648, Dorothy Angola and her husband Emanuel Pietersen, who both held half-freedom, adopted their godson, a five-year-old boy named Anthonij, after his half-free parents died. When Anthonij became an adult in 1661, Angola and Pietersen were able to successfully petition the WIC for Anthonij's full freedom in part on the basis that he had been baptized in the Dutch Reformed Church as an infant and his parents and godparents supported him without help from the WIC. Despite the legal codification of enslavement as inheritable, these enslaved families used the concept of enslavement status as heritable and linked to religion to protect and advocate for their childrens' freedom.

Without family networks to advocate for their freedom, Black children were vulnerable to enslavement in a colonial legal system that believed women, children, and people of color needed to be under the control of a male head of household. Europeans believed that a household headed by a male authority figure was necessary to maintain family and social order. In 1663, a young free Black woman named Lisbeth Anthonijsen was accused of stealing from the Dutch family where she was employed as a servant. When Lisbeth was accused of theft before 1663, her mother Mary was required to carry out the public beating required by the Dutch court. This gave Lisbeth a very small measure of protection but also showed the willingness of the Dutch judicial system to intervene in the lives of Black families if the community felt children were not being properly punished or disciplined. By 1663, however, Mary had passed away, leaving no one to advocate for Lisbeth. Accused of theft, Lisbeth was beaten by the Crieger family that employed her. When the Crieger family home burned down, Lisbeth was accused of arson and coerced into confessing to arson, sex outside of marriage, and thefts from a number of Dutch families. Alone and without an adult advocate, Lisbeth was first sentenced to be strangled to death at the stake with her sentence later changed to enslavement to the Criegers as a form of "mercy" from the court. This sentence placed Lisbeth back in the control of a male-headed household and was seen by the Dutch court as a restoration of social order. Without parents or godparents to advocate for her, Lisbeth's freedom was vulnerable.

Legislating Race

The codification of race in areas governed by English law created the system of racial classification that became prevalent in the United States. In English Virginia, enslaved Africans initially occupied a similar legal position as indentured servants brought from Europe. To provide labor for the rapidly growing tobacco plantations of the Chesapeake region, plantation owners paid ship captains for the debt bondage of European workers who could not afford passage to North America on their own. When the first enslaved Africans were sold at Jamestown in 1619, their indentures were first sold to English planters in this legal context, but over the next several decades their legal status would change.

English courts in Virginia and elsewhere began to distinguish between indentured people of African and European descent, often in gendered ways. In the first of these decisions in 1640, a man of African descent, John Punch, was sentenced to a term of life servitude for running away from the plantation where he was indentured, while the two European men who ran away with him were sentenced to additional years of service but not life servitude. The expectation that all people of African descent labored in servitude also emerged around this time. Under Virginia law beginning in the 1620s, plantation owners were required to pay taxes on all free and indentured people who worked in the fields under the presumption that this labor produced profitable tobacco. Women were implicitly excluded from this tax because English gender ideals of the time confined women's work to the home, garden, and dairy to produce food for household use, not profit. By 1645, a distinction between English and Black women was codified into law. To confront tax evasion by plantation owners who employed enslaved and indentured women in tobacco fields, colonial legislators defined taxable persons as all men between 16 and 60, as well as "all negro men and women" regardless of age. For the first time in English law, all people of African descent were defined as different from people of European descent. This racial distinction was made because of the kind of work women were presumed to do.

Some people of African descent navigated this system to attain similar economic and social status as free whites. In 1635, Angolans Mary and Anthony Johnson finished their terms of indentured servitude and by the 1650s they owned several hundred acres of plantation land as well as white and Black indentured servants and slaves. When a fire destroyed some of their property in 1652 and the Johnsons petitioned the courts for tax relief, Mary and her two daughters were exempted from the 1645 tax. This exemption placed them in a similar economic and social standing to white women. However, the fact that their tax status was only secured by petition shows that by this time Black women were assumed to be enslaved and laboring in tobacco fields, not running a plantation like the Johnson women.

This assumption would finally harden into law in 1662 in response to Virginian fears of increasing numbers of free Black people in the colony. Under English common law before the seventeenth century, children's social status derived from the status of their fathers. In 1655, a Black woman named Elizabeth Key successfully used English common law to legally secure her freedom and the freedom of her child. Key was the daughter of an enslaved African woman and a wealthy English planter, who under English law of the time was required to recognize any children born out of wedlock and provide for their support, including children born to enslaved women. Key was baptized as an infant, recognized in her father's will, and indentured to another English planter under terms that defined her as a free-born person whose indenture would end when she reached age 15. When Key reached age 25, the estate of the planter she had been indentured to as a child attempted to argue that Key was a slave for life because her mother had been enslaved. Key was able to successfully petition the Virginia General Assembly for her freedom and the freedom of her child, based in part on the fact that she and her son had both been baptized as infants and life enslavement of Christians was still prohibited, and the fact that Key's white English father had acknowledged her as his free child in his will.

Colonial legislatures passed a series of laws that gradually closed the paths to freedom used by Key, the Johnsons, and others. In Maryland in 1661, the legislature passed a law calling marriage between white and Black people a "disgrace not only of the English but also of many other Christian nations," and required any free English woman who married an enslaved man to "serve the master of such slave during the life of her husband; and that all the issues of such free-born women, so married, shall be slaves as their fathers were." This law aimed to prevent the birth of free people of color who could possibly blur the hardening line between free whites and enslaved Blacks. In 1662, the Virginia General Assembly defined slavery as a lifelong, inherited condition that passed from mother to child in a reversal of prior English common law. English fathers were no longer required to acknowledge their children born to enslaved mothers and English parentage was no longer grounds for freedom. In Virginia and other English colonies, baptism was explicitly outlawed as grounds for a freedom suit as well.

By 1700, many English colonies passed laws prohibiting marriage between enslaved people, marriage between people of African and European descent, unsupervised gatherings of enslaved people, and ownership of land and white indentured servants. Black women were defined within the law as reproductive bodies that created more enslaved people, both their labor and their reproductive potential commoditized. Combined with the construction of Black women as hypersexualized, animalistic, and inherently sexually available, this legal definition of race as carried through the sexual bodies of women lasted well into the twentieth- and twenty-first centuries.

English legal definitions of race and slavery solidified in a single generation in the seventeenth century. When Anthony Johnson died in Maryland in 1670, his land was awarded by the courts to a white colonist rather than Mary Johnson or their children because Anthony Johnson was determined to not be a citizen of the colony due to his race. Under English law, widows typically received one-third of their husbands' estates to support them for the rest of their lives. Mary Johnson was still exempt from taxes, but she did not receive her "widow's thirds" as white women expected were too. On her death in 1672, she only passed on two cows to her grandsons.

By the mid-eighteenth century, English law codified inherent differences between white and Black women's bodies and how they could be treated. In 1729, a free Black woman named Judith Spellman ran away from the North Carolina plantation where she was indentured to the English Joseph Stoakley. Spellman accused Stoakley of treating her as a slave rather than a free-born indentured servant who was born to a white mother. Spellman told the court that Stoakley had stripped her naked and whipped her, then kept her chained in irons so her feet swelled and she could not walk. Under the law in North Carolina and other English colonies, masters could only "moderately" correct free indentured servants with physical punishment, but enslaved people had no protection under the law. Stoakley's whipping and confinement of Spellman passed the bounds of acceptable punishment for free servants.

Judith Spellman's treatment by Stoakley shows that white plantation owners in the eighteenth century increasingly viewed race as the most important marker of safety from physical violence. English law followed and enshrined the idea of Black bodies as inherently different from white bodies as the brutality of punishments and masters' right to sexual access to enslaved and indentured women's bodies were defined by race.

As racial categories hardened throughout North America, colonial governments attempted to legislate sex, reproduction, and family formation. These laws attempted to prevent the birth of people like Judith Spellman whose mixed parentage had the potential to confuse her legal status. In 1691, Virginia made marriage between any white person and a Black or Indigenous person punishable by banishment from the colony. Interracial marriage, known as miscegenation, remained illegal in Virginia and many other states for another three hundred years until the 1967 Loving v. Virginia US Supreme Court case. The 1691 law made any children born to parents of different races by definition illegitimate and born outside of wedlock, itself a crime. Free white women who had children with enslaved Black men were punished with harsher fines than white women who had children outside of marriage with white men and their mixed-race children were sentenced to be indentured servants until 30 years of age, much longer than illegitimate white children. These disproportionate punishments were intended to discourage free white mothers like Judith Spellman's from giving birth to free people of color.

In areas of French colonization, the 1685 *Code Noir* similarly codified freedom status as passed from mother to child. On paper, the Code Noir initially gave some protection to enslaved women by punishing free men who had children with an enslaved woman with a large fine, and if the father was the enslaved woman's master, the woman and her children were to be taken from his ownership (but not freed). However, almost no fines for white men who impregnated enslaved women were ever recorded, illustrating the limitations of laws that were never enforced.

Some enslaved and free Black people were able to use the marriage provisions of the Code Noir to secure freedom for their families. The Code Noir recognized marriages between enslaved people with the permission of the enslaved person's master and prohibited the separation by sale of married couples and their children. In 1726, a Black man named John Mingo emancipated himself from enslavement in English Carolina by fleeing to French Louisiana where he was employed as a free laborer on a plantation. There he married an enslaved woman named Thérèse with the permission of her owner and later purchased her freedom. When Thérèse's former owner later disputed her free status, John and Thérèse's Catholic marriage and their contract to work for Thérèse's former owner, which stipulated that Thérèse would only "work at tasks suitable for women" and not work in the fields with other enslaved women, prevented Thérèse's re-enslavement.

Good Wives and Disruptive Women

Thérèse and John Mingo's efforts to secure both Thérèse's freedom and her gendered labor within their household reflects the importance of women's labor and their role in families throughout many North American colonies. European gender roles informed the creation of racial categories and shaped the experiences of free, enslaved, white, and Black women and men.

Women's lives throughout North American colonies were affected in part by demographic change and sex ratios. Indigenous communities affected by epidemic diseases faced declining populations or stabilizing populations, like the nations of the Haudenosaunee (Iroquois) Confederacy who numbered around 12,000 people in 1630 and stabilized around 7000 people in 1700 after several outbreaks of epidemic disease. Through the birth of children and adoption of European settlers and other Indigenous people, the population of the Haudenosaunee Confederacy climbed to at least 11,000 people by 1770. Haudenosaunee women's labor sustained their communities and included responsibility for growing and storing food, raising children, and choosing war captives to integrate into families and matrilineal clans.

All women's ability to regulate their reproduction depended on their health, access to food, and knowledge of reproduction and medicine in their communities. Maternal and infant mortality rates were very high during periods of epidemic disease for Indigenous communities and for enslaved women who faced brutal labor and inadequate food. European families in New England and New France were able to access more food and encountered less crowded, diseased conditions than in Europe, causing birthrates in those areas to climb compared to the colonies' source countries.

Individual women were also able to regulate their pregnancies. Some Indigenous women practiced long periods of breastfeeding for two to three years to help prevent a subsequent pregnancy, and timed pregnancies through a combination of contraceptives and abstention from sex that surprised Europeans. In Europe and North American colonies, cookbooks, and home remedy books commonly included herbal remedies to "clear the uterus," "regulate the menses," or "bring on bleeding," which were euphemistic terms for what we would now call a medically induced abortion. Under European and colonial law, a pregnancy was not recognized until "quickening," or when fetal movement was felt by the mother in about the fourth or fifth month of pregnancy because the fetus was not believed to have a soul until that point. Herbal remedies to end a pregnancy were widely known, commonly used, and did not carry social stigma for free women.

However, enslaved women who used abortifacients angered plantation owners who saw them and their reproductive potential as a source of wealth. The German botanist Maria Sibylla Merian reported that enslaved women told her they used "the seeds [of the peacock flower] to abort their children, so that they will not become slaves like themselves." Other European observers condemned enslaved women's "ill intentions" in ending pregnancies because it denied their owners' further wealth. In a system that dehumanized and commodified enslaved women, refusing to carry a pregnancy was a political act of resistance.

Almost all European colonies encouraged the growth of the free white population through the immigration of European women, who policymakers hoped would raise large families. Narratives of growing settler populations, declining Indigenous populations, the dehumanization of Indigenous people, and the disappearance or integration of Indigenous groups were used by Europeans to justify settler colonialism. Settler women's presence in European colonies was an important part of these narratives because their presence enabled the creation of families through the birth of children. Many Europeans believed that men with families would work harder, that women's household labor would reduce colonial expenses, and that the creation of familial households would ensure social control. However, women's experiences and social and legal status varied greatly across colonies due to race, labor conditions, religion, and class.

Region	Year	Settler, Non-Enslaved Population
Chesapeake	1624	1200
	1700	132,000
New England	1642	21,000
	1700	91,000
French Canada	1650	700
	1700	25,000
French Louisiana	1700	5000
Spanish Mexico	1570	7000
	1700	200,000
Spanish New Mexico	1610	1100
	1700	3000

In the English Chesapeake, both free white and enslaved Black family growth was hindered by the high mortality rate and harsh labor regime of the emerging tobacco plantation system. As early as 1619, the Virginia Company attempted to encourage the formation of white families by bringing dozens of poor, fatherless young women from England to be auctioned to free men as "tobacco brides." Because demand for male indentured servants to work in tobacco fields was so high, men outnumbered women by four or five to one. Female and male indentured servants were prohibited from marrying during the term of their indenture. The skewed sex ratio and inability of indentured servants, who formed a large part of the population, to marry significantly reduced marriage rates. This resulted in a relatively late average age at first marriage, in the mid to late twenties for both men and women, as well as an average marriage lasting only eight years due to the death of one or both spouses.

These imbalanced conditions had major effects on household formation and gender roles. In early Virginia in the absence of English women and social pressure against liaisons with enslaved Black and Indigenous women, some English men paired together to create all-male households that shared the traditionally feminine domestic labor of cooking, cleaning, and laundry in addition to agricultural work. At least some of these arrangements likely included sex between men, either as a temporary arrangement between men who typically preferred sex with women or as a relationship that would otherwise have been more socially sanctioned. There are only records for the prosecution and execution of one man, Richard Cornish, for same-sex contact in the early Chesapeake, when indentured servant William Couse accused Cornish of rape in 1624. The seeming absence of other prosecutions suggests a willingness to turn a blind eye to same-gender sex that may not have been tolerated elsewhere.

Gender imbalance also created social and legal space for some women to seize opportunities that were not available in England, while leaving other women profoundly vulnerable to sexual and legal exploitation. English women's property and legal rights typically came under the control of her husband after marriage. In English legal theory, after marriage, a husband and wife became one person under law, a concept known as coverture in which the woman became a *femme covert*. Widows and women who never married were *femme sole* and wealthy femme sole were able to exercise legal and social rights not available to other women. In 1648, the wealthy Margaret Brent petitioned the Maryland assembly for the right to vote as a landowner. Her petition was denied but Brent continued to represent herself under coverture.

Rank also allowed some married women to exercise political privileges denied to other women. Lady Frances Berkeley, the wife of three colonial governors, played a major role in the politics of the period. Berkeley was one of the wealthiest people in British North America with major wealth based in plantations and enslaved people that she managed on her own. When her cousin Nathaniel Bacon led a rebellion against her second husband Governor William Berkely, Frances Berkeley was influential in denouncing Bacon's Rebellion to both the leading white families of Virginia and the English government. After Bacon's Rebellion and imposition of stricter crown controls on the Virginia colony, Frances Berkeley used her political influence to first out-maneuver crown-appointed governors, and then later maneuver her cousin Thomas Colepeper into the governorship of Virginia and her third husband Philip Ludwell into the governorship of North Carolina. Although criticized by her political enemies, Berkeley's right to the political privileges of petitioning the King and influencing colonial politics on the basis of her gender was not denied by her contemporaries.

Indentured and enslaved women often found themselves especially vulnerable due to the intersection of gender, class, and race even if they were technically femme sole. When Denise Holland was indentured to Henry Smith in 1670, Smith coerced her into sex that eventually resulted in pregnancy. When Holland was prosecuted for the crime of bastardy, she was punished with the relatively light sentence of 20 additional days of indenture, which suggests that the court believed she had been raped. Smith, however, faced no punishment and was not held responsible for supporting the infant Hannah, who was herself indentured to another planter until age 16. When Hannah Holland finished her indenture and was herself charged for the crime of bastardy for becoming pregnant outside of wedlock with the child of a court official's son, she was publicly whipped and re-indentured to pay a fine she could not afford, and her child sentenced to indenture until age 30. The Maryland court called Hannah's pregnancy a "dishonor of Almighty God, scandal & evil example to all the good people of this province."

Like indentured white women, enslaved Black and Indigenous women were vulnerable to sexual coercion and assault with even less legal protection. Enslaved women resisted this coercion in a variety of ways, including self-emancipation by running away alone or with their children, or by practicing contraception or abortion to prevent pregnancy. In doing so, they asserted agency and control over their own bodies and reproduction even within a system designed to deny them these most basic rights.

Gender and Social Order

The sentences of Denise and Hannah Holland for pregnancy outside of marriage reflected English beliefs that households governed by a married man and woman were the foundation of a stable social order and the fear that children born outside of marriage would be a burden on public funds if not supported by a father. Although formally excluded from most legal privileges under coverture, women were involved in upholding this patriarchal social order. Midwives were required to report births outside of marriage and were required to ask for the father's name during labor in the belief that women in childbirth were unable to lie due to the pain.

Midwives were also called upon when communities believed individuals disrupted the gendered social order, as in the 1629 case of a person who went by both Thomasine and Thomas Hall. Hall was baptized Thomasine Hall in London and assumed female at birth. For the early part of their life, Hall dressed as a girl and was trained to do needlework and lace making. In the 1620s, Hall dressed in men's clothing, cut their hair, and assumed the name Thomas to join the military and serve as a soldier in Europe. After a brief return to female gender presentation and the name Thomasine for a few years in London, Hall again took on the name Thomas and male dress to depart for Virginia as an indentured servant.

In Jamestown, Hall dressed in men's and women's clothes at different times and was eventually accused of engaging in sex with women while dressed as both a man and a woman. Hall was accused of engaging in sex with men while dressed as a woman and sex with women while dressed as a man. Hall's naked body and genitals were examined multiple times without consent by both the male planter Hall was indentured to and several married midwives, who were asked to examine Hall and testify to the court about Hall's appearance as authorities on female bodies. The women who examined Hall, Alice Long, Dorothy Rodes, and Barbara Hall, testified that Hall lacked a vagina or vulva, while Hall's master John Atkins testified that he had seen both a vagina and a small penis. In the recorded testimony, Hall themselves was never asked how they identified; Hall testified that they had both a vagina and a nonfunctional penis and chose to dress in men's and women's clothing at different times.

Hall has been interpreted by modern scholars in changing ways over time. Hall has been interpreted as a cis woman who wore men's clothing for social and economic advantage; as a trans man who was assumed female at birth and who socially transitioned as an adult; and as an intersex, gender-fluid person who moved between male and female roles. Current concepts like nonbinary, transgender, and gender fluid did not exist in the seventeenth century in the way people understand them in the twenty-first century even though individuals like Hall have always existed.

In the seventeenth century, Hall's behavior was seen as disruptive both because they engaged in sex outside of marriage and because they destabilized what English people thought of as a natural binary between male and female. Hall was ultimately sentenced to wear a combination of men's and women's clothing to advertise their ambiguous gender status. The authority of the married women who examined Hall in defining gendered bodies was an important factor in this sentence.

The enforcement of binary gender roles and sexual order was likewise important in New England and other English colonies. As in the Chesapeake, bastardy or sex outside of marriage was considered a crime, but the punishments were reduced for couples who married before the birth of the child. In some New England, Puritan congregations as many as one-third of all children born to church members were conceived before their parents married. The prevalence of sex before marriage did not lessen its social stigma, however. Women who gave birth outside of marriage still faced fines, whippings, indenture, and "warning out" or banishment from communities that did not want to financially support illegitimate children. Behavior that violated gender norms was likewise punished, as in the 1642 case of Elizabeth Johnson, a servant in Massachusetts who was whipped and fined for sex with another woman, or Mary Henly, who was arrested in Massachusetts in 1692 for wearing men's clothing.

Henly and Johnson disrupted expectations for women to be good wives and responsible mothers under the control of a male head of the household. Unlike the Chesapeake, mortality rates in New England were much lower than in Europe, and sex ratios were closer to even because Puritan families tended to migrate together, rather than as unmarried indentured servants. As a result, women married much earlier, at an average age of 22, and had many more children. Lower maternal and child mortality, the "great migration" of the 1630s, and the decline of Indigenous populations due to war and disease resulted in rapidly growing settler populations in New England.

Puritan families left England because they rejected the authority of the Church of England. They believed the Church of England held a "covenant of works," in which people received salvation through their actions. The Puritans rejected this and embraced a "covenant of grace," in which individuals were predestined for salvation or damnation and searched for outward signs of salvation such as good fortune and church membership. Women and men were held to be spiritually equal, but women were nonetheless barred from speaking in church or religious leadership. Submission to a husband's authority was held to be a sign of a woman's piety.

Some women embraced these gender roles. The poet Anne Bradstreet celebrated her own writing skill and her role as wife and mother, writing in one poem "I am obnoxious to each carping tongue Who says my hand a needle better fits," and in another "If ever two were one, then surely we," about her husband. Bradstreet initially intended her writing for an audience of family and friends as part of the emerging Puritan genre of reflective writing that searched for God's influence and signs of salvation. Bradstreet's poetry was first published in 1678 by her male family members to show that an educated and godly woman elevated her role as wife and mother without stepping outside the proscribed bounds of the household.

Women who stepped outside these bounds of feminine behavior were severely punished. Although the Puritans settled in New England to ensure their own ability to worship freely, dissent and the practice of other religions, including other Protestant denominations, was prohibited. In 1636, Anne Hutchinson provoked a spiritual crisis in Massachusetts Bay Colony that ended with her banishment because of the way her preaching disrupted the gender hierarchy in the colony. An elite, educated woman and a midwife, Hutchinson held weekly meetings with other women at her house where she offered commentary on recent sermons. These initial meetings were considered within the bounds of respectable women's spiritual duties because the gatherings were all female and as an older woman, Hutchinson offered spiritual guidance to younger women. However, Hutchinson's gatherings soon grew to include men as well as women and Hutchinson became more outspoken in her critique of Puritan ministers, whom she accused of preaching a covenant of works.

Many of Hutchinson's teachings, including that salvation, was a direct gift from God, aligned with Protestant doctrine, but her gender and critique of male ministers were considered an immoral disruption. Hutchinson was put on civil trial for sedition, or expressing opinions dangerous to authority, for holding meetings that were neither "comely in the sight of God nor fitting to [her] sex." Hutchinson was ultimately banished from the colony, and having been pregnant during her trial, gave birth soon after. At 47 years of age, Hutchinson had a difficult pregnancy and delivered a preterm, nonviable mass of fetal tissue. Many Europeans in the seventeenth century believed that "monstrous births" of disabled or nonviable infants were a sign of God's displeasure. The governor of Massachusetts Bay Colony John Winthrop wrote of Hutchinson's delivery "see how the wisdom of God fitted this judgment to her sin every way, for look—as she had vented misshapen opinions, so she must bring forth deformed monsters." Puritan leaders believed Hutchinson's violation of English gender norms was so dangerous that God had punished her directly.

Gender and Legal Rights

Although gender roles were enforced so strictly because many Europeans believed them to be natural, women's legal and social rights varied greatly across colonies. In areas governed by Spanish law, women retained their own property after marriage, including an *arras*, or gift made by the prospective husband that became the sole property of the wife. Divorce was exceptionally rare in all colonies, but legal divorce or religious annulment was occasionally granted in cases of abandonment or severe abuse. Wealthy women had more options for ending a marriage, as in the 1700 divorce of María del Pino Argote from Josef Caballero. After Pino Argote fled with her daughters to a convent, Caballero petitioned the courts for custody of the children and the estate. Pino Argote successfully retained both her estate and custody of her children because the estate had been part of her dowry and arras; Caballero's mismanagement of her property was part of the grounds for the annulment of the marriage.

Spanish women were nonetheless expected to submit to male authority. Mexican nun Sor Juana Inés de la Cruz sought out convent life to avoid the household labor of marriage and motherhood. Like many nuns, Sor Juana wrote secular and religious poetry, music, and plays, but exceptionally for her time, her work was published and circulated during her lifetime. Although her order of nuns did not allow women to leave the convent, Sor Juana corresponded widely with male philosophers, mathematicians, and scientists, and one of her best-known poems examined the nature of the cosmos and theorizes the shape of the universe. She penned a number of poems and letters advocating for women's right to education and spiritual authority, writing "Thick-headed men who, so unfair,/ Bemoan the faults of women,/ Not seeing as you do that they're/ Exactly what you've made them." Her critique of church hierarchy eventually received censure from the Archbishop of Mexico, but even after her censure she subtly critiqued the church, signing one formulaic account of her penance with the ironic "I, the worst of women."

Like Spanish women, French and Dutch settler women also held a degree of economic independence. Like New England, Dutch New Netherland had much more balanced gender ratios because families tended to immigrate together, but women had a much greater legal independence. Marriage was still ultimately expected for most women, but in New Netherland prenuptial agreements were common and often written to protect women's property rights in marriage. In a *manus* marriage, a woman assumed the status of a legal minor under the guardianship of her husband similar to English coverture. Wealthy women like Margaret Hardenbroeck Philipse often opted for an *usus* marriage, in which a woman retained her property and legal status separate from her husband. Philipse built a major import/export business before her marriage and continued to amass wealth and real estate stretching from Albany to plantations in Barbados while managing her affairs separately from her husband.

Women in an *usus* marriage assumed all legal and financial responsibility for their own actions. In 1654, tavernkeeper Maria Jansz was charged with the crime of selling alcohol to an Indigenous woman. New Netherland's laws against alcohol sales were intended to prevent social mixing between Dutch settlers and Indigenous people, and Jansz's sentence of banishment from the colony was much harsher than the sentences men typically received for selling alcohol. Dutch women's economic and legal independence on paper was balanced by the social sanction for behavior that violated social norms. Jansz's husband was able to successfully sue for divorce rather than follow her in banishment, suggesting the danger of losing social support for women who violated the law.

In New France, an extremely skewed gender ratio of nearly 12 men to every one woman created a great deal of anxiety about the future of the colony for officials. Without French women available to marry, many French men either viewed their time in the colony as temporary or entered relationships with Indigenous women. Many of these Indigenous women came from nations with matrilineal descent and expectations that husbands and children would live with the wife's family. French officials encouraged these marriages at the same time that they feared them, hoping for the *francization* (frenchification) of Indigenous wives on one hand and fearing the *ensauvegment* (becoming savage) of French husbands on the other.

French officials approached this perceived problem in two ways. To encourage the *francization* of Indigenous women, the French government financed a convent school headed by Ursuline nun Mother Marie de l'Incarnation beginning in 1639. The Ursuline convent school enrolled French girls, girls from Indigenous nations allied to New France, and girls taken as hostages from Indigenous nations hostile to New France like the Haudenosaunee. Together, these girls were educated to be French wives and mothers and encouraged to marry French men. Many of the Indigenous girls, like an Oneida woman named Felicité who practiced Catholicism throughout her life, returned to their nations without marrying. Ultimately fewer than 20 Indigenous alumnae of this school married French men out of several dozen who attended.

French officials also attempted to encourage marriages between French women and French men by bringing more French women to the colony. These *filles du roi*, or daughters of the king, were young women or widows who lacked financial resources or family connections and were granted large dowries if they married in New France. Women like Marie Grandin opted for this arrangement because it allowed them to significantly improve their financial circumstances and offered a measure of leverage in negotiating an advantageous marriage. Under French law, women retained their property, but it came under the management of their husbands. When Grandin married eel fisherman and former indentured servant Jean Beaudet in 1670, she was able to negotiate a prenuptial agreement in which she would retain her dowry and half of the wealth she brought to the marriage. Grandin and Beaudet together grew their wealth enough to bequeath land to all three of their sons, something that would have been unattainable for their family in France. Although Grandin came from an impoverished background and had few opportunities in France, in New France she was able to secure a measure of financial security not otherwise available to her due to the skewed gender ratios of the new colony.

Conclusion

Women like Anne Hutchinson, Hannah Holland, Sor Juana, Judith Spellman, and Lisbeth Anthonijsen shared a common experience of restriction on their social and legal rights due to their gender. However, the bounds of those rights differed greatly based on location, class, and race. Black women like Judith Spellman and Lisbeth

Anthonijsen were much more vulnerable to sexual and legal violence due to their race, which emerged as a concept linked to the sexual availability of Black women's bodies. People like T Hall faced legal and social sanctions because they were not neatly defined as male or female. Elite women of European descent like Sor Juana and Anne Hutchinson did face sanctions for explicit critique of male leaders, but their elite status afforded them a measure of freedom to lead other women. Understanding the intersectionality between the multiple aspects of any individual's identity is an important part of understanding that although some women shared some experiences due to gender, not all women shared all experiences. Gender shaped the experience of race, class, and colonialism just as much as race and class shaped the experience of gender.

Bibliography

Block, Sharon. *Colonial Complexions: Race and Bodies in Eighteenth-Century America.* University of Pennsylvania Press, 2018.

Breen, T H, and Stephen Innes. *"Myne Owne Ground": Race and Freedom on Virginia's Eastern Shore, 1640-1676.* Oxford University Press, 2004.

Brown, Kathleen. *Good Wives, Nasty Wenches, and Anxious Patriarchs: Gender, Race, and Power in Colonial Virginia.* University of North Carolina Press, 1996.

Carrera, Magali M. *Imagining Identity in New Spain: Race, Lineage, and the Colonial Body in Portraiture and Casta Paintings.* University of Texas Press, 2003.

Earle, Rebecca. "The Pleasures of Taxonomy: Casta Paintings, Classification, and Colonialism." *The William and Mary Quarterly* 73, no. 3 (2016): 427–466. **https://doi.org/10.5309/willmaryquar.73.3.0427**.

Fischer, Kirsten. *Suspect Relations: Sex, Race, and Resistance in Colonial North Carolina.* Cornell University Press, 2002.

Guasco, Michael. *Slaves and Englishmen: Human Bondage in the Early Modern Atlantic World.* University of Pennsylvania Press, 2014.

Kopelson, Heather Miyano. *Faithful Bodies: Performing Religion and Race in the Puritan Atlantic.* New York University Press, 2016.

Morgan, Jennifer L. "'Some Could Suckle Over Their Shoulder': Male Travelers, Female Bodies, and the Gendering of Racial Ideology, 1500-1770." *The William and Mary Quarterly* 54, no. 1 (1997): 167–192. **https://doi.org/10.2307/2953316**.

Mosterman, Andrea C. *Spaces of Enslavement: A History of Slavery and Resistance in Dutch New York.* Cornell University Press, 2021.

Mustakeem, Sowande M. *Slavery at Sea: Terror, Sex, and Sickness in the Middle Passage.* Illinois University Press, 2016.

Noel, Jan. *Along a River: The First French-Canadian Women.* University of Toronto Press, 2013.

Norton, Mary Beth. *Separated by their Sex: Women in Public and Private in the Colonial Atlantic World.* Cornell University Press, 2011.

Schiebinger, Londa L. *Plants and Empire: Colonial Bioprospecting in the Atlantic World.* Harvard University Press, 2004.

Spear, Jennifer. *Race, Sex and Social Order in Early New Orleans.* Johns Hopkins University Press, 2009.

Turner, Sasha. *Contested Bodies: Pregnancy, Childrearing, and Slavery in Jamaica.* University of Pennsylvania Press, 2017.

Ulrich, Laurel. *Good Wives: Image and Reality in the Lives of Women in Northern New England, 1650-1750.* Random House, 1982.

White, Sophie. *Voices of the Enslaved: Love, Labor, and Longing in French Louisiana.* University of North Carolina Press Books, 2019.

CHAPTER 4

Atlantic Connections, 1690–1750

Women's experiences of war, cross-cultural contact, and the growing Atlantic economy in the early eighteenth century were shaped in large part by their gender. Women actively navigated and shaped the changes of the late seventeenth and early eighteenth centuries as leaders, diplomats, traders, wives, consumers, and producers. In British colonies, gender ideology of women as passive, chaste, and domestic in contrast to men as active and engaged in the public sphere of politics, diplomacy, war, and the market economy was not always reflected in daily life. It was nonetheless used to define many women, including Indigenous, Black, and poor white women, as outside the protections of true womanhood. In war, understandings of gender shaped hostilities between Indigenous and settler groups, while in peaceful negotiations, shared understandings of women as non-military actors allowed some women to take on diplomatic roles. The Salem witchcraft trials are one example of how gender shaped settlers' understanding of war with Indigenous groups, while the marriages of Indigenous women to settler men illustrate how nation and culture shaped the experience of marriage and motherhood.

Gender is a primary way of signifying power and creating social order, and therefore also a primary way of constructing individual and community identity. Previous chapters have discussed the way gender was used to impose hierarchies of race, but people have also used gender to define their own identities and communities against oppressive systems. Indigenous, Black, and settler women all used material goods and their own labor during this period to define themselves and their communities. Enslaved and free Black women participated in urban market economies to create and maintain community connections, while white lawmakers grew concerned about the solidarity and organization those connections enabled. Despite European settler attempts to impose their own gender roles, Indigenous and African people maintained some control within their communities despite the pressures of colonialism and enslavement.

American Women's History: A New Narrative History, First Edition. Melissa E. Blair, Vanessa M. Holden, and Maeve Kane.
© 2024 John Wiley & Sons, Inc. Published 2024 by John Wiley & Sons, Inc.

Gender and Warfare

The lives of many Indigenous, Black, and white settler women were shaped by warfare during the seventeenth and eighteenth centuries. The expansion of European settlements caused many of these conflicts as Indigenous nations defended their territories and homelands. In the Chesapeake, Matoaka's marriage to John Rolfe brought a temporary peace between what is now called the first and second Anglo-Powhatan Wars as a confederacy led by Matoaka's uncle Opechancanough attempted to push back encroaching English settlements. In Dutch, New Netherland, Dutch settlers fought a series of wars with Munsee-speaking Indigenous groups over land encroachments, including the Peach Tree War, which was set off by the murder of a young Munsee woman by a Dutch settler for picking fruit from a peach tree. These escalating seventeenth-century conflicts show the increasing pressure on Indigenous peoples' land as European populations grew.

In New England, a series of escalating wars in the seventeenth and eighteenth centuries were shaped by Indigenous and settler understandings of gender. Indigenous and settler groups shared an understanding of war and diplomacy as a masculine domain, and this shaped their attacks against one another during times of war. During the Pequot War (1636–1638) between the Pequot and the allied English, Mohegan, and Narragansett, the success of Pequot attacks against English towns triggered an unprecedented English attack on the Pequot town of Mistick. During this nighttime attack, English militia set fire to the sleeping town and killed more than 500 Pequot women, children, and men. The English-allied Narragansett and Mohegan expressed horror at the method and scale of the attack. Both the English and the Pequot attacks on one another's towns show a mutual understanding of the devastating effects of attacking non-combatants like women and children who helped both Indigenous and settler populations grow. Following the war, many Pequot women and children were sold into slavery in the Caribbean, a deliberate tactic by the English to further harm the ability of the survivors to reproduce and sustain themselves. Despite this, the Pequots survive in the twenty-first century as the Mashantucket Pequot Nation and the Eastern Pequot Tribal Nation.

The experiences of two women during King Philip's War (1675–1678) a generation later illustrate the shared and differing experiences of Indigenous and white settler women in New England warfare. Weetamoo was a sachem, or leader, of the Pocasset nation, a member of the Wampanoag Confederacy in what is now eastern Massachusetts. She and her sister Woonekanuske solidified their nation's diplomatic alliances with a series of strategic marriages, and by 1675 the Pocasset were allied to every Indigenous nation in the region and a major power within the Wampanoag Confederacy. Unlike English and other settler women, Wampanoag women retained their leadership positions after marriage. When English settlers began to violate previous peace treaties by confiscating guns from Wampanoags and asserting criminal jurisdiction over issues in Wampanoag territory, Weetamoo led attacks against English settlements alongside her husband Quinnapin and her brother-in-law Metacom (known to the English as King Philip). Weetamoo was feared widely by the English both because of her military and diplomatic success and because her leadership violated English gender roles. When she was found dead by English soldiers at the end of the war, her body was decapitated and her head displayed on a pole as proof that she was dead.

Much of what historians know about Weetamoo comes from the account of an English settler woman, Mary Rowlandson, who was held captive by Weetamoo and her husband for three months. Rowlandson and three of her children were taken captive in 1676 and ultimately ransomed back. After her ransom, Rowlandson documented her period of captivity in a pamphlet titled *The Sovereignty and Goodness of God*. Rowlandson's account is widely regarded by scholars as among the first English-language "captivity narratives," a genre of writing that became very popular in the seventeenth, eighteenth, and nineteenth centuries as a way for settlers to construct Indigenous people as a racialized other. Rowlandson's account drew on the Puritan belief that trials in the physical world were signs sent by God and she narrated her captivity and ransom as evidence of her deliverance by God. Rowlandson complained bitterly that Weetamoo forced her to perform manual labor and treated her as a slave, highlighting what Rowlandson believed was an unnatural hierarchy at a time when white settlers were coming to see themselves as inherently different from Indigenous people and enslaved Africans.

Captivity narratives were one way that white womanhood was constructed in contrast to Indigenous or Black womanhood. Rowlandson's narrative emphasized that she had not been sexually assaulted by any Indigenous men during her captivity, countering a rumor that she had willingly become pregnant during her captivity and protecting her sexual reputation. Sexual assault of settler women by Indigenous men was never reported in these captivity narratives and many writers during the seventeenth and eighteenth centuries frequently noted that Indigenous groups found the idea of sexually coercing female prisoners abhorrent. Rape was often harshly punished among Indigenous communities, and for groups that adopted prisoners, sexual coercion of a female prisoner could amount to incest if she was later adopted. Rowlandson and other settler writers' surprise at the absence of sexual assault of female prisoners suggests that they expected it. The unspoken assumption in Rowlandson's denial of sexual assault is that women at the bottom of the social hierarchy like enslaved Indigenous and Black women, who Rowlandson compared herself to elsewhere in her narrative, were expected to be sexually vulnerable to their captors.

Women's captivity narratives were also used to define what gendered behavior was acceptable, and what was acceptable in contrast to racial others. Hannah Dustan, who was taken captive a decade later during King William's War (1688–1697), was widely celebrated for her account of her murders of her Abenaki captors while they slept. Puritan wives were expected to be silent and submissive within marriage, and the published accounts about Rowlandson and Dustan that presented them in a heroic light seem to contradict these ideals. However, Dustan's violence and Rowlandson's narrative of her deliverance were celebrated by Puritan New Englanders as evidence of Christian women's strength against what they saw as literally Devil-worshipping racial others.

Indigenous communities saw settler captives very differently. Some, like Rowlandson, were taken captive for their value in ransom or for their use in negotiations. Others, like Eunice Williams, were intended to be adopted into Indigenous families. The seven-year-old Williams was taken captive by Kahnawake Mohawks in 1704 during Queen Anne's War (1702–1713). Mohawk families and some other Indigenous groups practiced the adoption of Indigenous and settler captives as a way to replace relatives who were lost from sickness or war. In this way, population losses were stabilized and clans could maintain the relationships of obligation and reciprocal duty that held together their communities. Mohawk and other Haudenosaunee women chose which captives would be adopted as part of a cultural belief in women's power over life and death. When Williams was adopted by her Mohawk family, they viewed her as Mohawk from that point forward. Williams seems to have viewed herself that way as well. Williams was baptized Catholic and took on the name Kanenstenhawi Marguerite, and at the age of 16 she married a Catholic Mohawk man named François-Xavier Arosen. Williams' father and brother continued to attempt to ransom her from her Mohawk family for the rest of her life, but her Mohawk family refused, saying they "would as soon part with their hearts as the child." Williams' birth family continued to view her as an English Puritan held captive by Indians, but Williams herself refused to allow them to ransom her away from her adopted family even when she went to visit them in Massachusetts as an adult.

Women like Weetamoo, Eunice Williams, Hannah Dustan, and Mary Rowlandson all experienced the upheavals of war during the seventeenth and eighteenth centuries in ways that were shaped by their gender. However, their cultural backgrounds, religion, and choices shaped how they navigated and made sense of those wars. English gender ideology that constructed the ideal for white women to be passive, chaste, and domestic was put to the test in extreme circumstances like Williams', Dustan's, and Rowlandson's captivity and constructed Indigenous women like Weetamoo as outside the protections of womanhood. Because gender was a foundational part of how colonial society was organized, individuals like Weetamoo and others who disrupted the supposedly natural gender and racial hierarchy were seen as particularly dangerous.

Salem Witch Trials

The Salem witchcraft trials in 1692 were a crisis of English gendered social order. The witchcraft crisis has been explained by scholars in many ways, and the events at Salem from the first accusations through the executions of 14 women and 5 men were considered strange and extreme by others at the time. Witchcraft accusations and executions reached their peak in Europe between 1580 and 1630 during the height of the Counter Reformation and the upheavals of religious wars. By the end of the seventeenth century, however, witchcraft accusations and trials had declined significantly. The Salem witchcraft trials were the product of an intersection between race, gender, religion, and warfare as the people of Salem tried to explain recent losses in war against Indigenous groups.

Puritan settlers' understanding of their place in the world at the time of the Salem witchcraft trials was shaped by their religious understanding of recent wars in New England. As discussed in the previous chapter, Puritan doctrine held that God had predetermined all events and the salvation or damnation of all people. Puritans believed that God sent signs in the physical world that could be understood by people to determine if they were saved. They attempted to understand their wars with Indigenous groups in this way as well. King Philip's War (1675–1678) had destroyed nearly one-third of all New England towns and killed 10% of the adult male settler population. As the Wampanoag Confederacy successfully pushed back the borders of white settlements at the height of the war, many settlers feared that the war and their losses had been sent by God as a punishment. A decade later, when Massachusetts settlers attempted to move north into what is now Maine, the Wabanaki Confederacy and their French allies succeeded in pushing out New Englanders back into Massachusetts. By 1692, many of the surviving Maine settlers were refugees returned back to Massachusetts. The frontier of fighting in what is now known as King William's

War (1688–1697) was as close as 50 miles to Salem, sparking fears that the losses of King Philip's War would be repeated.

The returned Maine refugees strained resources in Salem and exacerbated existing tensions about property lines, livestock grazing rights, and the appointment of a minister to the town church. This was the religious and political context when the first witchcraft accusations were made in January 1692. Two young girls in the controversial minister's household, Elizabeth Parris and Abigail Williams, ages 9 and 11, began having screaming fits and contortions and they were soon joined by 12-year-old Abigail Putnam, whose family was involved in a major property dispute. The girls accused Tituba, Sarah Good, and Sarah Osborne of harming them with witchcraft.

Tituba, Good, and Osborne differed in many ways, but what they shared was a disruption to the gendered order of Puritan New England. Tituba was an enslaved West Indian woman in the Parris household, while Good and Osborne were disreputable older women who had rejected what many Puritan New Englanders believed were their proper gender roles as nurturing mothers. Good had been left impoverished by her first husband's debts and was seen by many as a burden to the town because of her reliance on charity. Osborne was wealthy and upset the gendered social order by keeping her first husband's property and managing it with her second husband, rather than allowing her sons by her first marriage to inherit the property; she was also involved in a property dispute with the family of accuser Abigail Putnam at the time of the accusations. As an enslaved woman marked by her race, Tituba was especially vulnerable during a time of increasingly hard racial lines and fears of racialized Indian attacks. All three women were social outsiders who fit the typical mold expected for witches, and the Salem witchcraft accusations might have been unremarkable in the longer history of witchcraft accusations if they had been the only accused.

However, the accusations soon amplified and escalated. Good and Osborne protested their innocence, but Tituba was beaten until she was coerced into confessing. Tituba's coerced confession implicated Good, Osborne, and many others sparking a wave of paranoia and further accusations. By May 1692, 60 more people had been accused of witchcraft by 8 girls and implicated in other forced confessions. The accused included Sarah Good's four-year-old daughter Dorothy and the 70-year-old former minister at Salem, George Burroughs. Dorothy's accusation was taken as a sign of the widespread network of witches in Salem, while Burroughs was accused as the leader of the witches.

Although Burroughs was male, he shared some characteristics with Tituba, Good, and Osborne. He was in debt to the family of Ann Putnam, one of the accusers, for the burial of his first wife, who he was believed to have abused to death. His cruelty to his first and second wives and his failure to have his children baptized was seen as a violation of Puritan gendered order, in which husbands were supposed to be guides and protectors of their wives and children. As a former minister, Burroughs' failure to have his children baptized was also taken as a sign of his rejection of the Puritan church and God. This became especially important in how many at Salem understood his time on the Maine frontier. After his time as the minister at Salem, Burroughs and his family had moved north to Maine, where Burroughs served as the leader of a militia defending against Wabanaki attacks. There, he commanded at several battles where Massachusetts settlers suffered significant casualties, while Burroughs himself retreated without injury. Many of the girls who accused others of witchcraft had lost fathers and other family members to Indian attacks in Maine.

By 1693, 106 women and 38 men of all ages had been accused of witchcraft by the time the trials ended. Many of those initially accused, like Tituba, Burroughs, Good, and Osbourne, in some way violated expectations for their gender. Burroughs violated expectations for men to perform restrained, protective masculinity, while Tituba, Good, and Osbourne were seen as burdensome or overly aggressive for women. The vast majority of the accused witches were women, reflecting Puritan belief that women were inherently more sinful and susceptible to temptation than were men. Fifty-four of the accused had confessed under torture or to save their own lives, because witches who confessed were not executed. The accusers and accused eventually came to include those from all levels of society as more of the accused confessed under torture and accused others in order to save themselves from execution. Scholars have attempted to explain the events at Salem as the result of ergot poisoning, viral encephalitis, malice by the girls who made the accusations, and mass hysteria. However, the focus on Burroughs as the leader of the witches suggests that disruption to the gendered social order and a fear of losses to the Wabanaki and other Indigenous groups fueled many of the Salem witchcraft accusations.

Intermarriage and Intermediaries

Although war shaped the lives of many women in early America, women also took an active role in negotiating diplomacy and cross-cultural connections during both war and peace. They did so as diplomats, translators, traders, and wives. Their success often depended on shared European and Indigenous understandings of women's gender roles.

In negotiations between different European colonies, a shared understanding of women as non-political actors sometimes allowed them to navigate diplomatic roles that would otherwise be closed to them. When English ships sailed into the harbor of Dutch Manhattan in 1664, Lydia de Meyer and Hillegond van Ruyven were able to narrowly avoid a bloody takeover. The Dutch director of the colony had declared his intention to fight the English, but his militia and governing council wished to surrender because they lacked gunpowder. During the tense standoff between the outgunned Dutch and the more well-supplied English, the wives of two Dutch council members, de Meyer and van Ruyven, were able to visit the English camp and negotiate a peaceful meeting between the Dutch council and the English to negotiate a surrender. Their high status as council members' wives gained them entry to the English camp, while their status as women meant that they could unofficially reach out to the English without committing treason against the Dutch director-general.

In intercultural diplomacy between Indigenous and European groups, understandings of women's roles in each community were especially important. Hilletie Van Olinda, the daughter of a Mohawk woman and a Dutch trader, and Sarah Roelfs Kierstede, who was born in the Netherlands and learned to translate the Munsee language, were able to act as trusted negotiators and translators because of their gender. Both the Dutch and later English governments of New Netherland/New York paid both women to act as translators and negotiators. Van Olinda was a member of her mother's Mohawk clan and a member of the Dutch Reformed Church at Albany, NY, making her a trusted negotiator to both the Mohawk and the Dutch. Her gender helped her maintain her ties to her birth family and clan after her marriage to a Dutch trader because Mohawk clan belonging descends through the mother's family.

Kierstede was trusted as a negotiator and translator by the Munsee chief Oratam because as a woman, Kierstede was barred from holding a formal political or military position among the Dutch, meaning Oratam trusted her to not negotiate for her own gain. Kierstede was trusted as a negotiator among the Dutch because she was related by birth or marriage to many of the most influential families in the colonies. Both women's gender positioned them to be trusted as intercultural mediators in ways distinct from men.

Other women formed cross-cultural connections through intermarriage. White settler women rarely married Indigenous men, but Indigenous women frequently married settler men for various reasons. Like Hilletie Van Olinda, the children of these marriages were often raised by their mothers' families and retained their mothers' cultural connections. Colonial governments endorsed these marriages to a greater or lesser extent. As discussed in the previous chapter, some areas under English law began to bar intermarriage between white, Black, and Indigenous peoples to enforce racial hierarchies, while areas under French and Spanish law recognized these marriages. After Russian settlement of the North American west coast began in 1733, the Russian government formally encouraged the marriage of both Russian women and men to Indigenous men and women in what is now the state of Alaska, but only 10 of these marriages took place by 1794.

Scholars have argued that Indigenous women sought out these relationships for a variety of reasons, including a rejection of polygamy or abuse in their home communities, a desire for economic connections with European traders who imported manufactured goods, or a desire to convert to Christianity and marry a Christian husband. Individual women made their choices for their own reasons. One such woman was Marie Rouensa, the daughter of a Kaskaskia chief in what is now Illinois. The Illiniwek cultural group that the Kaskaskia were part of practiced patrilineal descent, marriage of men to multiple wives, and allowed men who accused their wife of adultery to cut off the wife's nose. For some Illiniwek women like Rouensa, the French Jesuit missionary emphasis on monogamy and the importance of the Virgin Mary made Catholic conversion attractive. Rouensa successfully appealed to the local Jesuit priest to avoid an unsatisfactory marriage and leveraged this support to require her first husband to convert to Catholicism with her. By her second marriage, Rouensa was a socially and economically influential woman in her own right under French property law and stood as a godmother for many Indigenous and French children. By the time of her death in 1725, she was one of the wealthiest people in the region.

Other Indigenous women like Maurgerite Faffert used their Indigenous family connections to escape abusive settler husbands. In 1709, Faffert married French trader Jean Baptiste Turpin in a union that was supposed to combine both their families' extensive business networks. Shortly after their marriage, Turpin beat her and their son, almost killing Faffert twice. Under French law, women could not obtain a divorce unless they could show that their husband was damaging their finances. However, in the Algonquin culture Faffert had been raised in, women had the right to divorce simply by leaving. In 1717, Faffert left her husband in French Detroit and took their son to live with her aunt, the noted diplomat Madame Montour, in what is now New York. Faffert ultimately married a Mohawk husband and rose to prominence as a fur trader in her own right and a diplomat working alongside her aunt. While Rouensa used Catholic conversion to negotiate her own marriages, Faffert used her Indigenous kinship connections to remove herself from an unsatisfactory marriage.

Women and the Atlantic World of Goods

Rouensa and Faffert's positions as influential traders were not exceptional. Many Indigenous, settler, and Black women throughout the Atlantic world acted as traders, consumers, and producers in ways that defined themselves and their communities. During what scholars now call the consumer revolution, consumers throughout Europe and North America gained access to a wider range of goods through the expansion of manufacturing, long-distance trade, and plantation slavery. Many women from many backgrounds participated in this new world of goods, but how they engaged with it was defined by culture, class, and race.

The growth of European and American markets for the products of plantation slavery like sugar, tea, coffee, chocolate, and tobacco drove the expansion of slave economies and cemented the racial hierarchies discussed in the previous chapter. The vast consumer demand and profitability of these products were believed to justify the brutal dehumanization of enslaved people required to produce these luxury goods. In England and English North American colonies, tea and coffee culture quickly became gendered. Coffee was popularly served in coffeehouses, where men gathered to gossip, share newspapers, conduct business, and engage in political debate. Many women worked in and even owned coffeehouses, but because coffeehouses were seen as public spaces where financial and political business was done, they were not seen as proper spaces for respectable women.

Tea, on the other hand, was seen as proper for both men and women because the tea table occupied a domestic space within the home. Eighteenth century English and French tea etiquette was used as a marker of refinement and social class in a space controlled by women. Many of the objects on a tea table displayed the household's access to the products of long-distance trade and colonial plantation slavery, including imported or imitation porcelain, tea and sugar, and the imported silk or calico worn by those sitting at the tea table. As an informal, domestic space, the tea table was seen as an appropriate place for women and men to gather and even discuss news.

As an extension of European women's traditional roles in market shopping for their families, retail shopping was seen as a feminine activity. In addition to acting as business owners in ways previously discussed, many settler women were primarily responsible for their family's purchases and developed wide information networks that brought them news about imports and shipments. Upper- and middle-class settler women used these connections to secure their families' class position, while lower class settler women used these networks just to get by. Women like Rhode Island tavernkeeper Abigail Stoneman kept careful track of the debts owed to her for food, lodging, alcohol, and laundry on a stack of playing cards. When she was called to court to pay her own debts, Stoneman produced these playing cards as proof of her ability to pay her debts, showing both her own wide commercial network and her tenuous economic place as a woman providing the reproductive labor of cooking and cleaning for others.

Enslaved women's position in this market economy was even more tenuous. Some enslaved women who grew their own produce were allowed to sell it at public markets, supplementing both their families' food and providing them with a connection to other enslaved and free women. Other enslaved women were part of urban market economies because their labor was hired out by their enslavers. Some large cities like Savannah, Georgia, and Charleston, South Carolina had entire streets and neighborhoods dedicated to housing enslaved people who lived separately from their enslavers and hired out their labor. The wages these women received from work like laundering, basketmaking, prostitution, sewing, nursing, and selling plantation agricultural products went back to their enslavers. Enslaved women and men in urban areas had more flexibility to meet and form connections with other enslaved and free Black people through buying and selling at markets, church, and marriage. Black churches formed the center of social life for many free and enslaved Black people in Southern cities and became an important focus for later abolitionist and social justice protest. Leadership in Black churches was gendered, with men taking on formal religious roles and women taking on the care work of visiting and aiding sick neighbors. The networks created between enslaved and free Black people worried white lawmakers, who protested that many enslaved people presented themselves and were treated by others as free when they were allowed to hire out their own labor without direct supervision. To counteract this, many urban areas like Charleston required enslaved people who hired out their labor to wear badges advertising their enslaved status.

Women used their network of connections to pursue their own economic benefit. In the Mohawk settlement of Kahnawake along the Saint Lawrence River, French sisters Marie-Magdalene, Marguerite, and Marie-Anne Desauniers ran a fur trade business that relied on their connection to Kahnawake Mohawk women like their business partners Agnese and Theresse. Under French law, trade between French residents and the English colony of New York to the south was illegal, but traders in Albany, New York, paid much better prices for furs than French exporters did. Indigenous women like Agnese and Theresse were not subject to French law, so the Desauniers sisters partnered with Mohawk women and men to carry furs south and sell them at a profit. Agnese and Theresse exchanged these furs for high-demand red cloth, which they and the Desauniers used to buy yet more furs from other Indigenous traders. Haudenosaunee women were able to move freely through their nations' territories because colonial powers like New France and New York could not enforce their laws in Indigenous territories.

Haudenosaunee and other Indigenous women like Agnese and Theresse bought a significant amount of European cloth. Clothing was a powerful cultural symbol throughout early America. Although by the eighteenth century many Indigenous women bought most of the materials for their clothing from settler traders, they reworked purchased cloth into distinctly Indigenous garments like wrapped skirts and wool leggings that accommodate their continued agricultural work. Settler men's and women's clothing was increasingly gendered during the seventeenth and eighteenth centuries. In the sixteenth and seventeenth centuries, many European men wore bright colors and extravagant lace. Over the course of the seventeenth and eighteenth centuries, light colors and floral designs were increasingly associated with femininity, while plain garments in dark colors were increasingly associated with the restraint and sobriety necessary to do men's business.

As a social construct, these gendered clothing associations varied between places and changed over time. Clothing was sometimes used to enforce gendered social order, as seen in the previous chapter with the case of T Hall. However, sumptuary laws, or laws regulating what kind of clothing people could or could not wear, were not widely passed or enforced in any North American colonies. One notable exception to this were the *tignon* laws of Spanish Louisiana and the French Caribbean. Enslaved Black women in these areas typically wore their hair wrapped with a piece of cloth called a *tignon*, to help protect it while they worked. In an effort to visually mark free Black women as similar to enslaved women and different from white women, *tignon* laws required Black women to wrap their hair the same way enslaved women did. Free Black women complied with the law by wrapping their hair, but defied it by wearing expensive fabrics, jewelry, and extravagant styles. The laws were rarely enforced, and the style was later adopted by fashionable white women as well.

Free and enslaved Black women and men resisted unjust treatment in large and small ways. Enslaved people from many national backgrounds, speaking many different languages, created a common community through their use of holidays and material objects. Sometimes enslavement brought together people from different backgrounds by chance, but slave owners sometimes deliberately purchased enslaved people who spoke different African languages to discourage slave rebellions. In New York, enslaved people created a diasporic identity through shared burial rituals and holidays. At the African Burial Ground in Manhattan, the largest known burial ground of enslaved people, a number of people were buried with the West African sankofa symbol, which symbolized a tie between past, present, and future. The enslaved and free Black communities in New York and Albany also celebrated Pinkster, a holiday with ties to both the Dutch and Kongo celebrations of Pentecost. Through these shared rituals and holidays, an ethnically diverse enslaved population created shared communities and families.

Conclusion

Women throughout early America navigated peace and war as active agents who made their own decisions on behalf of themselves, their children, and their communities. They did so as buyers who chose what to wear and how, and as producers who chose how to use their labor to support their families. In cross-cultural interactions, they made connections through marriage, trade, and diplomatic negotiations. The way both women and men understood these interactions were shaped by shared and diverging understandings of women's roles in Indigenous, Black, and settler communities.

Bibliography

Brooks, Lisa. *Our Beloved Kin: A New History of King Philip's War.* Yale University Press, 2018.

Carney, Judith A. *Black Rice: The African Origins of Rice Cultivation in the Americas.* Harvard University Press, 2002.

Fickes, Michael L. "'They Could Not Endure That Yoke': The Captivity of Pequot Women and Children after the War of 1637." *New England Quarterly* 73, no. 1 (2000): 58–81.

Hartigan-O'Connor, Ellen. *The Ties That Buy : Women and Commerce in Revolutionary America.* University of Pennsylvania Press, 2009.

Johnson, Jessica Marie. *Wicked Flesh: Black Women, Intimacy, and Freedom in the Atlantic World.* University of Pennsylvania Press, 2020.

Little, Ann M. *Abraham in Arms : War and Gender in Colonial New England.* University of Pennsylvania Press, 2007.

Merritt, Jane T. *The Trouble with Tea: The Politics of Consumption in the Eighteenth-Century Global Economy.* Johns Hopkins University Press, 2017.

Morrissey, Robert Michael. "Kaskaskia Social Network: Kinship and Assimilation in the French-Illinois Borderlands, 1695–1735." *The William and Mary Quarterly* 70, no. 1 (2013): 103–46. **https://doi.org/10.5309/willmaryquar.70.1.0103**.

Norton, Mary Beth. *In the Devil's Snare : The Salem Witchcraft Crisis of 1692*. Alfred A. Knopf, 2002.

Romney, Susanah Shaw. *New Netherland Connections: Intimate Networks and Atlantic Ties in Seventeenth-Century America*. University of North Carolina Press, 2014.

Simpson, Audra. "From White into Red: Captivity Narratives as Alchemies of Race and Citizenship." *American Quarterly* 60, no. 2 (2008): 251–257.

Sleeper-Smith, Susan. *Indian Women and French Men: Rethinking Cultural Encounter in the Western Great Lakes*. University of Massachusetts Press, 2001.

Toulouse, Teresa A. *The Captive's Position: Female Narrative, Male Identity, and Royal Authority in Colonial New England*. University of Pennsylvania Press, 2006.

CHAPTER 5

Rebellion and Revolution, 1750–1800

The American Revolution and the ideals of liberty and equality it was fought for had deeper historical roots in conflict over land, gendered political rights, and racial hierarchy. Enslaved communities struggled for freedom from the first arrival of kidnapped Africans in North America through the successful Haitian Revolution in 1794, while Indigenous nations resisted settler encroachment on their lands and infringement of their sovereignty through both diplomacy and war. White settler entitlement to both enslaved Black labor and Indigenous lands laid the foundation for the political conflicts of the 1760s that led to the American Revolution.

British gender ideology informed American concepts of political rights. British gender roles that constructed white women as ideally weak, passive, chaste, and domestic were used as a tool of violence against Black, Indigenous, and poor white women who fell outside these bounds and used to justify violence against those who resisted. Gender excluded all women in British colonies from political participation and economic self-determination. White men's gender identity was directly connected to the privilege of land owning, political representation, and economic independence. Indigenous women who fought to retain their own lands, Black women who resisted enslavement, and poor white women who were unable to secure the protections of a marriage directly threatened the gendered social order these male privileges were built on. During the course of the American Revolution, Indigenous, Black, and settler women navigated many roles to advocate for themselves and their communities. The Declaration of Independence and the radicalism of the American Revolution grew out of a gendered understanding that women were to be excluded from the public sphere of politics and representation, and an attack on men's political participation was an attack on their masculinity as well. Gender was central to the question of what the Revolution was fought for and who would belong to the new nation.

American Women's History: A New Narrative History, First Edition. Melissa E. Blair, Vanessa M. Holden, and Maeve Kane.
© 2024 John Wiley & Sons, Inc. Published 2024 by John Wiley & Sons, Inc.

Resistance Before Revolution

Enslaved women and men struggled for their freedom in many ways before, during, and after the American Revolution. Africans enslaved at one of the very first North American colonies, the failed Spanish colony of San Miguel de Gualdape in what is now South Carolina, rebelled in 1526 by burning several Spanish houses and seeking refuge with the nearby Guale Indigenous nation, where they may have intermarried with Indigenous people. Resistance and rebellion were always part of the experience of enslavement.

Enslavers punished resistance and rebellion harshly. In order for the system of slavery to function, constant violence was necessary to extract unpaid labor and justify the continued dehumanization of enslaved people. Writing much later in 1829 as the United States began to struggle with the question of ending slavery, North Carolina Supreme Court justice Thomas Ruffin wrote that "the power of the master must be absolute to render the submission of the slave perfect." Ruffin ruled in one of many legal decisions that declared that enslaved people had no right to physical safety or even life itself. Enslaved people who attempted to resist in large and small ways were punished with everything from execution, execution of loved ones, sale away from family, beating, sexual violence, and amputation of ears, noses, fingers, and limbs.

White women participated in this enforcement through violence in ways that reinforced their own place in the intersecting hierarchy of race and gender. When Alida Livingston suspected the enslaved Joe of faking sickness, she punished him by using her role as the female head of household in her husband's absence. White women, especially elite and middle-class women who supervised large households that included enslaved people and servants, were expected to provide medical care for those in their households. When Joe protested that he could not work because of illness, Livingston prescribed bleeding, sweating, and a course of medication to make him vomit. All of these remedies were common in the eighteenth century but forced vomiting and the draining of blood would have left Joe as weakened as if he had been beaten. As a woman, Livingston did not directly inflict physical violence on Joe when she suspected his resistance, but she used female-gendered medical care to inflict retaliatory violence against him until he returned to work "reasonably healthy." Violence was necessary to uphold the system of slavery and white supremacy, and the way people like Alida Livingston upheld it was shaped by their own place in the racial and gender social order.

Enslaved women's ability to resist and navigate their enslavement was shaped by their gender. Few enslaved women directly took part in the largest North American armed slave rebellions like the 1739 Stono Rebellion in South Carolina or the 1712 New York City slave revolt, although some did, like the unnamed pregnant woman who was executed for her part in the New York revolt. Enslaved women's duty of care for children and elders, as well as their vulnerability to sexual assault, made them more likely to participate in other forms of resistance like visiting family without permission, working slowly, ruining crops or breaking tools, or ending unwanted pregnancies. In the aftermath of both the 1712 and 1739 revolts, enslaved women with children self-emancipated at greater rates as colonial legislatures placed ever more restrictions on enslaved peoples' lives and the possibility of manumission.

Pregnancy and childbirth restricted enslaved women's ability to self-emancipate. Enslaved women were most able to escape slavery alone, early in pregnancy, with small newborns, or with older children who could walk on their own. The later stages of pregnancy or carrying an older infant may have made it too difficult or dangerous for many enslaved women to self-emancipate until their children were older. Women with small children who did escape tended to do so in family groups, like Dinah and her husband Cudjoe, who escaped from a South Carolina plantation with their eight-year-old and two-year-old children, along with another couple, Quane and Mingo and their three-year-old child. With more adults, it may have been easier for this family group to carry small children long distances to freedom.

Some of these families found refuge in remote, difficult to reach areas like the Great Dismal Swamp in what is now Virginia and North Carolina. Communities of self-emancipated former enslaved people were able to form in areas like this because they were poor for agriculture and difficult to navigate. This made the area unattractive for the expansion of plantation slavery and difficult to reach for slave catchers. Archeologists estimate that several hundred to several thousand people made homes in the Great Dismal Swamp in the eighteenth and nineteenth centuries. Conditions in the Great Dismal Swamp were harsh, with many venomous snakes, swarms of mosquitoes, and frequent flooding. The harsh conditions made it possible for self-emancipated people to form communities there without the threat of losing their families or freedom to the growing North American slave trade.

Women's Land and Women's Lives

By the mid-eighteenth century, gender roles in many Indigenous nations had changed significantly. European imperial land claims and white squatters increasingly threatened the security of many Indigenous women's lands. For New England Indigenous groups, debt, precarious day labor, and indenture to English settlers increasingly shaped family life after the loss of their territories from the wars of the seventeenth century.

One young Mohegan woman, Hannah Nonesuch, was indentured to English neighbors in Connecticut starting in 1751 at age 4. These indentureships were intended to teach young English and Indigenous girls and boys the skills necessary for farm and housework, but over the course of the eighteenth century, Indigenous children's indentures grew much longer than English childrens' indentures, often lasting long into adulthood. At age 14, Hannah's parents with the assistance of a white missionary had her sent to Moor's Indian Charity School, one of the first Indian boarding schools in what is now the United States. At Moor's, Hannah learned to read and write, but she again served an indentureship with a white family until age 19, when she married a fellow Mohegan student. Moor's had been founded to train New England Indigenous men as missionaries to the Haudenosaunee and train Indigenous women to be missionaries' wives. For a year, Hannah and her husband David evangelized in an Oneida community before returning home to Mohegan. There, they supported themselves through a precarious combination of David's day labor for English farmers and Hannah's sewing and broommaking. Although their experience as missionaries was unusual, their experience of childhood indentureship and adulthood poverty was common for many New England Indigenous people who lacked the security of national territories.

Other Indigenous groups were very aware of the gendered changes experienced by New England Indigenous groups and worked to prevent such changes in their own communities. When Moor's proposed sending more missionaries to Seneca territory in 1761, Seneca speaker for the women Onghwadeckha rejected the proposal because of the changes to gendered labor missionaries wished to make in Seneca communities. Among the Seneca and other Haudenosaunee nations, the speaker for the women was a male speaker who was tasked with expressing the wishes of the clan mothers in negotiations with Europeans. On behalf of the clan mothers, Onghwadeckha asked "how many remnants of tribes to the East are so reduced, that they pound sticks to make brooms, to buy a loaf of Bread or it may be a shirt . . .. This will be the condition of our children in a short time if we change or renounce our religion for that of the white people . . .. We shall be sunk so low as to chop wood, stoop down and milk cows like negroes among the Dutch people." Seneca clan mothers barred the missionaries from their communities because they were well aware of the English racialized hierarchy and the changes to gendered labor it would bring in their communities.

Some Indigenous women opposed settler intrusions more directly. British settler surveying of the Ohio Valley and increasing numbers of British American settlers squatting on Indigenous land in the 1750s caused conflict with groups like the Shawnee who objected to illegal settlement on their lands. The Seven Years' War (1754–1763) resolved competing British and French imperial claims when France ceded its North American territories to Great Britain in order to keep its lucrative plantation slave colonies in the Caribbean. However, settler pressure on formerly French-allied nations like the Shawnee only increased after the war. In the late years of the war, the Delaware Prophet Neolin preached a prophetic vision that rejecting European agriculture, returning to traditional gender roles, and removing white settlers from the Ohio Valley would protect Shawnee and Delaware lands. A female Shawnee chief named Nonhelema Hokolesqua led warriors alongside her brother Cornstalk and her husband Moluntha to eject British forts and settlers from the Ohio Valley. She earned a reputation as a feared warrior that she would carry into the American Revolution. Nonhelema Hokolesqua's direct military leadership was unusual for Indigenous women, but her opposition to settler expansion was not. Other women protested the presence of white traders, missionaries, and settlers in their territories by complaining to British government officials, refusing to allow the intruders in their territories, and by supporting wars like the one Nonhelema Hokolesqua led.

Gender and Liberty

To prevent further conflict with western Indigenous nations, in 1763 the British government prohibited further white settlement west of the Appalachian mountains, known as the Proclamation Line. This was among the first of a series of conflicts between British Americans and the British government that would eventually lead to the American Revolution. On their surface, the conflicts of the 1760s and 1770s were not overtly about gender, but many of them were informed by British American gender ideology. Settler, Indigenous, and free and enslaved Black women of all levels of society also participated in the conflicts of the Revolutionary era in ways informed by intersections of gender, race, class, and nation.

White settler anger over the Proclamation Line was informed by gendered expectations for the expansion of the British colonies. In almost all British colonies, property was a requirement to vote along with age and gender. The amount of property required to vote varied in different colonies, but in all colonies, an adult white man who owned no property could not vote, placing him in a similar political position to white women, children, and free Black men. Property was seen as proof that a man was not dependent on anyone else for his livelihood, as women and children were seen as dependent, and therefore his political opinions were not shaped by anyone else. As the population of the British colonies grew, land became more difficult for men to acquire. Settlement further west had been a solution to this issue but seizing land from Indigenous groups like the Shawnee who did not wish to sell provoked bloody, protracted border wars throughout the eighteenth century. As in the seventeenth century, these conflicts escalated.

For settler families, the presence of women and children helped establish a legal claim to land and obliged the British and colonial governments to protect settler families from the Indian attack. For the Shawnee and other Indigenous nations, the presence of settler women and children on their land indicated an intention for permanent seizure of their land that previous male-only, itinerant fur traders did not threaten. Indigenous attacks against white women and children were taken by settlers as symbolic of Indian "savagery" and used to justify settler attacks against Indigenous women and children in an attempt to eliminate the ability of Indigenous communities to reproduce themselves.

When the British government prohibited white settlement past the Proclamation Line in 1763, it signaled to many British Americans who wished to seize Indigenous lands that it would become ever more difficult for men to acquire land and become voters and that the British government would not protect their families against Indian attacks. This fear of Indian attacks would later be listed as the final, and greatest, grievance of the colonists against the British government that allowed the "undistinguished destruction of all ages, sexes and conditions" on the frontier.

The gendered fear of political disenfranchisement was intensified by conflicts over taxation in the 1760s and 1770s, beginning with the Sugar Act in 1764 and the Stamp Act in 1765. Earlier in the seventeenth and eighteenth centuries, British Parliament had occasionally imposed import or export taxes on certain goods to encourage colonial consumption of British manufactures or prohibit trade with colonies of other European powers. These measures were rarely enforced; however, colonial assemblies exercised authority over taxation and spending within their own colonies.

With the imposition of the Sugar and Stamp Acts and later Townshend Duties, many British Americans believed that the British Parliament had placed even property-owning, voting white men in a dependent political position. Under the doctrine of virtual representation, the British House of Commons within Parliament was believed to represent every resident of the British empire, including those who could not vote like the poor, women, or residents of major British cities like Manchester who were traditionally not represented by a House of Commons district. However, colonial property-owning men had grown used to more direct representation in their own colonial assemblies and objected to indirect, dependent political representation.

Remember the Ladies

As the tensions of the 1760s escalated, women at all levels of society participated in political discourse. Elite and middle-class women who were against the new taxes boycotted goods, while poorer women participated in street protests and riots. Although barred by custom from publicly participating in political debate, some women expressed their discontent in print as well. After the 1770 Boston Massacre, Mercy Otis Warren anonymously published a play titled *The Adulateur* in a Boston newspaper, which harshly criticized the British government and the British governor of Massachusetts' handling of the incident. Warren's writing was anonymous not only because of her political opinion but also because of her gender. Many British women in the seventeenth and eighteenth centuries published anonymously or under pseudonyms due to disapproval of women speaking in public spaces.

This stemmed in part from a belief in women's inherent intellectual inferiority to men. This was used to justify women's political exclusion, women's legal and economic coverture in marriage, and the lack of opportunities for women's education. This did not prevent many women like Warren from writing or prevent other women from pursuing education, running businesses, or managing their families' property. The ideals of the revolutionary era caused many women to begin questioning traditional gender roles, including women's responsibility to carry many pregnancies and raise large families. Although herbal remedies to regulate menstruation were known, as discussed in chapter three, the ideology of settler colonialism encouraged large white families and many women practiced lifelong childbearing in which they bore as many pregnancies as they were able to. Beginning in the 1760s, this began to change for middle and upper class free white women who increasingly limited their pregnancies through contraception and family planning. Elite women like Esther De Berdt Reed began to limit their pregnancies through the use of contraceptives, part of a broader argument that women were rational, restrained, and in control of their own bodies. Upper- and middle-class women increasingly positioned themselves as rational thinkers in contrast to the arguments that women were emotional, unrestrained, and unsuited for business and politics, and regulating their fertility was part of this.

Despite these changes, women remained limited in their social and legal rights and opportunities, and the upheavals of the Revolutionary era brought these limitations into focus for many women. Especially for families where husbands were called away for business, politics, or war, wives managed their families' property as "deputy husbands." During the war, Abigail Smith Adams, the wife of revolutionary John Adams, managed the couple's property in John's absence. In her letters, she began to refer to the property as her own, rather than his or their joint property, indicating her growing sense of ownership over it.

It was in this context that Adams admonished her husband to "remember the ladies" in 1776 as the Second Continental Congress began drafting the Declaration of Independence. The right to vote was not yet a major concern for American women. Adam's letter to her husband instead focused on the precarious legal place of women, who lacked formal education and were barred from managing their own property. In the eighteenth-century ideal of companionate marriage, husbands were supposed to protect their wives in a relationship based on mutual love, but married women had next to no legal protection from financial or physical abuse. Married women had no protection from rape or physical violence from their husbands and no access to divorce except on grounds of abandonment. Adams asked her husband to increase women's protection under the new laws, telling him to "not put such unlimited power into the hands of the husbands. Remember all men would be tyrants if they could."

Abigail Adams' reminder to remember the ladies was not a radical one. She made the suggestion to her husband in a private letter, not a public forum, and she suggested only that married women should have some protection from financial, sexual, and physical abuse. She did not mention rights like voting, divorce, education, child custody, or ownership of property that would later become central to the suffrage and women's rights movements. Her private suggestion for legal reform followed logically from both the cultural ideal of companionate marriage and the ideals of the American Revolution, but did not seek to wholly reshape marriage. In response, her husband John wrote that he could not "but laugh" at the absurdity of her suggestion and joked that he feared the "Despotism of the Peticoat" if such reforms were enacted because men were already subject to women in every respect except legally. John Adams' dismissive rejection of Abigail Adams' reminder to remember the ladies would echo through the following decades and the marginalization of women's rights for much of the early years of the new nation.

Cannons Roaring

In many ways, the American Revolution and the Declaration of Independence were truly radical in ways that would have long-term consequences throughout the world by proposing the absolute equality of all people. In other ways, the Revolution and Declaration were very much products of their time, especially with respect to gender and the position of women. The Declaration of Independence did not mention women in its opening statement that "all *men* are created equal." This absence and the way the radicalism of the revolution fell short of its ideals would become ever more apparent as the new government of the United States failed to change the legal position of women, to the point that the 1848 Declaration of Sentiments on women's rights used the rhetoric and structure of the Declaration of Independence to propose the radical sentiment that "all men *and women* are created equal." The only place women were mentioned explicitly in the Declaration of Independence was in the most serious colonial accusation against the British government, that they had failed to protect white women and families from Indian attacks. White women were used in this way as a rhetorical tool to emphasize the racial danger of Indigenous people, even as women were excluded from the political rights they were used to claim.

This inherent contradiction at the foundation of the Revolution did not prevent individual women from making their own declarations or participating in the war. Newspaper printer Mary Katherine Goddard was the first printer to publish the Declaration in full in her paper *The Maryland Journal*, and in her printing, Goddard added her name alongside the male signers of the Declaration. In doing so, she both risked a charge of treason and sedition against the British Crown and symbolically positioned herself as a signatory of the Declaration.

With the outbreak of fighting at Lexington and Concord in 1775 and the deepening of armed conflict in 1776, women participated in the war both willingly and unwillingly. Fighting near towns forced families to either shelter in place or try to flee to safety regardless of which side they supported, while sieges such as the British bombardment of New York City in 1776 trapped families in their homes. One New York mother wrote to her daughter that she sheltered from "cannons roaring, drums beating to arms all things in confusion . . . [while] the bullets flew thick over our heads."

War disrupted the lives of many women, from the danger of battle to disruptions in trade to family divisions. Many Americans experienced the Revolution as a civil war, with neighbors and family members turned against one another. When 18-year-old Lucy Flucker, daughter of prominent Loyalist and Crown-appointed Massachusetts secretary Thomas Fluker, secretly married a man her family believed to be beneath her social station, she was disowned. During the war, Lucy Flucker Knox was isolated from her Loyalist family while her husband Henry Knox led the Continental Army's artillery. Politics and war divided her family, and Lucy Knox wrote frequently of the difficulty in choosing between her husband and her family.

Some elite women like Lucy Knox and Abigail Adams were able to choose whether to stay in their homes or follow their husbands as Martha Washington, wife of George Washington, did. Gender allowed some of these women to serve the Continental and Loyalist causes in ways that were more difficult or dangerous than for men. Angelica Schuyler, who would later be a sister-in-law of Alexander Hamilton, passed information on British troop movements and supplies to her father Philip Schuyler, a Continental Army officer. As a woman, Schuyler was able to attend balls and hear information through gossip networks that were not otherwise available to the Continental Army. Loyalist Lorena Holmes slipped past Continental Army guards intended to stop messages to the British Army, confident that soldiers would not shoot a woman even when she was spotted. When she was later caught by a mob and accused of carrying letters between the British Army and other Loyalists, her punishment was also gendered. The local Committee of Safety stripped her and forced her to pose naked in a window as punishment, intending to humiliate and violate her for stepping outside the bounds of proper feminine behavior. Holmes continued to carry information for the British throughout the war and later received a pension for her service.

Other women followed their husbands during the war. Many poorer women followed their husbands who enlisted with the Continental Army or as Loyalist volunteers for lack of other economic options. Known as followers of the army, these women and their children provided important services for their male family members and other soldiers. Before the nineteenth century, armies were logistically unable to provide essential services like laundry, nursing, and cooking to enlisted soldiers. Female followers were often stereotyped as prostitutes, but most were married to soldiers and supported themselves and their families by receiving money or rations in exchange for the logistical support they provided the army.

During battle, these women often provided additional logistical support such as carrying ammunition and water to soldiers and tending to the wounded. A handful of these women, including Margaret Cochran Corbin and Mary Ludwig Hays (the basis for the "Molly Pitcher" story) were granted pensions by the later United States government in recognition of their service during battle. Other people who were assumed female at birth, including white soldiers Deborah Sampson and Anna Maria Lane and a free solider of African descent named Sally St. Clair, assumed men's dress and served as soldiers during the war. Sampson and Lane both received veterans' pensions for their military service and both returned to women's dress and gender roles after the war, while St. Clair died during battle. Some women may have temporarily assumed male dress for economic or patriotic reasons; other people assumed female at birth may have taken the opportunity to present as male. Due to the necessity of hiding their assumed gender, it is unknown how many other people who were assumed female at birth may have assumed male roles during the war or continued to live as men after the war. The outbreak of war created both difficulties and opportunities that people like Corbin, Hays, Sampson, Lane, and St. Clair chose to navigate in different ways. War created a temporary space in which gender roles could be relaxed or altered or the boundary between male and female genders could be crossed with less social disapproval than in times of peace.

Enslaved women also seized some opportunities presented by war. In 1775, the British governor of Virginia John Moore, Earl of Dunmore, declared martial law and deemed all colonists who took up arms against the government traitors, a capital offense. In an effort to economically damage wealthy plantation owners, create fear of slave rebellions, and bolster his own small force of only 300 soldiers, Lord Dunmore's Proclamation also granted freedom to any enslaved or indentured person who could reach British lines and bear arms. Explicitly limited to only enslaved men, Lord Dunmore's Proclamation was not an altruistic or moral stance against slavery.

Nonetheless, thousands of enslaved women, men, and children self-emancipated by fleeing to British-held territory. By the end of the war in 1783, more than one hundred thousand formerly enslaved people had freed themselves. Free Black and formerly enslaved men served in both Continental and Loyalist units in large numbers throughout the war. As of 1772, slavery was illegal in Britain itself and setting foot in Britain automatically freed an enslaved person under British law, leading many self-emancipated people to hope that the British government would confirm the freedom promised by Lord Dunmore's Proclamation.

Formerly enslaved women found that their situation was much more precarious than formerly enslaved men's. Without the option to enlist as soldiers, self-emancipated women found themselves working for little or no pay in British camps. Sixteen-year-old Deborah Squash fled from George Washington's plantation Mount Vernon in 1781, only to find that the British Army camp had little food and an outbreak of smallpox. By some estimates, as many as half of all formerly enslaved people who fled to the British died before the end of the war. Squash survived, and at the end of the war she and her husband Henry successfully evacuated from New York City with the British to freedom in British Canada.

The Society of Patriotic Ladies

The widespread availability of newspapers helped some women seize new legal rights and advocate for themselves. Women's political activity also received increasing pushback in the press. As the American public wrestled with the question of women's place in the new nation, the gendered image of the new nation changed as well.

Printings and readings of the Declaration of Independence and new state constitutions led some women to question their legal rights. In 1780, an enslaved woman named Elizabeth Freeman heard the new Massachusetts state constitution read. Although herself illiterate, Freeman took her case to a lawyer and said, "I heard that paper read yesterday, that says, all men are created equal, and that every man has a right to freedom. I'm not a dumb critter; won't the law give me my freedom?" When Freeman won her 1781 suit for freedom, her case set the important legal precedent that slavery was illegal in Massachusetts and she became the first Black person to sue for freedom in the new United States.

Elite white women used newspapers and broadsides to argue for women's involvement in both the war effort and public life more broadly. Wealthy women like Esther de Berdt Reed and Martha Washington organized ladies' associations to collect cash donations and sew clothing for soldiers, organized through a network of Continental Army officers' wives and governors' wives. De Berdt Reed published an anonymous broadside publicizing the effort, in which she argued that "if the weakness of our Constitution, if opinion and manners did not forbid us to march to glory by the same paths as the Men, we should at least equal, and sometimes surpass them in our love for the public good." In a single summer, the ladies' associations raised more than $300,000 (the equivalent of more than six million dollars in 2020). Both Freeman and De Berdt Reed's advocacy for the equality of women and men raised the question of what women's place in the new republic would be.

Women's political efforts were not welcomed by all. While newspapers could be used as a tool for advocacy, they were also used to mock women's political acts. When the real ladies' association of Edenton, North Carolina met to agree on a tea boycott in 1774, they exercised one of the few political tools available to them as women and joined many other women and men in refusing to buy taxed goods as a form of protest. A political cartoon circulated in England caricatured the meeting by depicting the women as ugly, neglectful mothers ("A society of patriotic ladies, at Edenton in North Carolina, 1775" **https://www.loc.gov/resource/ppmsca.19468**). The cartoon satirized women of all classes as foolish, showing lower class women in the background drinking from a punch bowl, middle class women being tricked by merchants, and elite women playing at politics while neglecting the child under the table and the dog who urinates on their feet. The presence of a Black enslaved woman in the background further satirized the white women as hypocrites who supported the political cause of liberty while enslaving others.

As Americans wrestled with the question of women's place in political life, images of women symbolizing the new nation evolved as well. Symbolic depictions of "America" in the seventeenth and early eighteenth century depicted North America in "Indian" dress as a nude woman with a feathered headdress and skirt. These depictions emphasized the supposed exoticism, availability, and fertility of the continent. (Previously discussed in chapter two with the engraving "Allegory of America.") Over the course of the American Revolution, symbolic depictions of a female America evolved. In 1774, the political cartoon "The able doctor, or, America swallowing the bitter draught," (**https://www.loc.gov/resource/cph.3g05289**) depicted the American colonies as a white American woman being held down and sexually assaulted by British politicians who poured tea (symbolizing unjust taxes) down her throat.

Symbolic depictions of America as an exoticized Indian woman continued to coexist alongside newer portrayals, but the United States was increasingly symbolized by "Columbia." Columbia was depicted as a white woman in a toga, positioning the new nation as the inheritor of Greco-Roman democratic traditions. In 1775, the enslaved poet Phillis Wheatley described Columbia as "The Goddess comes, she moves divinely fair / Olive and laurel binds Her golden hair." Wheatley's poem alluded to her belief that the promises of American liberty had not yet been fulfilled for enslaved people when she wrote, "Fix'd are the eyes of nations on the scales / For in their hopes Columbia's arm prevails." Wheatley had been born in what is now Senegal or Gambia and kidnapped into slavery at age seven and later wrote and published poetry with the support of the white Boston family that enslaved her. Wheatly criticized the hypocrisy and barbarity of slavery in 1772 when she wrote "Remember, *Christians, Negroes*, black as *Cain*, /May be refin'd and join th' angelic train," tying together ideas of religious and political equality she would later allude to in her Columbia poem.

A War Against Vegetables

Indigenous women and their nations faced many difficult choices during the Revolutionary era. For many groups, neutrality seemed the best course early in the war. Indigenous people knew the British Americans who declared independence as neighbors or illegal squatters, but many Indigenous nations had long-standing treaty relationships with the British government. This led many groups to attempt to stay neutral, framing the conflict as a family disagreement between the British father and his American children. As pressure to formally ally with the British or Americans mounted and some Indigenous nations sought to secure title to their lands, many groups found their nations divided about the best course to take.

Many New England Indigenous groups allied with and fought for the Continental Army early in the war. Many believed this to be the best course to secure recognition of their nations that had been under threat since the seventeenth century. One Mohegan widow, Rebecca Tanner, lost all five of her sons to battle during the course of the war. Losses like these put enormous strain on economically and legally marginalized Indigenous nations like the Mohegan.

The question of neutrality or war deeply divided many nations. Nonhelema, discussed earlier in this chapter, favored neutrality for her nation during the Revolution. During the earlier French and Indian War, the Shawnee had been allied against the British with the French to eject British settlers from their territory. With the outbreak of the Revolution, many Shawnee hoped that allying with the British against the Americans would finally oust American squatters from their territories. Nonhelema and her brother Cornstalk instead sought neutrality as a path to negotiation for recognition of their lands with the Continental Congress. This ended disastrously for Cornstalk when he was held hostage and killed by Continental soldiers angry about attacks made by British-allied Shawnee. Nonhelema herself lived through the war but lived to see American settlers, angry over continued Shawnee resistance to illegal squatters, destroy the town of Maquachake her family had established as a refuge from the earlier upheavals of the Seven Years' War.

Further south, Shawnee allies the Cherokee faced a similar choice between neutrality and war. In the 1750s, Nanyehi Nancy Ward had been named a Beloved Woman of the Cherokee for her leadership in war against the Creek and Choctaw nations, a title that gave her a vote and a significant political voice in the Cherokee General Council. Ward, like many other Cherokee women, had taken an Irish American husband and integrated some elements of settler material culture, like raising cows for dairy and weaving cotton. As a leader of her people, Ward attempted to navigate a difficult position. She opposed land sales but believed European style farming would secure title to her nation's lands. Other Cherokee, led by her cousin Tsiyu Gansini Dragging Canoe, allied with the Shawnee, Delaware, and other groups who believed American settlers had to be ejected from their lands at all costs. In negotiations with Americans, Ward appealed to American women as fellow mothers and guardians of life. "Let your women hear our words," she asked at the 1781 peace treaty between the United States and the Cherokee.

Choices for neutrality or alliance like those made by Ward, Nonhelema, and other Indigenous leaders made a significant difference to British and Continental war efforts because of the significant resources Indigenous women controlled. Like many other nations, the Six Nations of the Haudenosaunee were divided on the question of neutrality, British alliance, or American alliance in the early stages of the war. Many Oneida and Tuscarora eventually sided with the Continental Army, swayed by promises that their lands would be secure from encroachment and illegal seizures after the war. Those lands, and the women who worked them, proved pivotal to the American war effort. In the first harsh winter of the Revolution during 1777–1778, George Washington's army at Valley Forge faced severe hardships and food shortages as the new army's logistical capabilities were stretched to breaking.

About 1 in 10 Continental soldiers died of starvation or disease while encamped at Valley Forge for the winter. A group of 50 American-allied Oneida, led by Polly Cooper, relieved Washington's troops by delivering hundreds of bushels of corn to the starving soldiers.

In recognition of the military and economic significance of Haudenosaunee women's lands and the food they could supply, the following fall of 1779, Washington ordered a months-long campaign against the previously neutral Seneca, Cayuga, and other western communities of the Haudenosaunee who refused to ally with the Americans. This campaign was widely described as a "war against vegetables" because the campaign burned hundreds of thousands of acres of cornfields, orchards, and vegetable fields. Washington ordered that "parties should be detached to lay waste all the settlements around, with injunctions to do it in the most effectual manner, that the country may not be merely overrun, but destroyed." Rather than a war against vegetables, the campaign was a war against women. The campaign's explicit intent was to terrorize neutral Indigenous communities, which the Americans believed to be supplying food and information to the British. One leader of the campaign wrote that "should we be so fortunate as to take a considerable number of the women and children of the Indians I conceive that we should then have the means of preventing them from acting hostilely against us." Although Seneca and Cayuga towns successfully evacuated ahead of the Continental Army, resulting in few deaths, clan lineage lands were devastated and food supplies destroyed just before harvest time. In the early years of the American Republic, the Haudenosaunee lands that became western New York were celebrated as the breadbasket of the new nation.

Infant Liberty Nursed by Mother Mob

With the 1783 treaty of peace between the new United States and Great Britain, residents of the new American nation struggled with the fundamental tension between the ideals of liberty and equality and the continuing political disenfranchisement of women, dehumanization of enslaved people, and dispossession of Indigenous nations. The Articles of Confederation (1781–1789) and the Constitution (1789) attempted to resolve the tension between federal authority, state authority, and individual liberty, but did not fundamentally change the status of women or enslaved people within the nation. As had been the case before the Revolution, the basic building block of society was viewed as the household, rather than the individual, in which women were politically represented by their husbands or fathers and therefore were not invested with votes of their own.

White women nonetheless navigated these restrictions to advocate for new roles for themselves, both politically and socially. Judith Sargeant Murray's 1790 essay "On the Equality of the Sexes" argued for the spiritual and intellectual equality of men and women and criticized the lack of educational opportunities for women. When women had voted in the Elizabeth, New Jersey election of 1797, they were criticized by one male writer who argued that "it is evident, that women, generally, are neither, by nature, nor habit, nor education, nor by their necessary condition in society, fitted to perform this duty with credit to themselves, or advantage to the public." Murray's essay criticized this widely held belief by drawing on beliefs of spiritual equality that spread with the populist religious movements of the First and Second Great Awakenings. Murray argued that the difference in women and men's abilities were the product of education, since even between a brother and a sister, "one is taught to aspire, and the other is early confined and limited." In 1790, New Jersey had become the first state to explicitly allow unmarried white women and free people of color who owned property to vote. The 1797 election in Elizabeth was decided by a narrow margin of only 93 votes, making it clear that the inclusion of women and people of color as voters could swing an election. In 1807, the New Jersey legislature restricted the vote to only white men who met the property qualification as part of a broader national backlash against the political inclusion of white women and free people of color, but like Abigail Adams' earlier admonishment to remember the ladies and Phillis Wheatley's critique of slavery, Murray's essay and women's voting in New Jersey suggest that many people were reevaluating the political roles of women in the revolutionary era.

Murray and other women argued for education for women and girls both for their own sake, and for the sake of the sons they would educate. Most children's education was provided in the home before the advent of widespread public schooling. Citizenship in the early American republic was believed to require informed, educated male citizens who could understand political issues rather than blindly following populist politicians. Women's education was therefore seen as increasingly necessary to raise sons who would understand and uphold republican virtues. Historians call this concept "republican motherhood." Although republican motherhood reinforced the idea of women's domestic sphere separate from men's public sphere and was mainly restricted to middle- and upper-class white women, it nonetheless laid the foundation for the expansion of women's political and social rights in later years.

American emphasis on separate spheres created tension in negotiating foundational treaties with Indigenous nations. At the 1794 Treaty of Canandaigua between the United States and the Six Nations of the Haudenosaunee, which still governs US-Haudenosaunee relations today, disagreement over women's voice in public spaces was a central point of conflict. The US Commissioner negotiating the treaty, Timothy Pickering, attempted to bar all Haudenosaunee women from even attending the treaty. Pickering lacked the power to enforce this. At the treaty, negotiations were interrupted by the Public Universal Friend. The Friend had been named Jemima Wilkinson and assumed female at birth, but by 1794 identified as a genderless embodiment of the holy spirit.

The Friend asked the Haudenosaunee to grant their religious community of unmarried women a tract of land on which to build a settlement. The Friend's appearance was part of a broader upswelling of populist preaching by both women and men during the Second Great Awakening. Pickering apologized to the Haudenosaunee for the interruption, saying that he had only allowed the Friend to speak out of American politeness to women. In response, three Oneida clan mothers stood to respond to both Pickering and the Friend. They called on the Americans to repent, using the religious language the Friend had used, and took Pickering to task for attempting to exclude Haudenosaunee women from the meeting. The Oneida clan matrons argued that it was "they that made the men," and controlled Haudenosaunee lands, so it was only proper that the Americans should hear from Haudenosaunee women. The terms of the treaty that were negotiated ultimately secured a large portion of Haudenosaunee lands and recognized the sovereignty of the Haudenosaunee set their own laws, and remains in effect. This disagreement over women's diplomatic roles between an Indigenous group, the American government, and an American assumed female at birth encapsulates the conflicting understandings of women's place in public in the early years of the republic.

These gendered and racialized tensions about liberty, democracy, and equality came to the fore with the beginning of the Haitian Revolution in 1791. The French colony of Haiti was one of the most brutal and most profitable slave economies of the Atlantic world. The island produced the majority of the coffee and sugar imported into Europe, and enslaved people outnumbered free people eight to one. The brutal labor demanded for sugar and coffee production caused a very high death rate among the enslaved population. The 1789 French Revolution and the French Declaration of the Rights of Man and of the Citizen caused many white plantation owners in Haiti to fear that slavery would be abolished in the colony. Free Black men who demanded the right to vote and full citizenship were brutally executed, while white planters discussed independence from France as necessary to protect the legality of slavery. Many enslaved people feared full independence for the colony, which would leave the already harsh treatment of the planters unchecked by public opinion in France and believed that the execution of free Black men showed that white planter power on the island had to be destroyed, not negotiated with.

In August 1791, an enslaved woman named Cécile Fatiman and a self-emancipated man named Dutty Boukman performed a religious ceremony that brought together enslaved people from a number of neighboring plantations. The ceremony at once affirmed the participants' African heritage and gave them an opportunity to organize mass resistance across multiple plantations. Within 10 days, the successful slave revolt took control of the northern portion of the island. Black women like Marie-Jeanne Lamartinière, Victoria Montou, and Sanité Belair participated in many roles in the Haitian Revolution, from caring for the sick to taking up arms.

As the successful revolt took control of more parts of the island, white planters fled to other colonies, including the new United States and the Spanish colony of Louisiana. For many Americans, news of the Haitian Revolution's success stoked fears of slave rebellions and unchecked mob democracy. Political cartoons circulated with images of Black revolutionaries holding the heads of white women and children, while plantation owners in the United States harshly punished any perceived rebellion for fear of spreading slave revolts. These political cartoons played on stereotypes of violent Black men and vulnerable white women who needed to be protected from them. These stereotypes had grown out of and justified the brutality of slavery by at once rationalizing white violence and dehumanization of Black men, and by erasing the sexual assault and violence committed against Black women by white men. These stereotypes remain current and have often used in American history to justify violence in the twentieth and twenty-first centuries.

These fears filtered into domestic political conflicts as well. The 1807 political cartoon "Infant Liberty Nursed by Mother Mob" (**https://www.loc.gov/ item/2002705935**) expressed the combined American fears of unchecked democracy, women's political education, and Black freedom. In it, a white woman caricatured with African facial features and wearing a *tignon* cap nurses the "Infant Liberty" from breasts marked whiskey and rum. At her feet, one winged imp burns law books while another dries a dirty diaper marked "Mortals avant! 11,500," alluding to the 11,500 American prisoners of war who had died aboard British prison ships during the Revolution and who were remembered as martyrs to the cause of liberty. In the background, a mob pulls down a building in a scene echoing the demolition of the Bastille, one of the incidents that precipitated the French Revolution. This cartoon was published in a Federalist paper to attack the Jeffersonian Democratic-Republicans then in power. The Federalists supported a strong federal government with limited influence from everyday voters. This cartoon satirized the more populist

Democratic-Republicans as a danger to the laws of the United States and the legacy of the Revolution, drawing on fears of women's influence and the Haitian and French Revolutions.

Conclusion

The era of the American Revolution brought upheavals and changes to many women's lives. Indigenous women guided their nations to secure their communities' land and sovereignty. Enslaved and free Black women seized opportunities to self-emancipate and secure their freedom before, during, and after the Revolution. Settler, Black, and Indigenous women navigated the violence of war in many roles and participated in political discourse about what women's roles and the new nation would look like. Gender ideology underlays many of the political and diplomatic conflicts and fears of this period. Although the Revolution was fought for the ideals of liberty and equality, the unequal treatment of white women and both free and enslaved Black people under the law left fundamental questions of the extent of liberty unresolved.

Bibliography

Berkin, Carol. *Revolutionary Mothers: Women in the Struggle for America's Independence.* Vintage, 2006.

Brekus, Catherine A. *Strangers and Pilgrims: Female Preaching in America, 1740–1845.* University of North Carolina Press, 1998.

Cleves, Rachel Hope. *The Reign of Terror in America: Visions of Violence from Anti-Jacobinism to Antislavery.* Cambridge University Press, 2009.

Girard, Philippe. "Rebelles with a Cause: Women in the Haitian War of Independence, 1802–04." *Gender & History* 21, no. 1 (2009): 60–85. **https://doi.org/10.1111/j.1468-0424.2009.01535.x.**

Haulman, Kate. *The Politics of Fashion in Eighteenth-Century America. Gender and American Culture.* University of North Carolina Press, 2011.

Kane, Maeve. *Shirts Powdered Red: Haudenosaunee Gender, Trade, and Exchange Across Three Centuries.* Cornell University Press, 2023.

Kelley, Mary. *Learning to Stand and Speak: Women, Education, and Public Life in America's Republic.* University of North Carolina Press, 2008.

Kerber, Linda K. *Women of the Republic: Intellect and Ideology in Revolutionary America.* University of North Carolina Press, 1980.

Klepp, Susan E. *Revolutionary Conceptions: Women, Fertility, and Family Limitation in America, 1760–1820.* University of North Carolina Press, 2017.

Maskiell, Nicole. *Bound by Bondage: Slavery and the Creation of a Northern Gentry.* Cornell University Press, 2022.

Pearsall, Sarah. "Recentering Indian Women in the American Revolution." In *Why You Can't Teach United States History without American Indians,* 57–70, edited by Sleeper-Smith, Susan, Juliana Barr, Jean M O'Brien, Nancy Shoemaker, and Scott Manning Stevens. The University of North Carolina Press, 2015.

Perdue, Theda. *Cherokee Women: Gender and Culture Change 1700–1835.* University of Nebraska Press, 1998.

Sayers, Daniel O. *A Desolate Place for a Defiant People: The Archaeology of Maroons, Indigenous Americans, and Enslaved Laborers in the Great Dismal Swamp.* University Press of Florida, 2016.

PART II

Vanessa M. Holden

CHAPTER 6

Expansion and Division: The Women's Market Revolution, 1800–1820s

By January 1800, the original 13 United States had become 15. Just over the Appalachian Mountains, two news states, Kentucky, and Tennessee, were now a part of the union. In the imaginations of European Americans, they were the first of many states that other European Americans would carve out of a vast wilderness in the West. In the early decades of the nineteenth century, the West included all territories west of the Appalachian Mountains, the Far West lay west of the Mississippi River. In their imaginations, Euro-American leaders saw the West as an ever-expanding territory that pushed well beyond even the northern and southern border of the United States. Would the new nation be a hemispheric power? Would the Caribbean become the US? For them, American imperial aims were boundless. But in the early nineteenth century, the Northwest Territory (now Ohio, Michigan, Indiana, Wisconsin, and Minnesota) and the Old Southwest (now, Alabama, Mississippi, and parts of Florida) were in the sites of the Federal government and Euro-American migrants. There, in an imagined empty wilderness, leaders in Washington expected that white immigrants, middling white farmers, and intrepid men with wealth and business acumen would expand the nation.

But the lands in the west of the original 13 states, the two new western additions, and vast areas of territory on US maps were not empty. Instead, Americans of all colors and classes knew well enough that Indigenous people had been combatting European incursion for centuries, that in Tennessee and Kentucky Indigenous people were present, and that violence, not a mysterious destiny, would shape American expansion. By the time John Louis O'Sullivan coined the term "Manifest Destiny" in 1845, Americans knew that violence, forced migration, the internal slave trade, and war were what shaped the Old Southwest and were shaping the Northwest territory into states. But the allure of destiny as justification for the reality of a sustained violent campaigns and the brutality of human bondage made for a better happier national myth.

American Women's History: A New Narrative History, First Edition. Melissa E. Blair, Vanessa M. Holden, and Maeve Kane.
© 2024 John Wiley & Sons, Inc. Published 2024 by John Wiley & Sons, Inc.

Many Euro-Americans ascribed to the belief that it was the God-ordained destiny of the United States to spread democracy westward one white settlement at a time to explain why they should be the rightful inhabitants of Indigenous people's homelands. At the start of the nineteenth century, European Americans who had previously identified by their ethnicity, colony or state, or status as free or indentured increasingly identified as white. This racial category flattened ethnic differences and differences between the place of origin in favor of physical markers like skin color. In the eighteenth century, Americans used social categories that denoted religion or place of origin like Christian or Englishman interchangeably with the racial classification of white. They defined whiteness against Blackness and Indigeneity and assigned rights and privileges to white people that were not available to Black people. For example, white people could not be enslaved, while Black and Indigenous people were always vulnerable to enslavement. At the start of the nineteenth century, white supremacy, the belief that white people are rightfully superior to all other people, permeated all aspects of society from the law to social custom. White supremacy was the most important building block of Manifest Destiny.

Expansion was not solely the result of white men's labor. Women, of all classes and races, shaped the American economy and America's land-based empire. The market economy and the beginning of the Industrial Revolution mitigated some of middle- and upper-class women's traditional labor and opened new types of employment to poor and working-class women. The federally supported push to "settle" the West enabled Euro-American settlers to violently remove Indigenous women from homelands and those women resisted incursion and labored to survive forced migration. Enslaved women labored into the cotton frontier under the lash and contributed to the vast cash crop system that made enslavers and the global cotton trade lucrative. For some women, missionary work, migration west, and the distance from eastern social conventions provided them with room to carve out roles that challenged gender norms. Some free people of color and fugitives from slavery went to the Far West and established their own practice of freedom. Looking at the changing economy and its connection to contestation over western land illustrates the many ways that women's wage labor, domestic labor, and reproductive labor were central to the largest political, economic, and social questions of the day.

Maria Stewart: Women of Color, Activism, and the Rising Middle Class

When Maria Stewart stood up before a promiscuous audience, one composed men and women, among Boston's burgeoning free Black community to deliver her own treatise she stood decades ahead of the many women engaged in reform work throughout the United States. "African rights and liberty," she proclaimed, "is a subject that ought to fire the breast of every free man of color in the United States, and excite in his bosom a lively, deep, decided and heart-felt interest." The speech that followed admonished free Black men for their vices and challenged them to become community leaders who would demand that America, and its institutions, live up to its Revolutionary Era ideals and promise. Stewart, like her political mentor David Walker, publicly called for community leaders and community organizations to demand freedom for all African Americans, social equality, and equal access to economic opportunity. For Stewart, public protest, organizing, and shrewd strategy would allow Black women to grasp at their rightful share of the American Dream.

The rising industrial economy of the early and mid-nineteenth century reshaped women's work and place in society. It also transformed into social class. In previous generations, class stratification left little room for a middle class between the poor and the wealthy. One major shift, which began before the American Revolution but came to fruition in the early nineteenth century, was the expansion of the American middle class. Initially made up of artisans and tradesmen and their families, by the early nineteenth century the middle class included low- and high-level administrators such as clerks, managers, and accountants. Clergy, factory owners, and self-made men in professions like medicine and the law along with their families, were also included. Not wealthy or heirs to vast fortunes but comfortable enough not to engage in physical labor, American middle-class status was based on wealth and more permeable than European class systems that included an aristocracy and nobility. This expanding class of Americans had the power to purchase goods, services, and the labor of others. Women, whose class status depended on the status of their male kin, were expected to uphold class values and conform to class norms. Society upheld white middle-class womanhood as the gender ideal for all women. But that did not mean that women of color did not achieve middle-class status or ascribe to middle-class values.

"What if I am a woman; is not the God of ancient times the God of these modern days?" Maria Stewart asked of her audience in Boston, Massachusetts, in 1833, in the middle of her, "Farewell Address to Her Friends in the City of Boston." She was leaving because her brand of activism did not receive warm support in the free Black community of Boston. Born free in Hartford, Connecticut, as Maria Miller in 1803, Stewart was part of the expanding population of free people of color after the American Revolution. Orphaned by age five, Stewart would become an indentured servant like many children, Black and white, with no kin to take them in. Later, after aging out of her indenture, Stewart worked as a domestic servant to support herself. When she married James W. Stewart, a shipping agent and veteran of the War of 1812, in 1823, her life and status changed with her husband's. Suddenly, she was a member of the small but growing Black middle class of Boston, MA.

Initially, her activism was well within the bounds of a respectable married women's purview like many middle-class women in the early nineteenth century. She taught in sabbath schools and was active in the church. She supported local Black institutions that advocated for the abolition of slavery and supported members of the Black community. But when her husband died in 1832, her fortunes changed just as suddenly as when she got married. Her husband's white business associates swindled her rightful inheritance away and she was left with nothing. Vulnerable because of her status as a woman and an African American, Maria Stewart confronted both the racism and sexism of her era head-on.

It was out of this tragedy that Stewart's activism began to challenge conventional middle-class gender norms. Instead of sticking to religious topics and children's education, she took on social and political issues within the Black community of Boston. Mentored by the famous radical, David Walker, and spurred on by William Lloyd Garrison's call for Black women to submit writing to his newly founded abolitionist newspaper, *The Liberator,* in 1831, Stewart began carving out a public life for herself. She spoke in front of mixed male and female audiences, claimed authority using scripture, and pressed for uplift efforts among free Black people, particularly critiquing Black men's behavior, and male privilege.

And so, in April 1832, Stewart found herself in need of a new place to call home because not even Black Boston, hotbed of abolition and reform, was ready for her radical vision. She moved to New York City and taught school to support herself. She shifted her writing to religious topics. Down but not out, yet again, she remade herself and endured.

Stewart's lifetime, her work, and the story of her ouster from Black Boston mirror the many changes women faced in the early decades of the nineteenth century. Economic changes, technical advances, and the consequences of violent westward expansion left many nineteenth-century women with means asking where they could and should fit into the young republic? The rise of the market economy, an exploding population fueled by immigration, and Euro-American hunger for Indigenous lands characterized the early decades of the nineteenth century. By the time of Stewart's early antebellum speech, America's pursuit of a land-based empire expanded political rights for free white men but excluded everyone else. Her fervor for political action was ahead of most male radicals let a lone female reformers. But her vision would prove right as the consequences of expansion, slavery, and a rapidly changing economy came to bear.

A Land-Based Empire: Women's Migrations

Indigenous women shaped what European Americans called the West for generations before the arrival of settler colonialism in North America. Indigenous peoples lived, traded, fought, and negotiated with each other and with many groups of Europeans before Americans entered the arena. The Spanish, French, Dutch, and English had each pushed into Native lands and many Americans had experience with European versions of colonialism before the United States was independent from England. At the start of the nineteenth century, leaders in the US Federal Government knew that those same European nations would be all too happy to claim for themselves the vast Indian Territory they claimed from England at the end of the Revolutionary War. Westward expansion occupied politicians at the state and federal level almost immediately. Of course, maps and treaties may have staked out claims between nations, but they rarely reflected the reality of lived experiences on the ground. What cartographers rendered as empty space with rivers, mountains, trees, and the promise of natural resources were really the homelands of multiple Indigenous groups. And despite what Euro-Americans desired, those Indigenous nations remained ready to resist American incursion.

Indigenous people faced new waves of Euro-American settlers after the American Revolution. The early United States relied on land cessions from Britain at the end of the Revolutionary War to raise revenue, pay veterans, and project power in the world. The United States was a land-based empire that relied on settling its citizens on lands ceased from Indigenous people to expand its power and influence in the world. Settlement of white migrants was paramount to the American national progress. In the Northwest Ordinance (1787), legislators imagined states north of the Ohio River before the lands included in the Northwest territory had enough free white male settlers to begin to approach statehood. Below the Ohio, Kentucky, and Tennessee were established before the turn of the century as states that allowed slavery. Below them, a vast territory controlled by powerful Indigenous groups left Southern planters and middling farmers envious. Those lands too were in Euro-Americans' sights.

Euro-Americans did not desire untouched wilderness. They wanted lands shaped by generations of Indigenous women's command of agriculture, their knowledge of the migratory patterns of game animals, and their savvy trading with partners both European and Indigenous. That is, Euro-Americans wanted the land that Indigenous women had carefully cultivated for generations and made prosperous. While national myths in popular American culture tried to render Indigenous people as "disappearing," "uncivilized," and worthy of pity, those Euro-Americans who decided to venture into Indigenous lands learned quickly that the people whose land they desperately wanted were politically sophisticated, tactically savvy, and very much present.

In 1803, federal intentions could not have been made clearer than with then President Thomas Jefferson's Louisiana Purchase that included the modern-day state of Louisiana but, beyond it, a vast tract of land that reached from west of the Mississippi all the way to the Pacific Ocean. Jefferson had no real idea of who lived on those lands or what the lands were like ecologically. He had to fund a famous expedition, the Corps of Discovery, led by Meriweather Lewis and William Clark from the summer of 1803-fall of 1806 to scout what exactly lay up the Missouri River and who future generations would need to confront to take it. Even before settlers or the federal army could make it so, America's leaders were clear that they wanted Indigenous lands and they intended to take them.

The West – the Northwest Territory, the Old Southwest, and the Louisiana Territory – would figure heavily in an imagined empire for Euro-Americans. To them, land and property were ways to claim citizenship and bolster democracy. At the turn of the century, most states required property ownership for men to qualify as voters, and women of all races were almost universally excluded from the franchise. Lands in the west could be used as a pressure valve for poor and middling white men in search of their own place in the young democracy. Selling federally claimed lands, with or without the involvement Indigenous people, would shore up the new nation's coffers and help it remain fiscally viable given the population's hatred of taxes. But those dreams of wealth, prosperity, and a thriving democracy necessitated suffering, displacement, and the exclusion of Indigenous people, free Black people, and enslaved people.

For Indigenous people, who lived in all the territories that cartographers depicted as empty, savvy politics, violent resistance, and incredible displacement would characterize their nineteenth century. For Black Americans, free and enslaved, the West would hold *less* rather than more freedom as the cotton gin, the market economy, and industrial advancement fueled a booming economy based on slavery. Euro-Americans in the South would grow more convinced that slavery's profitability was a necessity for their vision of democratic society. Outside of the South, most Euro-Americans would either become involved in economic activity that benefited from the continuance of slavery or choose apathy rather than outrage.

Migrations and the Women's Market Economy: Feminine Ideals, Domestic Labor, and Wage Labor Opportunities

Women had long played a vital role in the American economy. While wealthy women often had help with domestic labor, their role as managers bolstered households. They also frequently managed property including enslaved people. For many women, work processing produce into food, natural fibers into cloth and clothing, and planning carefully for winter occupied their working lives. Domestic labor was often arduous and required years of training with older women to learn how to manage a household. Open hearths, heavy cookware, the ever-present task of child minding, and a long list of daily tasks made women significant contributors to household economies as daughters, wives, kin, and hired or enslaved help. Even women who had to work outside of their own homes to ensure their families survival or because they were enslaved were expected to take up domestic work for their own families and communities.

While Euro-Americans tended to view heavy agricultural labor as the responsibility of men, they tended to see problem viewing women of color as uniquely suited to hard labor. Enslaved women played an important role in household economies both as valuable human property and as productive and reproductive laborers. Their enslavers relied on them to work primarily as laborers in fields of cash crops. Some also worked at domestic tasks for their enslavers such as dairy work, animal husbandry, gardening, cooking, and housekeeping. But very few enslavers had the wealth to keep some enslaved people exclusively for domestic work. Most had to rotate as needed into agricultural labor and processing labor like tobacco grading, cotton ginning, and rice pounding – all hard physical tasks. When forced to do domestic tasks by their enslavers, they often had to labor alongside and under the close watch and management of Euro-American women. Only the wealthiest of Euro-American women could completely avoid farm labor. Working along hired help, indentured women, and enslaved women became a part of their domestic labor.

Indigenous women played a vital role in their societies' agricultural endeavors. Women were often in charge of cultivating staple crops among the peoples of the Eastern Woodlands. They also processed produce to preserve it for winter months, processed natural fibers into clothing, and carefully managed households and communities. Eastern Woodlands groups also trusted the task of seasonal migration to women who knew when in the agricultural cycle to rotate between winter and summer settlements.

Population shifts and migrations, both forced and voluntary, shaped gender norms and expectations. Transportation innovations, Federal land claims in the West and Far West, and the rise of the Market economy shaped how the dominant Euro-American culture defined early nineteenth-century gender roles. The statesman Henry Clay of Kentucky laid out a careful plan, the American Plan to make the most of America's holdings west of the Appalachian Mountains. The problem of making and transporting goods from US coasts to the interior where most Euro-Americans fully expected to infiltrate Indigenous lands became key to the America's imperial plans. Along with tariffs and a national bank, Clay proposed subsidies for roads, canals, and internal improvements – all a way to move raw materials to manufacturing and trade centers while funneling finished goods back into the interior. The West and Far West, in Clay's mind, would function as a colony of the East. America's land-based empire would make use of the interior just as other nations made use of their colonies to produce raw materials and to purchase finished goods.

This system of interconnected roads, canals, rivers, and shipping lanes brought more than household goods to faraway markets and raw materials to developing factories and international trade partners. It brought immigrants, planter migrants, and enslaved people into the interior. It moved news from the coasts more swiftly into the interior and print media from faraway locations to the frontier. Women with access to basic literacy connected with family and friends via regular correspondence. But the proliferation of print culture also brought women images of idealized physical beauty, fashion trends, and even housekeeping advice.

In the North and later the Upper Midwest, internal improvements would revolutionize women's labor and access to finished goods by the 1820s and 1830s. The market economy of the early nineteenth century, an economy based on the purchase of goods rather than in-home economic production, gradually shifted the work that women did within households processing raw materials to manufacturing centers. What women once processed themselves to clothe their communities and feed their households would begin to shift to laborers outside of their homes and eventually into industrially produced products for purchase. Domestic management would shift from managing production to managing purchases. Those purchases would include books and women's magazines, religious tracts, and even news of charitable projects and causes.

Middle-class women's economic role may have been in flux as they moved from producers to consumers, but socially, the Market Revolution carefully prescribed gender norms that had not changed much. Rapid urbanization, goaded on by the increased trade with the interior, would provide their male counterparts with the ability to live away from their families and enter a vast developing culture of young single men with jobs as clerks, managers, and other white-collar professions. With their newfound urban freedom and money, vice became a concern for parents and potential marriage partners. Young women were expected to prepare for marriage and motherhood, remain chaste, and do their best to influence the men in their lives to live moral lives. With a moral mandate, but little civil or legal recourse, middle-class and wealthy women were encouraged by their elders, advice literature, and religious institutions to look to ways outside of politics and the masculine world of commerce to influence their society.

Women's prospects and class identifies were not always tied to men, though the law tried to make it so. Wealthy and middle-class women may have attended to appearances and considered propriety, but they often took up commercial activities to support themselves and their families. Euro-American women held, traded, and managed enslaved people. Women of all races started and managed businesses. They took work into their homes to supplement the income of male relatives and spouses. In the absence of husbands, fathers, brothers, and male kin, women took over men's businesses and economic activities to ensure the survival of their families. Race also played a role in class status. Women like Maria Stewart, a free woman of color and domestic servant, would have been considered middle class in her own free Black community, though white women would have seen her as working class, if they considered her status at all.

Working-class women and poor women navigated the new economy but enjoyed few of its benefits. As consumers, they often lived hand to mouth subsisting on very little. The poor purchased cheap bread full of fillers, fuel, and necessities day by day. Relegated by men to work deemed feminine like laundry work or domestic work, poor and working women often labored in concert with all of their family members to make ends meet. Women and children supplemented men's wages within families to eke out survival in America's growing urban centers. Women became laundresses, worked as maids and cooks, and marketed goods on the street. Some became sex workers, referred to at the time as prostitutes and with other prerogative language, either fulltime or to make ends meet when times were particularly hard. After pooling their family's wages, working-class and poor women had little if any left over for fashionable attire or the trappings of idealized womanhood.

By the 1820s, some of the innovations that made Europe's industrial revolution prosperous made their way across the Atlantic and unmarried women were able to take jobs as industrial textile workers. But, like other work that women could get, millwork was dangerous and paid low wages. Poverty persisted and women and children remained particularly vulnerable. In rural areas, poor women worked just as their mothers and grandmothers had, to make and process raw produce for their family's survival. Often, wage work in developing urban centers was an attractive alternative to farm labor and poor girls jumped at the chance to leave home and build a modest savings.

Steam technology made river travel a viable mode of transportation both up and down American rivers. In the US South, river travel made the movement of cash crops and raw materials to market in the same way that man-made canals had aided the market economy in the North and Upper-Midwest. When, after the War of 1812, the Federal Government solidified its claim on Indigenous people's homelands against the British, and successive violent campaigns against powerful Indigenous groups like the Creek ushered in the violent seizure of their lands, what was once the cotton frontier, rapidly developed into new states like Mississippi and Alabama by a flood of Euro-American planters migrating from states in the east. They brought slavery and enslaved people with them. Along with Georgia and Louisiana, Mississippi and Alabama would become producers of upland short-staple cotton for global trading partners and mills in the northern United States. Steamboats would transport raw cotton to Southern ports and finished goods to farms and plantations all over the region. The market economy would enable southern enslavers to purchase all that they needed to subsist and produce the raw goods that fueled mills in Europe and the Northern United States.

Making the South: *Southern Women* and Planter Migration

The Northern economy relied on the labor of poor and working-class men, women, and children, who were increasingly from immigrant groups. By the early nineteenth century, most northern states had abolished slavery or had started manumission campaigns to gradually abolish slavery. New Jersey, the final state to do so, began gradual emancipation in 1804. The South continued to rely on enslaved people's labor and exploitation to make cotton, tobacco, and rice culture profitable. Euro-Americans in the South pushed Indigenous people out and moved enslaved people into their lands in a tandem process of forced migration to expand and sustain cash crop agriculture. Always violent, without regard for Black or Indigenous families or cultures, this region's American Plan also came with an exorbitant human cost.

Initially, Southern women migrated into the Cotton Frontier from established southeastern states as a part of a trend called planter migration. Already established male farmers and plantation owners moved with their households into the Mississippi Territory. Under the law, their households included their wives and children in addition to all the African Americans they enslaved. Enslaved women were expected to help clear land, establish fields of cotton and produce, and bear children who added to their enslaver's wealth. Some of the settlers in earlier generations of Euro-American migrants hoped to establish themselves as enslavers once they arrived and built wealth in landholdings. In those days, before powerful Indigenous groups were forced to the negotiating table by frontier violence, men of small to middling means had a better chance at grasping for land. But, after the War of 1812, the land market was only accessible by those who already had money to purchase land at sometimes wildly rising prices thanks to rampant speculation.

In 1790, even as post-Revolutionary enslavers freed some enslaved people and northern states began enacting manumission, enslaved people numbered about 700 thousand in a population of roughly 3.7 million. The population of free people of color grew in the early nineteenth century. But the population of enslaved people in the United States far outnumbered free Black people. Enslaved people's numbers rose because of the Atlantic slave trade that remained in operation and enslaved women's reproductive labor: enslaved children followed their enslaved mothers' condition and were born slaves. After 1808, with the close of legal American participation in the trans-Atlantic slave trade, enslaved people's value rose sharply and purchasing enslaved people to work became even more out of reach for those who were not already established. Black women's reproductive labor also increased in value to enslavers. Longstanding slave law dictated that children were enslaved or free at birth according to their mother's status. Enslavers regarded enslaved women's children as "natural increase," as if mother and child were cow and calf. According to the law, enslaved children equaled an increase in an enslaver's wealth incentivizing enslavers to further commodify Black women's reproductive capacity. According to US Census data, by 1830, as the intrastate slave trade flourished, over two million enslaved people, 14% of the US population, lived in the country. Black women's reproductive and productive labor kept the economic system of slavery viable.

When the Mississippi Territory became the states of Mississippi (1817), and Alabama (1819), joined the Union planters were already amassing wealth using enslaved people to farm cotton. Within their borders, large populations of Cherokee, Creek, Chickasaw, Seminole, and Choctaw remained on lands they negotiated with the Federal government to keep. Thanks to revolutionary steam technology and the success of industrial looms, cotton only became more profitable. The Indigenous people who remained in the cotton South, remained on lands that Euro-Americans would not cease to covet. Federal policy dictated a campaign of "civilization" among Indigenous people groups. For Euro-Americans, "civilization" meant sedentary agriculture, conversion to Christianity, and assimilation into Euro-American cultural norms such as the adoption of Euro-American clothing and gender roles. If Indigenous people "civilized," the US Government promised, then they would stay on their lands unmolested by Federal troops and American citizens.

Christian missionaries were active among Indigenous groups from the arrival of Catholicism with early Spanish colonizers in the 1400s. Similarly, Protestant missionaries were the religious arm of English colonialism. In the early nation, missionaries, including women, supported Federal "civilizing" policy and served as the spiritual arm of American imperialism. Society generally accepted that it was appropriate for middle-class white women to do missionary work alongside their male kin. White women aided male clergy in enforcing the values of Protestant Christianity and Euro-American gender and societal norms. White Christians from diverse Protestant sects, including Methodists, Baptists, Presbyterians, and Moravians, lived among southeastern Indigenous groups to convert and "civilize" them. They set up churches and schools while pressing Indigenous people to assimilate into white American culture and encouraging to renounce their traditional way of life. The tension between Federal promises and local Euro-American interests would in the decades to come push Indigenous women and their communities front and center in National politics. Women's work as missionaries bolstered their role as arbiters of spiritual and moral rectitude among Euro-Americans and made them direct actors in the effort to eradicate Indigenous peoples.

Making the North: European Immigration and Women's Labor

After the American Revolution and again in the years after the War of 1812, European immigration increased to the United States. The largest immigrant groups came from central Europe (present day Germany) and the British Isles. Many immigrants saw the United States as the best place to purchase land of their own, to escape religious persecution, or to escape systems of inequality in their homelands. Ethnic German and Irish communities already existed in the United States. Some immigrants had high hopes for better prospects in the United States, others just wanted respite from religious persecution or war back home. When they arrived, they encountered discrimination, particularly if they were Roman Catholic, and many were caught in exploitative cycles of poverty and debt in America's east coast urban centers.

Immigrants often became part of the expanding class of working poor in America's growing cities. New York, Philadelphia, Boston, and Baltimore all grew in the early decades of the nineteenth century in large part because of increased immigration. There, all members of immigrant families needed to find wage labor to piece together funds for their basic needs: shelter and food.

Women worked outside of their homes in marketplaces selling goods they made. Some took in piece work, needlework they were paid by the piece for, or worked as seamstresses, a skilled profession. Some became laundresses and others engaged in part-time or full-time sex work. Sex work is the practice of selling sexual favors for goods or money historically called prostitution. Irish women, who immigrated alone instead of as members of family units in higher numbers than other immigrant groups, worked as domestics who lived in their employers' homes. The same economic calculations that lead factory owners to open factory work to American-born Euro-American women also encouraged them to look to immigrant women, who could be paid even lower wages to replace the first generation of female factory workers. Paid less than men but more than children, many immigrant women relied on wage labor to contribute to their households' subsistence. Exchanging wages for poor housing and cheap food, the urban working poor sometimes made ends meet and often did not.

Immigration would continue to increase from Europe throughout the nineteenth century. And immigrant women and families would continue to worry American-born middle- and upper-class Protestant women. Whether prejudiced against immigrants' religion or their inability to attain feminine ideals because of poverty, American women of better means began to think of new arrivals as fertile ground in which to sow the seeds of their own middle- and upper-class social and religious values. Like Maria Stewart who taught Sunday School, a combination of basic academic and religious instruction, many women saw work among America's growing population of impoverished workers as an appropriately feminine way to serve their communities.

The West and Far West: Imagining Empire on Indigenous Lands

Many poor and middling Euro-Americans hoped that the West would provide them with the chance at prosperity that they were locked out of by elites in their home states. Young men established small-time farmers, and even men with families held out hope that the Federal government would make their dream of equality for all men like them possible. And the government delivered, though in half-measures. The Northwest Ordinance promised Euro-American men five to seven new states with good farmland and a ban on slavery that would keep wealthy planters out. While the Mississippi Territory and the Louisiana Territory held out hope for would-be planters that they too could purchase enslaved people and build sprawling plantations of their very own, men from regions where subsistence and not cash crop farming were the ideal wanted to leave the crowded land markets of the East for the West. Migration into America's western territories did not provide poor and middling Euro-Americans immediate prosperity.

The federal government could not universally guarantee settlers' safety from Indigenous people defending their homelands. In the Northwest, just as in the Southwest, Indigenous groups did not intend to leave their homelands open to Euro-American settlement without resistance. Wealthy investors and land speculators made westward movement and landownership expensive and difficult for poor and middle-class farmers. And war with England in 1812 significantly destabilized the American interior as Indigenous nations, competing colonial powers, and England all vied for control in the Northwest and Southwest. The Ohio River Valley and the Great Lakes Region, prosperous when held by Indigenous groups, remained coveted by Euro-American settlers in the early nineteenth century.

Like their Southern counterparts, Euro-American migrants to the Northwest, often moved in family units. Women ventured with their husbands and fathers in hopes of better prospects than their homes in New England and the Mid-Atlantic could offer them. They were expected to do the grueling domestic labor necessary to start successful farms and businesses. Like women in the East and South, improved transportation systems, the availability of finished goods, and the proliferation of periodicals would keep them connected to the kin they left behind and a new American women's culture grounded in Euro-American women's standards of femininity.

Conclusion

Euro-American women participated in settler colonialism, reform movements, and as workers in the rapidly industrializing market economy. Print culture and improved transportation made it easier for women to connect with each other across long distances. By the middle of the antebellum period, popular literature, periodicals, and mass-produced prints would have the same impact on women's lives as other finished products: they would provide and reinforce universalized standards of femininity. Of course, excluded from these dominant standards were women of color, poor and working-class women, and immigrant women who did not have access to the financial resources that Euro-American women had. Tensions between these hard to attain gender ideals, with neatly separated public and private spheres, and women's lives that were hardly ever so neatly lived experiences would be a source of conflict for generations between women.

Maria Stewart, a domestic servant, and teacher would never have met the bar for womanhood that white middle-class women set. A Black woman, she worked to support herself. While she was respectable and middle class in her own community, white women's activism in the antebellum period would not readily distinguish women like Stewart as leaders with definitions of womanhood that were valid. Her activism anticipated forms and tactics that prominent white female reformers would take up in decades to come. But her race kept her from most white reformer's notice. Black women like Stewart continued to advocate as they saw fit and fissures between them and white abolitionists did not diminish their resolve. Theirs was a groundbreaking stance as abolitionist well before the movement became mainstream and women activists and reformers became commonplace in Northern cities.

Bibliography

Caughfield, Adrienne. *True Women and Westward Expansion*. 1st edition. College Station: Texas A&M University Press, 2005.

Dublin, Thomas. *Transforming Women's Work: New England Lives in the Industrial Revolution*. New edition. Ithaca: Cornell University Press, 1995.

Johnston, Carolyn Ross, ed. *Voices of Cherokee Women*. Winston-Salem, North Carolina: Blair, 2013.

Jones, Jacqueline. *Labor of Love, Labor of Sorrow: Black Women, Work, and the Family, from Slavery to the Present*. 2nd edition. New York, NY: Basic Books, 2009.

"Lowell National Historical Park (U.S. National Park Service)." Accessed January 11, 2023. **https://www.nps.gov/lowe/index.htm**.

Lyons, Clare A. *Sex Among the Rabble: An Intimate History of Gender and Power in the Age of Revolution, Philadelphia, 1730–1830*. 1st edition. Chapel Hill: University of North Carolina Press, 2006.

Robinson, Harriet, ed. *Loom and Spindle: Or, Life Among the Early Mill Girls; with a Sketch of "The Lowell Offering" and Some of Its Contributors*. Carlisle, MA: Applewood Books, 2011.

Rockman, Seth. *Scraping by: Wage Labor, Slavery, and Survival in Early Baltimore*. 1st edition. Baltimore: The Johns Hopkins University Press, 2009.

CHAPTER 7

Reform, Revolt, and Women's Rights, 1830s–1860s

Catharine Beecher published *A Treatise on Domestic Economy, for the Use of Young Ladies at Home, and at School*, in 1841. In it, Beecher, a prominent educator and reformer, outlined her firm belief that women's role as homemakers, a role subordinate to their husbands, formed the cornerstone of a truly Democratic social order. Beecher empathized with American women who as young wives and mothers had to adapt to the sometimes rapid changes in the fortune of their spouses. In her guide, she purported to include helpful advice for American women weathering the changes of the evolving market economy and the expanding industrial economy. Popular women's advice literature assured women that their subordinate position to men was an important part of their role as women in a democracy. According to dominant gender norms, domestic economy, the sensible frugal management of household labor and resources, would provide women purpose and allow men to fulfill their role as voters and citizens. But unlike their mothers, antebellum women adapted to an industrializing economy that impacted the domestic role that advice literature like Beecher's mapped out for them.

In the early decades of the nineteenth century, the Market Revolution changed many Americans' access to finished and processed goods. The expansion of the American middle class was also an expansion of a class of consumers with the funds to purchase finished goods. Advances in transportation networks made the movement of both raw materials and finished goods cheaper and faster. Merchant Capitalism, the system in which merchants turned a profit by buying goods at a low price and selling them for a higher price, developed generations earlier and accelerated because of the Atlantic world's triangle trade. Industrial Capitalism, the production of large amounts of goods for sale on the market, was fueled by the emergence of the factory system and began its rise in the United States with the textile industry just as it had earlier in Europe.

American Women's History: A New Narrative History, First Edition. Melissa E. Blair, Vanessa M. Holden, and Maeve Kane.

For example, women were once relied upon to spin plant fiber and animal fiber into thread that either they or itinerant weavers wove into cloth that women then turned into items of clothing. The emergence of factories shifted production of finished goods from individual women within their households and traveling artisans to factories where wealthy owners used wage laborers to mass produce merchandize like cloth. When the mass production of cloth made factory-made textiles cheaper and continent to acquire than homespun fabric, women who could afford to, began to purchase ready-made cloth to make clothing for their families.

This shift was gradual. Not all women could afford ready-made cloth and the supply of affordable factory-made cloth required the expansion of factories, workforces of textile workers, and a ready supply of raw fiber over time. Other economic developments in the same time period made this shift from homespun to factory-made cloth possible. During the middle of the nineteenth century, immigration from Europe increased. Immigrants and poor white Americans supplied the cheap labor needed to make the factory system profitable for factory owners. At the same time, Euro-Americans increased the production of raw cotton using enslaved African Americans to grow, harvest, and process cotton, a durable and versatile fiber in newly formed states like Alabama and Mississippi.

The textile industry is one example of how the industrial economy changed women's lives with different impacts across different classes and racial groups. Poor and working-class women found labor opportunities in factories but risked injury and death in mechanical looms in mills, had low wages, and long hours. An emerging middle class of women found store-bought cloth to be a time saver. Time that women once spent spinning could now be dedicated to other domestic tasks or charitable work outside of their homes. While wealthy women had access to dressmakers, middle-class women often made their own clothing. Enslaved and poor women's labor as domestic servants, enslaved agricultural laborers, and factory workers allowed the wives and daughters of middle-class men to enjoy more leisure time and time to devote to interests outside of their households. The textile industry is one example of how the industrial economy changed women's lives. Though that change was not universally for the better.

Competing Womanhoods: Middle-Class Women and Emerging Definitions of Womanhood

Catherine Beecher came from a prominent middle-class family in New York. At the time, America's middle class exploded as industries and merchants demanded armies of clerks, lawyers, insurance agents, commodities factors, and professionals to administer the flow of goods and merchandize around the nation. Beecher was the daughter of Presbyterian minister and evangelist, Lyman Beecher. Her younger brother, Henry Ward Beecher, was also a well-known minister and reformer. Beecher's half-sister, Harriet Beecher Stowe, remains the most famous member of her family because of the success of her abolitionist novel, *Uncle Tom's Cabin*.

Catharine Beecher's advocacy for girls' education was of a piece with her family's political beliefs and considered appropriate by society for a woman of her social class.

She never married and did not necessarily believe that women needed to marry to play a vital role in society. For unmarried women, she supported employment such as teaching. For married women, their job as mothers remained the most important contribution to society in Beecher's eyes. While she lived outside of the dominant culture's domestic ideal as a single woman with a career, her writings encourage women to accept their separate sphere of influence over society. was a reformer, but she scoffed at many of the radical causes other female reformers of her generation took up. She was not interested in challenging gender inequality or prescribed gender roles. Beecher, instead, celebrated and affirmed them like many middle-class white women who benefited from the status of male members of their families.

Sarah Grimke and Angelina Grimke Weld had much less predictable path to reform work and concern for women's place in society than Catharine Beecher. Like Beecher, both women were part of the generation born right after America's founding. But unlike her, the Grimke sisters grew up surrounded by slavery and enslaved people on their father's plantation in South Carolina. They were wealthy women from an influential family in South Carolina. The two could have grown up to be esteemed women who were well-positioned to become enslavers themselves. Instead, the two broke radically with their childhood of privilege. Sarah Grimke was emboldened to defy her upbringing after she visited Philadelphia with her ailing father. There she was exposed to Quakerism and the vibrant reform community for which the city was known. Famous as a hub of medical innovation, Philadelphia was also home to a large, active, and visible free Black community. Philadelphia would have provided a sharp contrast to the world in which Grimké grew up.

In 1821, Grimké converted to Quakerism and moved to Philadelphia, leaving her life as a Southern elite behind. Quakers believed in spiritual gender equality, nonviolence, and had broadly moved to end their participation in slavery and advocate against it. When Sarah's younger sister, Angelina joined her there and became a Quaker they took a public stand against slavery. The Grimké sisters were radicals who challenged even the Friends, as Quakers called themselves. When the Grimkés boldly arrived at Quaker meeting, a Quaker religious gathering, and sat with Sarah Mapps Douglass, a prominent African American Quaker, and her mother, they caused a stir. Black and white Quakers until that point did not sit with each other despite the doctrines of spiritual equality that Quakers professed. The Grimkés and the Douglasses integrated seating in Quaker meeting pushing the Friends beyond anti-slavery and toward racial equality. They took on established religious leaders with their actions and their words. Sarah Grimké also took on the religious leaders of the South in her anti-slavery tract, *An Epistle to the Clergy of the Southern States* (1827).

In 1836, Angelina Grimke published her essay "An Appeal to the Christian Women of the South," with the American Anti-Slavery Society. In it, she both dismantled prominent arguments in support of slavery and called on women in the South specifically to stand up to men in political power to dismantle the slave economy. Catharine Beecher responded publicly to Grimke's essay with an essay of her own, "An Essay on Slavery and Abolitionism, With Reference to the Duty of American Females." At the same moment that the Grimkés were well on their way to articulating their vision of Women's Rights, Beecher staunchly rejected the idea of women's equality and was appalled that Grimké encouraged women to take explicitly political stances and actions. Instead, Beecher reiterated the belief that men and women were inherently different, that they had separate spheres of proper influence, and that women should not directly engage in politics. In the letters between Angeline Grimké and Beecher that followed the publication of Beecher's essay, the two articulated many of the major conflicts that would characterize women reformer's divisions in coming decades. Who was a true woman and what was true womanhood? How should women participate, or not, in public life? And what obligation did women have to influence the world around them? How should they go about influencing and making that change?

The sisters were celebrated by some and disparaged by others. At the invitation of the Massachusetts Anti-Slavery Society, both sisters went to Boston to work with anti-slavery activists. But not everyone was excited at their arrival. Nehemiah Adams, a Congregational Minister, authored the General Association of Congregational Ministers' annual Pastoral Letter in which he took Sarah Grimké to task for encouraging women to move into the masculine world of public life. In 1837, Sarah Grimké engaged in correspondence with Mary S. Parker, then the president of the Boston Female Anti-Slavery Society. In 1838, Sarah's letters were published together in a book titled, *Letters on the Equality of the Sexes, and the Condition of Woman.* In her letters, Sarah Grimké asserted women's equality to men using her faith and scripture to bolster her argument. In her third letter, a response to the Pastoral Letter, she confronts the rhetoric of male ministers head-on. "Men and women," she writes, "were CREATED EQUAL." The criticism the Grimké sisters faced illustrates the limits of many reformers' efforts. While the desired a better world, many of the Gremké's contemporaries were not willing to transgress middle-class social norms. American gender roles were dictated by race and social class. Americans constructed masculinity and femineity according to several social markers. Just as in the previous period, not all Americans were members of the dominant cultural group: white protestants with ancestors from the British Isles and the Netherlands. While dominant gender ideals certainly influenced the interaction between social groups, how individuals experienced, defined, and expressed gender was highly contingent. How did women define womanhood in the antebellum period? Who could be a woman and fell short of dominant ideals? Who did the dominant ideals of femininity leave out and exclude?

Until the Market Revolution and the dawn of industrialization, most women did not have the opportunity to work outside of their own homes for wages or at professions. Some middle-class white women found work as governesses or relied of extended family if they did not marry, or their immediate family fell on hard times. Later, teaching opened to some women who had access to the education needed to teach children. Often, society saw these options as viable only before marriage or as the last resort of women unable to find a husband. Society viewed middle-class white women compelled to work for wages because of the death of male kin as unfortunate. Marriage and domestic labor for their family remained the ideal for middle-class and wealthy white women. This did not stop some women from managing assets, owning businesses, and making their own way in the world. But dominant ideals encouraged society to pity rather than celebrate them.

Industrialization, increased urbanization, and rapidly expanding markets in the early years of the nineteenth century brought more poor white women out of domestic work to work in factories. Wages for poor women were lower than for poor men. Childrearing on a factory floor was often impossible. Women juggled the responsibility of rearing young children and providing for their families until children reached an age where they too could take up factory work, run errands, shine shoes, sell small goods, or fend for themselves while their parents worked. Some took in piecework that could be done from home or took in laundry work. Domestic service was closed to women with children in most cases. Industrialization made new types of wage labor available to women, but industrialization did not overturn the structural barriers to women's economic independence.

In some cases, working-class women from rural areas took up industrial work temporarily. Many of the early Lowell Mill girls of Lowell, MA, expected to earn cash in preparation for marriage, business owners quickly realized the benefits of hiring women and children: their wages were lower and owners and managers believed that their ability to resist unfair labor conditions was restricted. Lowell's mill girls, as they were called at the time, defied these expectations when, in 1834, they halted work and went on strike. In response to a market flooded with ready-made fabric and plummeting textile prices, management cut their female worker's wages. They used strategies that would be important in future labor activism: they organized petitions and, when management fired their leader, eight hundred women walked off the job. Management ultimately squashed this strike, but the women and girls at work in Lowell learned valuable lessons.

In 1836, the textile economy booming and the need for workers rising, there was trouble in Lowell once again. Many mill workers lived in mill-owned dormitories. In the early days of the mills, these living arrangements put the parents and family of young women and girls at ease. Mills assured worried family that their employees had safe, single-sex, living arrangements and that young women were safe from immoral temptation. The companies took money out of their pay to cover their room and board on company grounds. The mill also employed women to cook, clean, and care for these residences. When inflation made it difficult for domestic workers at the mills to survive, management decided to charge workers more from their pay to make up for the poor compensation they offered to the women who took care of mill dormitories. Mill workers founded The Factory Girls Association, planned for a lack of wages, and launched a strike that was more than 15,000 workers strong. Across Lowell's textile industry, mill workers won key victories in wages and accommodations while demonstrating how collective bargaining could deliver important results.

These working-class women and girls' goals and activism were in stark contrast to the priorities of middle-class reformers. As more young white women entered the workforce, even if for a short time, Americans became increasingly worried about what work outside of the home might mean for the moral and spiritual future of the nation. When, by the 1830s and 40s, more immigrant women came to the United States, anxieties among the dominant population grew. In the 1840s, the Irish women who arrived were often single and overwhelmingly Roman Catholic. Many went into domestic service. Middle- and upper-class white women benefited from Irish women's work as cooks, housekeepers, maids, nannies, and nurses. But they also worried about what women's wage labor would do to jeopardize nuclear family hierarchies. Would immigrant women exercise influence over their Protestant children. Would they bear more children and impose their cultural norms on society?

Of course, handwringing about working-class rural white women who sought opportunity in urban contexts ignored the reality that women labored constantly at all but the wealthiest levels of society. Poor women, of all races, labored to contribute to their household income. Enslavers owned enslaved women's labor and reproductive labor. The dominant culture consistently undercut the womanhood of enslaved women because they largely labored at "masculine" work in fields doing heavy labor. Indigenous women continued to take active roles in the economic lives of their communities and with increased settler colonial violence labored for survival under duress. Women's work outside of their homes did not spell an end to gendered hierarchies. Antebellum womanhood, what we would call gender roles, was important to antebellum Americans. Whether individual women could live up to the white Eurocentric ideals of the day or not, what antebellum society decided was feminine and what constituted womanhood impacted every stratum of society.

Some women outside of the dominant culture did strive to attain middle- and upper-class status by ascribing to dominant gender roles. Despite their striving, dominant norms simply shut other women out because of the immigrant status, race, ethnicity, or status as enslaved people. Black women, Indigenous women, poor women, and immigrant women wanted to survive subjugation, violence, poverty, and preserve their families. Many wanted the respect and protections afforded middle-class women. Others were far more worried about basic human rights and survival. Enslaved women wanted their freedom on their own terms, but that did not mean that they universally wanted white women's lives even if they practiced Christianity. Indigenous women fought daily to survive white incursion and displacement. They did not want to abandon their own traditions and definitions of womanhood. Poor women in America's expanding urban centers lived hand to mouth and often developed working-class culture that critiqued, made fun of, and scoffed at the social norms of the middle and upper classes. A particular vision of American womanhood may have dominated national print media, popular culture, and religious organizations, but many women consistently defined and redefined themselves within and outside of structures of gendered hierarchy. Rather than an antebellum womanhood, it is more accurate to investigate antebellum womanhoods. Some women fiercely upheld and believed in dominant cultural definitions of womanhood. Many others simply lived outside of them whether they wanted to or not.

Reform and Imperial Aims: Women and "Civilizing" Missions

The antebellum period brought with it two forced migrations: the movement of enslaved people from the coastal and upper South into the cotton frontier by planter migration or sale, and the forced violent removal of Indigenous people from much of those same lands in what became Mississippi and Alabama in the 1810s. After the War of 1812 ended in North America in 1815, America had established its dominance in the Old Southwest. The process took different courses depending on region, previous history with American federal troops and agents, and geography. Indigenous women faced not only the possibility of violence but also the specter of removal with greater urgency.

By the early antebellum period, the ideology of Manifest Destiny had dominated American policy and politics. Most white Americans believed that Euro-Americans best knew how to use the rich land in the Mississippi Territory. For them, the destiny of the United States was to dominate the Americas. Settling more white people in the West and Far West, sedentary farming communities, and the spread of Christianity would be their contribution to the nation's destiny. Sustained Federal campaigns against Indigenous groups in the Northwest Territory and the Old Southwest weakened the ability of Native people to fend off American incursion in the 1810s. By the 1820, both Alabama and Mississippi had officially joined the Union. Missouri, the first state after Louisiana to be admitted from the land of the Louisiana Territory, was on the brink of joining as well.

By the 1830s, the Cherokee had emerged as a test case for "civilizing" missions. An official extension of US Indian policy, "civilizing" Indigenous populations had its roots in centuries long colonial strategies to subjugate Native populations. In the United States, significant armed resistance on the part of Indigenous groups derailed the Federal policy of treating Indigenous groups as "conquered peoples." Instead, the Washington administration pivoted to a strategy of "civilizing" Indigenous people. In the late eighteenth century, "civilizing" meant Indigenous people were expected to assimilate to Euro-American cultural and economic norms. This included gender norms and roles. The policy of "civilizing" assumed that Indigenous people were uncivilized and, through cultural assimilation, could be integrated as citizens into American society.

Each qualification for "civilized" status stood in contrast to various Indigenous cultures and ways of life. Federal policy dictated that "civilized" people wore European-style gender-appropriate clothing, practiced Protestant Christianity, and practiced sedentary agriculture and animal husbandry. "Civilizing" missions insisted that women did domestic labor and men did agricultural labor. According to American laws, men held property, civil responsibility for their wives and children, and participated in political life and government. For many groups, these standards of "civilization" upended their traditional gender roles and Indigenous agricultural practices.

Many white missionaries and government officials considered the Cherokee to be the model that other Indigenous groups should follow. Not all groups agreed to the parameters of white "civilizing" missions. Both leaders and individuals rejected white attempts to strip them of their culture, religion, and way of life. Some groups rejected American cultural and land incursion. Others negotiated a precarious middle ground between assimilation and separatism. Though considered a model by white missionaries and reformers, the Cherokee did not acquiesce to "civilizing" missions without resistance. The Cherokee carefully negotiated their relationship to the US government and their American neighbors. Women's roles in Cherokee society did not change overnight and women continued to assert their traditional place in Cherokee society even at the advent of removal.

In traditional Cherokee society, as with many Indigenous groups of the Eastern Woodlands, women oversaw agriculture, men moved into women's homes upon marriage, and women played significant roles in decision-making in their local villages and more broadly across Cherokee lands. Inheritance moved through women's hereditary lines. All these traditions were in direct conflict with white standards of "civilization." When in 1808, male Cherokee leaders imbedded inheritance structures in male hereditary lines, and women encountered a significant shift in their political authority. Women's political role and economic authority diminished as men began to step into public and political roles more in line with Euro-American standards than long-held Cherokee tradition.

Cherokee women did not let go of their long-held connection to the land. In the 1810s, with settlers grasping at Cherokee lands in earnest, Cherokee women did come forward to protest the move from holding land collectively to holding land individually. They knew that Euro-Americans planned to use allotment to, one-by-one, pry Cherokee land from individual landholders and they knew that with allotment married women would be stripped of their property rights.

Cherokee women also resisted missionary groups and fought to retain authority over their children. Initially, Cherokee leaders were interested in the schools Christian missionaries promised to build. Christian missionaries planned to use schools to educate Indigenous children and hoped to convert the Cherokee to Christianity by converting their children first. Over time, both missionaries and government officials used schools to push their version of "civilization" and proper gender roles on the Cherokee. Some women removed their children from mission schools, incurring the distain of missionaries. By the early antebellum period, male Cherokee leaders centralized Cherokee government stripping local towns of political independence. The lifestyles of the men in leadership increasingly took on the trappings of Euro-American landowners, including the American system of enslavement of African Americans as chattels and not according to traditional systems of captivity in wartime. At the start of the 1820s, the Cherokee had their own alphabet and by the end of the decade their own periodical in their own language. Schools and schooling became an arm of the Cherokee nationalist project and contributed to assimilation.

By the start of the removal crisis, US officials and male Cherokee leaders had finished a decades long project of attempting to strip women of their traditional place in Cherokee life and government. An increasingly small number of men interfaced with US government officials who had long tried to persuade the Cherokee to voluntarily remove to the Far West. Power to negotiate land sale rested with the centralized Cherokee government and the fate of women's long-held homelands rested in the hands of men less resistant to assimilation.

Indigenous Women Strategize for Survival: Violence and Indian Removal

No one knew the benefit to violent expulsion better than Andrew Jackson. Famed as an "Indian Fighter" before his victory at New Orleans in 1815 solidified his fame as an American war hero, Jackson and other men of means knew the potential for agricultural expansion in the Old Southwest. Just as he fought furiously against Indigenous groups in Tennessee, Jackson rushed headlong into Florida in 1817. The Seminole, long the holders of land in Florida even with the lingering Spanish presence in the region, were his target. The Seminole, Jackson believed, posed a threat on America's southern border. They not only remained strong but they also famously took in fugitives from slavery. Jackson's aim was to push beyond the then President Monroe's direction to exercise restraint and caution along the border. He attacked forts that housed subjects of Spain and England along with Seminoles. John Quincy Adams, the secretary of state, cleaned up Jackson's mess and Europe, weary from the Napoleonic Wars, was in little position to challenge American actions on the far outer reaches of its empires. Jackson's foolhardy campaign earned him a reputation and a following that he would later exploit to campaign for President. The lesson learned was that white Americans wanted a Federal government that protected their rights and claims to land over those of Indigenous people. Their ideology of Manifest Destiny outweighed notions of "civilizing" missions and peaceful cohabitation with Indigenous people, in favor of outright removal and extermination.

The land that Indigenous groups lived on in the Deep South were lands that held significant natural resources. The Choctaw and Chickasaw had homelands on rich cotton land in Mississippi and Alabama. In Alabama, Creek and Cherokee lands were in proximity to gold finds. The same was true for the Cherokee in Georgia. The increasing number of Euro-Americans migrating to the Deep South throughout the

1810s exploded in the 1820s and 30s. They brought enslaved people with them and stoked a booming market to purchase more enslaved people to work cotton fields, clear land, and harvest timber bringing plantation agriculture to the region. Settlers overran Indigenous lands that had been in the sites of speculators, planters, and the government for decades.

The desire to remove Indigenous people from lands that white settlers coveted was not a new one in the 1830s. Treaties in the 1810s and 20s with Indigenous groups included provisions to encourage groups to leave their homelands for territory west of the Mississippi River. Some groups, including some Cherokee, even decided to leave. But many more Indigenous groups refused. Both Indigenous people who assimilated to Euro-American cultural and political norms, and those who did not, fully intended to continue to live on their homelands. When Andrew Jackson won election to the presidency in 1828, the coalition of Southern voters to championed him fully expected him to remove Indigenous people from their lands in the South. Voters knew and liked Jackson's stance that negotiating with Indigenous people was pointless and that violence between settlers and Indigenous people was a forgone conclusion. The Cherokee were Jackson's target community. If congress would back him on the issue of their removal, other Indigenous groups would be removed with less legislative trouble.

Indigenous people were not passive victims of white encroachment or ideology. They played an active role in defining their future even as US leaders levied American policy and military might against them. The Cherokee took to the courts to argue for their land rights. In defiance of Georgia legislation that stripped them of their civil rights and banished missionaries from their lands, the Cherokee began fighting a prolonged legal battel. In 1830, Gregoria instituted a land lottery that encouraged white incursion on Cherokee lands and lead to violence and turmoil. In 1834, when the Supreme Court of the United States ruled in favor of Cherokee land rights, Gregoria and Georgians, backed by President Jackson, simply ignored the court's authority.

Americans, particularly reformers in the northeast who had supported "civilizing" missions and missionaries, were appalled at Jackson's violent move to remove the Cherokee. Prominent figures like Jeremiah Evarts, of the American Board of Commissioners for Foreign Missions, wrote an impassioned dissent. Indian missions, a favorite cause of women's missionary societies, were supported by an incredible number of female donors. Many white women in these associations outside of the South thought removal were immoral and organized concerted political action to protest removal. Women collected signatures for petitions to national leaders in which they demanded respect for the rights of "civilized" Indigenous people. As Catharine Beecher expressed in her plea to American women to petition in support of the Cherokee, "The laws and regular forms of a civilized government are instituted; their simple and beautiful language, by the remarkable ingenuity of one of their race, has become written language with its own peculiar alphabet. . ." the Cherokee had done what they were asked, she argued, they assimilated to Euro-American standards and were worthy of white women's support.

Beecher's tone betrays a reality that all Indigenous groups had long confronted: American racism. Earlier white arguments for "civilizing" Indigenous people aimed at making them over in the image of Euro-American social and political standards relied on the idea that it was Native people's culture that needed to change. But all along, in confrontations over Natives' lands, Euro-Americans made clear that race, not ethnicity, was the most important social marker to them. What Andrew

Jackson brought with him to the White House was a hardened racist policy refined in violent campaigns against Indigenous people. What he expressed and pursued through legislation and military action as President reflected the views of many Americans who lived far away from reformer's drawing rooms and lecture halls. To them what mattered was that Indigenous people were not white and their lands were white people's destiny. They knew Beecher was wrong when she wrote, "the Indian nations have faded away. Their proud and powerful tribes have gone. . ." They knew Indigenous people were very present and stood in the way of their prosperity. And they wanted their state and federal governments to privilege them over Indigenous people who they believed could never be their equals.

The program to remove Indigenous people from the Southeast to the Far West cost thousands of Indigenous people's lives. Many died from exposure or from the violence of federal troops who forced Indigenous people from their homes and marched them to the Far West at gunpoint. The federal government removed tens of thousands of Indigenous people and white planters moved tens of thousands of enslaved people into the Deep South. Violent tandem forced migrations made Cotton king and left Black and Indigenous people to reformulate strategies for resistance and survival.

Regions Drift Apart: Womanhood, Labor, and Regionalism

During the antebellum period, regional cultural differences became increasingly more pronounced. In the North, urbanization, industrialization, the arrival of immigrant women, and a wave of revivals inspired white women to become activists and advocates of moral and spiritual causes. A rising population of free African Americans advocated for abolition and aided fugitives from slavery, sought social and political equality, and recognition as citizens. In the South, white women upheld slavery as an economic and social system and even couched their slaveholding as a type of social work. White Southern women organized and participated in reform movements at rates significantly lower than their Northern counterparts. Black women, free and enslaved, enacted strategies of resistance and survival in community. Their antiracist and antislavery activities shaped the South in significant ways even though they had little or no access to the reform movements that free Black women participated in outside of the South. In the West, missionary women and settlers alike saw their colonial activity as a type of social work as well. Indigenous women resisted incursion and braced for the havoc of American expansion. Some Black women sought freedom in the Far West. Whether they fled west from enslavers in the East or were born free, Black women in the Far West attempted to build their own freedom. Each region produced competing visions of idealized women and womanhood in line with the political sectionalism, politics based on regional concerns and identity, that developed during the period.

Most women of all classes and races spent their days consumed by labor. The increasing importance of the market economy and the wider availability of finished and processed goods did not immediately make women's work as domestic managers and producers obsolete. Women in all regions still performed much of the labor that turned raw goods and purchased goods into clothing and meals. Without refrigeration beyond root cellars, cool bodies of water, and, in some regions, ice for sale, women's labor preserving food kept their families alive through the agricultural cycle. What antebellum society considered appropriate women's labor was classed, raced, and dependent on region and immigration status. Their work outside of their domestic roles depended on the intersection of these other social markers. The market economy and rise of industrialization necessitated a rise in wage labor. The wage labor available to women was also contingent upon regionally constituted gender norms.

Earlier in the nineteenth century, immigration from Europe to the United States rose, particularly in American cities. By the 1830s, German and Irish immigrants numbered in the hundreds of thousands. In 1845, when a famine caused by British imperial policy began in Ireland, the number of Irish immigrants rose sharply. They joined the communities that previous waves of immigration founded. Irish women immigrated in large numbers to work as domestics. Irish men joined the ranks of previous generations of men who worked at hard labor and in rapidly industrializing urban centers. American factory owners, public works foreman, and any number of businesses were happy to have a ready supply of cheap labor. But many Protestant Americans worried about labor competition and the religious beliefs of the Irish and some German immigrants: Roman Catholicism.

As their numbers rose, and political parties saw an opportunity to build voting blocs among immigrant men, anti-immigrant sentiment among Protestant Americans rose. Immigrant communities shaped America's urban centers by carving out ethnic neighborhoods and building leisure and print cultures all their own. They founded benevolent societies. They built churches and synagogues. Their arrival inspired those Euro-Americans with means to flee inner cities for neighborhoods further from crowded and dirty commercial and trade districts. Horse drawn street cars and ferries made it possible for middle-class and wealthy American-born whites to leave immigrants to the squalor of crowded neighborhoods near the factories and seaports that employed them.

Jewish and Catholic immigrants suffered discrimination and violence. Women commanded lower wages than men and often had to piece together marketing, domestic work, and even factory work to help their households survive. Immigrant communities often competed with other immigrant communities and African Americans for jobs making it easy for business owners to pit groups against each other and keep wages low. Irish and Black women, for example competed for work as laundresses and domestic workers. Laundry was one of the most taxing types of labor. Most women with any money to spare sent their wash out or hired domestic servants to help with it. Difficult, hot, and hard on women's bodies and hands, laundry work was often the only work available for women who needed to earn wages and keep an eye on their children.

The work of poor, working class, and immigrant women made it possible for middle-class women to enjoy leisure time that had only been available to wealthy women in generations past. Work for pay outside of the home was generally seen as unsuitable for women of their class, particularly for married women. Middle-class women and wealthy women worried about the rise in urbanization, the teeming crowds of immigrants and single American-born white men who clerked, managed, and ran the economic juggernaut of industrial commerce. With wages in their pockets, young men away from the watchful eye of their families fell into vice: drinking, gambling, and frequenting brothels. How could young men fulfill their role as husbands and heads of household if they were lost to vice in their youth?

Middle- and upper-class white women feared that young women were in danger of falling prey to vices in American cities as well. Reforming social and economic ills with religious answers became the calling of many Northern women who, because of their class position, considered themselves arbiters of what womanhood should be and considered themselves holders of America's moral standards.

The American South remained far more rural than the American North. The problems and concerns of urban life in the South's urban centers were mitigated by chattel slavery. For example, immigrants and poor whites did not find employment opportunities outside of the most dangerous labor in Southern cities because southerners relied on enslaved people's labor. Even southerners who could not afford to own enslaved people hired them, sending their wages to their enslavers, for short periods of time for far less than a free white laborer would demand. Southerners, including southern white women, remained invested in the racial hierarchy and economic system that slavery provided.

In the South, most Euro-American women were never members of households wealthy enough to rely on enslaved women for all of the domestic labor needed to keep their farms and plantations running. Most enslaved women had to do field work for all or part of each year's agricultural cycle. On small- to mid-sized farms, enslaved women and their female enslavers may have done some domestic labor side-by-side when Black women could be spared from the fields. Farms and plantations often also had domesticated animals that could be used for meat and gardens and orchards for produce. In the South, enslavers often still made use of old cloth production techniques to clothe enslaved people. Free women of color found work throughout the rural South spinning cotton for cloth making and were often registered as spinsters in free person of color registries. "Slave cloth" required enslaved women and white women to spin and weave rough cloth. On small- and mid-sized farms and plantations, enslavers often hired in free people of color to supplement their small enslaved labor force. Free women of color, hired for a year at a time, often lived with enslaved people and performed similar labor. Black women were also involved in all facets of child rearing for both Black and white children. Only the wealthiest families could afford to enslave a woman solely to care for their children, but enslavers of lesser means did rely on enslaved women to tend and rear young children, Black and white, over their day's work.

Enslaved women cultivated cash crops like tobacco in Virginia and North Carolina, rice in South Carolina, and cotton in the Deep South. Enslavers used enslaved people to cultivate cash crops, unlike subsistence crops, in large amounts so that those crops could be sold at market. They then used the money made from the sale of the harvest to survive. Come harvest time, all hands were required to bring in cash crops like tobacco, rice, sugarcane, and cotton. On landholdings of all sizes, enslavers expected enslaved women to process cash crops for market. They dried, graded, and prepared tobacco for packaging in hogsheads. They pounded rice to separate its grains from its shell. They ginned cotton for baling.

Wealthy and middle-class white women acted as managers of their and their husband's domestic lives, but they were not bystanders to slavery. They actively participated in enslaving Black people at all class levels. Even women who could never afford to own a single enslaved person benefited from the existence of slavery and the flourishing economy slavery made possible. Enslaved people were not simply laborers. Their labor was valuable. But they were also valuable movable property. Enslavers could use them as collateral for loans, sell them to cover losses in an agricultural cycle, and those who enslaved women were entitled to their children as well. Black women's reproductive labor increased their value on the slave market *and* increased their enslaver's wealth. Some women were enslavers in their own right. The South's laws about marital property reflected the ruling class's interest in preserving women's inheritance and protecting them from fortune seeking husbands. In some cases, women continued to manage their dowries and enslaved property after marriage. They bought and sold enslaved people, they disciplined enslaved people using violence, and they thoroughly enjoyed the leisure that enslaving provided them. When Sarah and Angelina Grimke left the South to become radical Quaker abolitionists, the forsook what many white women were more than happy to enjoy: the luxury that enslaved people's labor provided. Southern women's vision of womanhood was far more self-aware and explicit about the exploitation that made it possible in contrast to their Northern counterparts.

Class Relations and Women's Activism: Constructing a Deserving Poor

Poverty in antebellum America accompanied the period's economic booms. The cycle of boom and bust often left investors destitute, workers unemployed, and poor houses overcrowded. There were few protections for investors and very little regulation of the nation's financial system. In the antebellum period, President Jackson destroyed the National Bank and financial crisis ensued. Financial wrangling led to a cycle of boom years followed by economic depressions that left investors and workers with nothing. Wages for works were low, for women, they were lower still. Very few working-class women achieved financial independence from their husbands and male family members. Most worked in family and extended kin groups, pooling resources to scrape by month to month. Working-class women continued to do much of the processing work like food prep, clothing production and maintenance, and household labor needed to save their cash poor households' resources for other expenses. Taking in wash, doing piece work (work by the piece) at home, and selling foodstuffs all allowed women to keep watch on children underfoot and earn supplemental income. Some did sex work, the practice of exchanging sexual favors for money or goods, either supplementally or full time. But scaping and scrimping did not always leave women and their families with enough at the end of each pay period. Some households relied on cheap food vendors from day to day, making only enough to feed themselves for one day at a time. If they could not work or bosses cut wages, they did not eat.

The North was the site of the most women's organizing and reform work.

Southern white women did not organize in the same numbers as their northern counterparts. In the South, well-to-do women also formed benevolent societies and auxiliaries to men's religious institutions. They shared with their Northern counterparts a sense that women's role as domestic mavens and moral arbiters included acts of charity. In antebellum period, female enslavers tried to characterize their relationship to enslaved people as innately benevolent and an extension of their Christianity. Like middle- and upper-class women in the North, Southern women did not challenge pervasive gender norms or slavery. The Grimké sisters had to leave South Carolina behind for a reason, anti-slavery sentiment would not have been tolerated, least of all by women of their own class.

In the North, poor and working-class women's lives and choices of behavior, comportment, and clothing were all influenced by their lack of resources and ready cash. Often what middle-class and wealthy white women read as the slovenly, amoral, or unseemly behavior of the poor, working-class women knew to be part of survival in the very brutal system of wage labor with few protections for workers that pervaded. When middle- and upper-class women bemoaned the immoral culture of cities and wrung their hands about vice, poor and working-class women were often their targets.

Antebellum middle- and upper-class white women defined vice as habits and behaviors they deemed to be immoral like gambling, consuming alcohol, and sex work. Vices held people and controlled. Love of vice made it impossible for the poor to escape poverty. The term vice has a moral and spiritual connotation. Dominant gender roles dictated that women were responsible for influencing men's behavior and raising morally upright children. The "deficiency" reformers ignored in poor and working-class women was financial and economic. In an economic system that exploited laborers and made it impossible for poor women's male kin to make wages large enough to support them, women could not forgo work outside of their homes and take up the life of middle-class women.

The most popular form of women's activism grew out of religious benevolence work meant to both save souls and address material concerns like shelter, clothing, and food for the most destitute. Dominant gender roles dictated that "respectable" women did not enter public life by having a profession or advocating for political causes. But reform work couched in the rhetoric of Protestant Christianity, morality, and framed as an extension of women's "proper" domestic care work, allowed many women to address social problems indirectly. Campaigns against alcohol consumption often cited alcohol as the root of marital physical and sexual abuse, for example. The Temperance movement provided women with a way to campaign against the many ways they were vulnerable to men without directly challenging gender roles.

As the nation's Northern cities grew, issues of poverty, sanitation, and vice also grew. Dominant Protestant ideals prescribed that hard work, virtue, and Christian ethics were the solution to the era's social issues. With prayer, diligence, and good home economics, most middle-class women believed, like Catharine Beecher, that poverty could be if not eradicated then at least alleviated. If a poor person could become rich by working hard, they reasoned, a poor person would remain poor only because they did not work hard enough. Reformers sought to reform the moral and cultural attitudes of the poor so that they could work to better their situations. This view ignored that the economic system, state and federal laws, and ethnic and racial prejudice hindered their ability to change their fortune. Direct relief was for the most deserving poor: those who had no part in their present circumstance like widows, children, the ill, and the disabled. But even for people in those categories, relief was rarely financial or focused on the structural conditions, like the lack of worker's protections, that lead to poverty. Instead, women focused on the material like shelter or clothing.

Dominant beliefs about gender held that women were more moral and nurturing than men. Many believed that women were innately suited to domestic tasks and childrearing. Dominant gender norms dictated that women be more pious and take up responsibility for the moral character of their households. Many middle-class women took the leisure time provided them by poor and working-class woman's labor and worked to benefit the moral good of their communities. They believed sincerely that poverty was the result of sin and middle-class and that wealthy women should work to make the world around them more morally correct. Early efforts by women included the tradition of well-to-do women visiting the poor to evangelize and offer aid. Women also worked to help fund asylums for the poor that helped "respectable" poor women and kept them from falling into immorality, like vice and sex-work, to make ends meet. Women did not see their charitable work with the poor as political and were not interested in upending the economic structures that contributed to urban poverty. Initially, the female aid societies that white women founded and their benevolent work did not challenge gender norms or economic conditions.

In contrast, Black women who resided in Northern urban areas took up the cause of anti-slavery in the earliest days of the United States. They worked with men in their communities to found benevolent societies and institutions like churches and schools. Middle-class Black women, who often worked as domestics or had some other form of business or employment, saw their work among the Black poor, fugitives from slavery, and within religious institutions as key components to their version of womanhood. Very few African Americans approached the wealth of well-to-do whites. But their commitment to community uplift was innately political as was their commitment to the cause of abolition. Black women and men knew that full citizenship was the mark of true freedom and their institutions reflected this.

Women began to branch out from earlier forms of benevolence by the end of the 1810s. In the 1820s, many reform-minded Americans, men included, blamed alcohol consumption for many of America's social ills. In a time and place where respectable women could never have spoken about sexual assault, domestic abuse, or the inequality of men's and women's wages, taking up the issue of alcoholism allowed them to engage in public discourse. Addiction was understood as a moral failing at the time. In what came to be known as the Temperance movement, women worked tirelessly to end alcohol consumption and Protestant religious denominations began to advocate for total abstinence from alcohol. Alcohol stood in for any number of social ills and women found space and purpose in combating alcohol consumption with prayer, pamphlets, and banning alcohol from their homes.

Women also supported and joined moral reform societies supporting efforts to curb sex-work and vice. They pitied female sex workers who they increasingly saw as victims of male lust, the absence of male family members to protect them, and vice. They prayed for "fallen women" and asserted the ways that men abused women's natural dependance on them. But rather than upend this power differential by arguing for women's independence from men, reformers pushed for efforts that would make men more moral. They supported Bible societies that handed Bibles out to young men and engaged in religious proselytizing meant to lead men and women to moral correctness. They also turned to prison reform to rehabilitate those who had fallen short of their moral ideals. Reformers hoped that prisons or penitentiaries would provide humane spaces for sinners to do penance, rehabilitate, and become moral productive members of the working class.

Reformers were not just focused on prisons but also on asylums, mental hospitals, and poorhouses. As moral arbiters, many reform-minded women considered the treatment of those incarcerated in these state-run facilities as under their purview. They wanted an end to the mistreatment of inmates and patients, provide good moral job training for inmates to encourage work rather than a life of crime, and advocated for compassionate care for the mentally ill. But despite their best intentions, as with other forms of reform, middle-class women often had a hard time with women and men who were not immediately grateful for their efforts and often ended up seeing inmates as "undeserving" of their energy, particularly those women jailed for crimes involving sex. Nevertheless, their focus on conditions in state-run facilities held state officials accountable.

This type of public work was just short of political involvement and the organizational skills women refined in early reform movements prepared them for the organizational work of the movement against slavery and for women's rights. The movement for abolition encompassed a broad coalition of Black and white activists and reformers. Women, both Black and white, played significant roles as organizers, thinkers, and risked their lives to deliver fugitives from slavery to freedom. Black women and white women made their fight for abolition moral *and* political, challenging gender conventions. Simultaneously, white female activists began to formulate their case for women's rights often echoing Black women's intellectual and activist labor, with and without acknowledging them. At the height of the antebellum period, anti-slavery and women's rights would challenge reformer's coalitions and impact national politics in incredible ways.

Conclusion

Women continued to argue within organizations about what women's proper place in society should be. At the time, "respectable" women did not address mixed-gender audiences and their work in mixed-gender organizations often related women to axillary or supportive roles and not leadership. Women formed their own organizations in which they took up leadership roles. Outside of formal world of reform organizations, work-class women, poor women, Black women, and Indigenous women were often at odds with the wealthy and middle-class women bent on reforming them and disparaging their ethnic, class, and regional definitions of womanhood.

The Grimké sisters boldly disavowed the trappings of enslaving and chose to work diligently to end slavery. They faced the threat of physical violence for their abolitionism. But at no time in their lives in Philadelphia did they ever worry that kidnappers would assault them and carry them to the South to sell them at auction like Black women in the same city feared. Similarly, Catharine Beecher worked to provide education to girls and to support America's housewives with sound advice on domestic economy. But she never knew poverty, and her righteous stance against women's rights in later decades assumed a level of privilege and financial means that few women enjoyed.

As America's political landscape was consumed by the fight over slavery and the violence of westward expansion, women would take the lessons they learned in reform movements and push into mainstream American political life in new ways. On the advent of the sectional crisis that led to the American Civil War, a small group of radicals insisted that women's political equality including the vote, not moral improvement, would truly change women's lives. Inconceivable and too radical for most, women's rights activists developed their politics over years of hard work in reform movements.

Bibliography

Berry, Daina Ramey. *The Price for Their Pound of Flesh: The Value of the Enslaved, from Womb to Grave, in the Building of a Nation.* Reprint edition. United States: Beacon Press, 2017.
Dorsey, Bruce. *Reforming Men and Women: Gender in the Antebellum City.* 1st edition. Ithaca, NY, London: Cornell University Press, 2006.

Ginzberg, Lori D. *Women in Antebellum Reform*. 1st edition. Wheeling, IL: Wiley-Blackwell, 2000.

Glymph, Thavolia. *Out of the House of Bondage: The Transformation of the Plantation Household*. 1st edition. Cambridge; New York: Cambridge University Press, 2008.

Johnson, Walter. *Soul by Soul: Life Inside the Antebellum Slave Market*. 58327th edition. Cambridge, MA: Harvard University Press, 1999.

Jones-Rogers, Stephanie E. *They Were Her Property: White Women as Slave Owners in the American South*. Illustrated edition. New Haven London: Yale University Press, 2020.

Painter, Nell Irvin. *Sojourner Truth: A Life, A Symbol*. Revised edition. New York, NY: W. W. Norton & Company, 1997.

Scheer, Mary L, ed. *Women and the Texas Revolution*. Reprint edition. Denton: University of North Texas Press, 2014.

Smith, Stacey L. *Freedom's Frontier: California and the Struggle over Unfree Labor, Emancipation, and Reconstruction*. Reprint edition. Chapel Hill, NC: The University of North Carolina Press, 2015.

Women's Rights National Historical Park (U.S. National Park Service). Accessed January 11, 2023. **https://www.nps.gov/wori/index.htm**.

CHAPTER 8

Disunion, 1850–1860

The antebellum period (1830–1860) brought old questions about the meaning of American liberty to bear on national politics. Women's activism of earlier decades shifted abolition, the immediate stop of American chattel slavery, from a fringe radical position to a mainstream concern. New legislation that built on decades of tacit support for the system of slavery made slavery, and the place of African American people in American society, a consideration for all Americans. In the far West, forms of unfree labor and slavery existed before American incursion. A white American public that at one point had been apathetic about slavery came to see the spread of American chattel slavery as an important moral and political question. Women's reform work helped to make this shift in mainstream politics possible.

Right after the American Revolution, enslaved people numbered about 680,000. By 1800, the enslaved population numbered just over one million, despite many northern states' manumission programs. Slavery, as some in the Revolutionary generation had hoped, was not simply fading away. It was expanding. Over the course of the early nineteenth century, enslavers sold tens of thousands of enslaved people to states further south. For example, in Virginia in 1790, enslaved people were just under 40% of the state's population. By 1860, on the eve of the Civil War, enslaved people made up about 30% of Virginia's population. Enslavers were intent on moving slavery and enslaved people everywhere they could west of the Mississippi River. Those who could not afford to purchase slaves and those who believed slavery was wrong did not remain apathetic and openly opposed enslavers. American territory west of the Mississippi River became the setting for a prelude to violence and the promises, and disappointments, of the Civil War and Reconstruction. American women did not simply experience these political, social, economic, and cultural changes, and they played an active role in making them – shaping the nation in the wake of unprecedented destruction.

American Women's History: A New Narrative History, First Edition. Melissa E. Blair, Vanessa M. Holden, and Maeve Kane.
© 2024 John Wiley & Sons, Inc. Published 2024 by John Wiley & Sons, Inc.

The Dred Scott Decision: Women's Intimate Lives, Marriage, and American's Crisis over Slavery

In 1847, an enslaved man named Dred Scott sued for his freedom from his enslaver. The case would take a decade to wind through appeals and different courts on its way to the Supreme Court of the United States. In 1857, Chief Justice Roger B. Taney authored the majority opinion of the Supreme Court and famously ruled that because Scott was Black, and he was not a citizen and had no right to sue his enslaver. Additionally, the court ruled that the 1820 Missouri compromise that limited the spread of slavery in US territories north of Missouri's southern border was unconstitutional and Federal legislation could not limit slavery in American territories. The landmark case, colloquially called the Dred Scott decision, was both a significant moment in US legal history and harbinger of bloodshed. While Scott and Taney's names remain famous, two others point to the intimate dimensions of the national argument about American chattel slavery deserves: Harriet Robinson Scott and Irene Emmerson Chaffee

The Dred Scott Decision exposes the connection between questions of intimacy, family, and the "private sphere" to the "public sphere" of nationwide public, political, and social quandaries. As historian Tera W. Hunter demonstrates, the heart of Scott's freedom suit was his marriage to Harriet Robinson that took place sometime in 1836 or 1837. Forced migration, Indian Removal, planter migration, and the internal slave trade all impacted women's lives, just as the impacted Harriet Robinson Scott, in both private and public ways. And women responded in kind, in private and public. Harriet Scott sued for her freedom, just like her husband, and did so claiming the rights and privileges of married womanhood. And the Scott's enslaver, the recently widowed Irene Emmerson Chaffee, negotiated life as a widow and an enslaver with a sharp sense of how her own status gave her some privileges while foreclosing others.

Mrs. Eliza Irene Emerson married John Emmerson 1838 close to the time that the Scott's married. Emerson's service as a military physician required travel. Previously, Emerson took Dred Scott to St. Louis, Illinois, and the Wisconsin Territory having purchased Scott from his original enslavers. In 1840, Emerson left his wife and enslaved property behind when transferred to serve in the Seminole Wars in Florida, an extension of the US government's violent removal program to expel the Seminole from their homelands. The Scotts remained with Irene Emmerson on her father's plantation near St. Louis, and she hired them out in the surrounding era. Like many female enslavers, Irene Emerson actively participated in managing her husband's human property. She, like other Euro-American women of her class, actively benefited from the labor of the Scotts by receiving the wages they earned. When her husband returned to Missouri after his honorable discharge in 1842, he moved to the Iowa Territory and by 1843 she followed her husband. The Scotts most likely remained in St. Louis, hired out by the Emersons, and received wages that in part or full went to their enslavers, even though the Emersons lived in a free US Territory. The personal story of the Emerson's marriage and their enslaved property intersected the major political questions of the day: expansion, Indian Removal, and slavery.

John Emerson died in December 1843. At the time, Emerson had hired the spouses to a grocer in St. Louis. Living independent of their enslavers, most likely keeping some of their wages for their basic needs and sending the rest to their enslavers, the Scotts had saved enough to purchase their freedom. But Mrs. Emerson's situation changed with the death of her husband. She now needed to support herself, and enslaving the Scotts provided her with a pathway to do so while remaining respectable. She chose to hire Dred Scott out to an Army captain, an arrangement that would inevitably take Scott away from his wife who was to remain with their enslaver. Mrs. Emmerson declined the Scotts' offer to purchase themselves. She, like many other widowed slaveholding women, intended to support herself with the wages from the Scotts' lifetime of labor.

While Dred Scott's name is associated with the suit, Harriet Scott brought her own suit against their enslaver as the historian Tera Hunter points out. When Emmerson refused their offer to purchase their own freedom, the Scotts turned to the courts to stay together. For the Scotts, their time in a free state and a free territory coupled with their marriage formed the grounds for their claim to freedom. For Mrs. Emerson, her social position as a white woman and widow of an army surgeon meant that slavery remained a lucrative way to stay solvent. Both women, Harriet Scott and Irene Emerson, made important claims to womanhood, married status, and citizenship, within gendered and raced limitations.

After years of appeals, the Scotts' suit failed, the Supreme Court dealt a crushing blow to slavery's opponents, and the expansion of America's system of chattel slavery continued to be profitable for white enslavers and the businesses that supported them. During the years that the Scotts' freedom suits made their way through the American legal system, Irene Emmerson remarried to Dr. Calvin Chaffee. Again, her status as a married woman determined her civil and financial reality. Her second husband was a supporter of anti-slavery and, at the time of the Supreme Court decision, he was a congressman from Massachusetts, a hotbed of abolitionist activism. He could not intervene in the court proceedings, but Irene's husband now controlled her property, including the Scotts. He transferred ownership of the Scotts to one of the sons of Dred Scott's former enslaver. Like many female enslavers, Irene Emmerson Chaffee was still a savvy businesswoman. She demanded the equivalent of the Scotts' wages in exchange for the transfer of the Scotts to their new enslaver. She still benefited from their labor even as she relinquished ownership. Taylor Blow, their new enslaver, manumitted the Scotts in short order. The couple lived in St. Louis joining the city's free Black population. Dred Scott worked as a porter and Harriet Scott took in wash. The reality of free Black life was still hard labor but importantly for the Scotts, freedom also meant a life together.

The Scotts' story spans the geographic realities of the expanding nation. They were caught up in the migratory trends of enslavers and Euro-Americans just like thousands of other African Americans and Indigenous people. Most Euro-Americans had long seen the West, to which St. Louis was the gateway and trailhead, as the solution to any number of class and social ills. In the West, middling and poor white men had a chance at land, self-sufficiency, and full citizenship as heads of household. Whenever Americans from other racial, ethnic, and genders strove for the same, both society and the government worked to squash them. The Scotts' freedom suits exemplified just how quickly the quarrels of the East determined the battlegrounds of the West. Whether in the Northwest Territory or the Old Southwest/Deep South, Euro-American men believed they were destined for mastery: of the land, of their wives and children, and, in the South, of enslaved people. Of course, the Scotts' story also points to another reality most holders of the fantasy of Manifest Destiny had to face: the West was not empty untouched wilderness. Their enslaver's military career demonstrated that violence, not destiny, "won" the West. Rather, the West was already populated by often prosperous and strong Indigenous groups. Enslaved by an Army surgeon and hired out to another Army officer, Dread Scott and his wife knew that violence against resistive Indigenous people was part and parcel of the "destiny" Euro-American's believed was their right.

From the Margins to the Center: Abolitionism and Women's Activism in the Antebellum Period

By the start of the 1850s, white women established active roles in benevolent societies, movements for anti-vice moral suasion, "civilizing" missions among Indigenous people, and the anti-slavery movement. In previous decades, some middle-class white women came to see their role in society in much the same way that many of women of color long had – as community leaders. Women were not voters, and basic civil rights were only afforded to them through their male spouses and kin. But for middle-class and wealthy women with the increased free time that the market economy and working-class women's labor afforded them were able to throw themselves into public life via religious and moral causes. Public speaking to mixed audiences remained taboo for respectable white women, and formal leadership roles within mixed-gender abolitionist organizations were often reserved for men in the early antebellum period. But the anti-slavery movement relied heavily on women's labor.

Black women, enslaved and free, demonstrated with their actions and participation in Black institutions their commitment to abolition and anti-slavery work. They took to their feet and fled their enslavers. They helped others along their journey to freedom. They worked with local vigilance societies to combat the kidnapping of free people of color from Northern cities. They organized within their local communities to resist slavery at every turn and advocated alongside the men in their community for abolition. Mary Ann Shad Cary, born free in Delaware, grew up in a household that aided fugitives from slavery on their journey north to freedom. As an adult, she committed her life to serving freedom seekers moving to Ontario, Canada, to set up a school for the children of those brave enough to flee to freedom. Black women were willing to take radical action to combat slavery and help freedom seekers.

White women mostly began their work in anti-slavery by first supporting the movement, led by men. Black activists, both men and women, often stood in conflict with the movement for moral suasion, because their experiences with racism and slavery taught them that moral suasion simply would not work. White women also found the established movement for abolition stifling and infantilizing. And so, like Black activists, they founded their own organizations.

In 1837, in New York City, the first Convention of American Anti-Slavery Women convened with nearly 200 women in attendance. It was a women's only event that explicitly rejected the auxiliary status most women worked under in the formal movement. Female speakers took to the podium to speak to both Black and white women packed into the Third Free Church. Many openly critiqued how women's roles in the anti-slavery and abolition movement did not include leadership. Not all women reformers joined them in their dissatisfaction. But for those who did it was clear, women could shift their role in the fight against slavery *and* their place in public life going forward.

"The Woman Question," became central to debates among abolitionist communities about their best way forward. The rise of the internal slave trade and significant victories for proponents of slavery forced men and women in the movement to reconsider the strategies of moral suasion, the belief that bad actors in society could be persuaded to change their sinful ways when activists ministered to them and convinced them that their actions were wrong and amoral. Some even reconsidered the tactics that Black abolitionist had long practiced in their own organizations and advocated for in interracial organizations such as political activism, self-defense, and even violence. What role women could play, particularly if strategies became more political, caused a major fissure in movement organizations.

In 1839, the Massachusetts Anti-Slavery Society made women full and equal members. While the change was applauded by some, other more traditional anti-slavery advocates were shocked and appalled. But women were not going to stop with changes in their membership status. In a range of social reformer movements, women had provided critical labor in petition drives, organizing meetings, hosting lecturers on the lecture circuit, and other support work. At the 1839 annual convention of the American Anti-Slavery Society, the organization appointed Abby Kelly to the business committee triggering moral panic from some of the more traditional members of the organization. Should women be in closed meetings with men? Was it appropriate to sit women on committees? Would these radical moves hurt the cause when presented to the public? The resolution led to conflict over women's participation in the society and caused a faction to break off and form their own organization: the American and Foreign Anti-Slavery Society. Their separate society would adhere to gender norms and refuse to entertain questions of women's rights. At the 1840 World's Antislavery Convention in London, most male delegates to the convention voted for separate seating for women from men and denied women the right to participate as delegates. The women who traveled to take part in the convention did not remain silent and their protest echoed across the Atlantic. Why, they challenged male leaders, could they not be leaders and equals in anti-slavery organizing? Out of their discontent, a new cause bubbled up into movement spaces: Women's Rights.

Facing exclusion from a movement their hours of labor built, the white women of the anti-slavery and abolitionist movements forged a new way forward. Much of their reform work in earlier decades centered domestic issues particular to women. While some women reformers would never advocate for expanding women's political and civil rights, the women who boldly worked in the radical movement to end slavery, Black and white, were well situated to take their reform work and develop the concept of women's rights for American women.

When Elizabeth Cady Stanton moved with her husband and children to Seneca Falls, New York, in 1847, the discontent and boredom with domestic drudgery that inspired her to seek out reform work and a circle of women who also did reform work, was a marker of her class status. Previous generations of working-class and poor women, Black women, and Indigenous women had forged types of womanhood for themselves that included outspokenness, advocacy, and labor. The middle- and upper-class, mostly white, women who built a movement from their anti-slavery and reform work often regarded women outside of their class and race as unfeminine, worthy of pity or scorn, and in need of reform. Some outliers among them did believe in true racial and class equality. But most had spent previous decades trying to reform the very women who could have given them a clear picture the lengths to which white middle- and upper-class men would go to preserve their power and status – even among radicals. For many, like Stanton, their winding path to Women's Rights wove through years of middle- and upper-class domestic labor, work as auxiliary members of reform movements, experience founding women's societies, and careful negotiations between "proper" femininity and their desire for meaningful work.

The network Stanton entered included powerhouse reformers and thinkers like Lucretia Mott, Mary Ann McClintock, and Martha Wright. They and their networks brought years of experience organizing to their newfound common cause. On 19 and 20 July 1848, they held a convention at Seneca Falls that drew about 300 people, including both men and women. By the time of the convention, the year 1848 had seen multiple republican revolutions in Europe. In present day Italy, Germany, and France, republican revolts challenged imperial rulers. The educated reform minded middle-class women who met to plan for the convention were aware of this climate of change and revolution. Before the Seneca Falls Convention, Elizabeth Cady Stanton and Mary Ann M'Clintock drafted the Declaration of Sentiments prior to convening the meeting and the document served as a guide for the convention. Intentionally using the language that Thomas Jefferson used in the Declaration of Independence, the women couched their claim to citizenship in the same God-given human writes. "We hold these truths to be self-evident: that all men and women are created equal; endowed by their Creator with certain inalienable rights. . ." they wrote.

Among the rights discussed at the convention were women's rights to their own wages and property, women's ability to speak and lead in religious spaces, and women's subjection to men's immoral behavior. But most stunning of all was the call for women's suffrage. With the vote, convention leaders believed, women could effect changes to the law to protect themselves and their children. Importantly, the convention did not challenge dominant gender norms or the belief that women's morality was inherently superior to men. They did not call for an overturn of the American economic system or class system. Instead, the reforms noted in their Declaration of Sentiments that they aligned with a staunch belief in individual responsibility and assumed access to education and professions that most Americans, men, and women, simply did not have.

The Convention implicitly most excluded poor women, working-class women, immigrant women, Black women, and Indigenous women though its organizers considered themselves to be magnanimous. Women outside of America's white middle class did not silently accept white middle-class women's visions for their rights. Black women, for example, continued their own advocacy for abolition and built wary coalitions with white women when expedient. Some Black leaders like Sojourner Truth and Frederick Douglass supported the cause, attended the convention, and saw potential for coalition.

Susan B. Anthony regarded the convention with amusement and at first did not understand the utility of calling for women's rights. She did not meet Stanton until 1851 and did not attend the convention in 1848, though her mother and sister did. But like many other women in reform movements, her ideas about women's rights would formulate over time. Anthony, born in 1820 in Massachusetts, grew up in a Quaker household primarily in upstate New York. Like many middle-class women of her generation, Anthony participated in multiple reform movements including the Temperance Movement and the Abolition Movement. Her family home in Rochester, NY, was often the meeting place of anti-slavery advocates. Just like many of the leaders at the Seneca Falls meeting, Anthony was eventually radicalized by the reform movements she supported. Not content to "listen and learn," while letting men speak and lead, Anthony came to her own understanding of women's rights and place in society. By 1854, Anthony made Stanton's acquaintance, attended a women's rights convention, and began her work as an advocate for women's suffrage and married women's property rights all while continuing to champion abolition.

The Crisis of 1850, Women in the West, and Women's Activism

When Harriet Beecher Stowe published Uncle Tom's Cabin in 1852, the decades long battle for abolition and manumission found a respectable cultural voice. Stowe was no Seneca Falls radical campaigning for women's rights, nor was she particularly interested in challenging antebellum gender roles or racial hierarchies. Her characters, Uncle Tom, Eliza, Topsy, and Little Eva, would go on to become American cultural architypes. Her Black characters, a wise and pious older enslaved man, a courageous and feminine mixed raced mother, and a mischievous enslaved girl each pulled at the heartstrings of Stowe's middle-class white readers. Unlike Dred and Harriet Scott, her imagined African American characters relied on white Americans to save and shelter them. Her white characters, both the unadulterated evil of the enslaver Simon Lagree and the pure innocence of Little Eva, a Southern white girl, provided white readers with clear villains and heroes. Her work conformed to the sentimental literary tropes of her time and encouraged white readers to think of American chattel slavery in deeply personal rather than economic terms.

What was once a fringe radical position, that slavery should be immediately abolished, slowly crept into mainstream American politics, and influenced major political party platforms. Women, like those who could afford to purchase and read Stowe's work, were integral to all facets of the movement for abolition. Both radical and moderate, women spoke up in clear and important ways on both sides of the most pressing American conflict: the political battle over slavery.

The battle over slavery reached beyond polite society's parlors and lecterns. Concerned with the fortunes of free white men, working-class communities increasingly saw enslaved laborers as unfair competition. If enslavers could bring enslaved people and slavery with them out West, would there be space for small-time landholders? If cities and towns made use of skilled enslaved laborers, what would become of white artisans and skilled workers? Many white Americans still could not bring themselves to advocate for immediate abolition. Very few but the most radical white activists believed in true racial equality. But mainstream apathy faded into vehement concern for many white northerners and westerners because the question of slavery's spread directly impacted them. This pushed women's voices into the public in ways that were previously unimaginable.

White women's cry for women's civil rights, while still radical, would greatly influence the mainstreaming of abolition and anti-slavery that boiled over into a national crisis in 1850. A few years earlier, in 1848, the same year that delegates met at Seneca Falls, the end of the Mexican War expanded America's empire significantly. In Europe, democratic revolutions against imperial powers. In North America, the

United States went to war with its democratic neighbor to the south when America annexed the border nation of Texas/Tejas. The Mexican War resulted in the United States claiming half of Mexico's territory and incorporating promising land in Texas and California into the new nation. But what could easily be represented on a map with the change of national borders was far messier on the ground. When at the end of 1848 gold was discovered in California, issues that politicians had hoped vast western territories would solve, catapulted to the center of political discourse. By 1850, California had a population of Euro-American settlers great enough to bid for statehood, and suddenly the question of free or slave status made lawmakers and enslavers back east fiercer in their defense of slavery.

California's history with unfree labor and American chattel slavery was fraught. Under Spanish and Mexican control, systems of unfree labor that enslaved Indigenous people flourished and remained in place when the United States gained control of the region. Through indentures, adoptions, and peonage, landowners and the Catholic church in Spanish and Mexican held California had long profited off the labor of Indigenous people. Women and children were particularly vulnerable to this form of slavery and were often exploited by colonizers. Indigenous people who had confronted colonizers before were faced with the increased migration of Euro-American settlers and their families with far more vast designs on settling in and claiming Native lands than their colonial predecessors. What wagon trains earlier in the century had predicted would soon be a settler population explosion.

Under Mexican law, women of European descent had property rights and some civil liberties. Women like Rosalia Vallejo de Leese woke up after the signing of the treaty of Guadalupe Hidalgo in 1848 to a world without those protections under American control. Suddenly, women had to rely on male kin in ways they previously had not. And, at every turn, Euro-American settlers angled to defraud them. Vallejo de Leese was a member of the prominent Vallejo family who were part of Mexican California's gentry, called Californios. Their land claims in northern California, and the Indigenous people who worked them made them wealthy. She witnessed and endured the Bear Flag Revolt of 1846, a revolt of Americans against Mexican control who aimed to take over California. By the time of the Mexican cession after the Mexican War, she was more than acquainted with American imperialism. Vallejo de Leese, like other women in her time, experienced her fortunes fall along with her male kin. First, she was abandoned by her husband. Then, in the ensuing decades of the nineteenth century, the Vallejo family lost their land to theft, US government policy, and financial hardship brought on by American incursion.

When Americans began to arrive in California in large numbers in 1849, some brought enslaved Black people with them to the gold fields to bolster their bid to strike it rich. Other white men viewed enslaved people as a threat to free white men's chances at making their fortunes and wanted enslaved labor outlawed in the territory and state. The choice of California to apply for statehood as a free state was far from easily made and remained a fraught sticking point among white settlers, both new and old. African American women in the Far West also advocated for their own freedom.

The Far West offered some Black women the chance to build lives that were not available to them back East. In 1848, Bridget "Biddy" Mason arrived in Salt Lake Valley in present-day Utah. Born enslaved in Mississippi, Mason walked nearly 2000 miles because her enslaver was a Mormon convert. Many Mormons looked to the West in the 1840s for refuge from religious persecution. Those who owned enslaved people, forced them to migrate with them. When her enslaver left Utah for

California in 1851, California had entered the United States as a free state because of the Compromise of 1850. With the help of other free Black people, Mason contested her enslavement and won her freedom and the freedom of multiple family members in 1856. Mason continued to work a midwife and nurse in southern California and used her earnings to purchase land in what is now downtown Los Angeles (LA), build the first African Methodist Episcopal Church in LA, and support her community through charitable work and giving.

Mary Ellen Pleasant was born sometime in the early nineteenth century. It is not clear if she was born free or enslaved but she did help the abolitionist cause in New England in the 1820s. When her first husband passed away, she took the wealth he left her, remarried in 1848, and sailed for California in 1850. Once in San Francisco she used her money to open boarding houses and laundries. As a successful business owner, Pleasant continued to support abolition and abolitionist. In 1859, she both funded John Brown's raid on Harper's Ferry *and* spent time recruiting for him in Virginia. She amassed a considerable real estate and business empire and used to fund her community, employ African Americans, and aid fugitives from slavery.

California had not entered the union as a free state without controversy. What historians call the Compromise of 1850, really five separate pieces of legislation, emboldened previously apathetic whites to take their cues from radicals. Women were empowered by the moral questions at the heart of anti-slavery – from free soil to immediate abolition. The compromise admitted California as a free state and abolished the slave trade in Washington, D.C. But it also established two territorial governments, one in New Mexico and one in Utah, brought Texas into the Union as a slave state, and gave the Fugitive Slave Act mechanisms for enforcement that made slavery, and the choice to uphold it, personally relevant to all Americans.

Conclusion

Immediate crisis was averted leaders in Washington, but many previously apathetic Euro-Americans, particularly those in free states and western territories, were inspired to think seriously about the moral, economic, and political question of slavery. For some, the cause of Free Soil, that is the containment of slavery and prohibition of its spread to US territories, was a way to bolster middle- and working-class white prospects. For others, the Fugitive Salve Act's mandate that all Americans, enslavers, and non-enslavers alike participate in returning fugitives from slavery back to a state of bondage went too far. Abolition, no longer such a radical proposition, was the only way they saw to curb Southern leader's overstepping their state boundaries. While only Black women and men and their most radical white allies would advocate for true social and political equality for emancipated people, far more white Americans than ever before were inclined to see slavery as both a moral ill and a central political issue.

Important cultural moments like the publication of Harriet Beecher Stowe's novel, significant judicial decisions like the Dread Scott decision, and the political crisis of 1850 made high politics in Washington, D.C. relevant in front parlors and pubs across the nation. No longer was the cause of anti-slavery a fringe radical concern, it was now in the mainstream. It was so mainstream that, with the vote split four ways, the Republican Abraham Lincoln, who ran on a free soil platform, stood election and won in 1860. Women may not have had the vote, but their long decades of activism greatly influenced the broader movement to end slavery. In the South, female enslavers stood staunch in their conviction that slavery should remain an option in all corners of newly gained US territories. In late 1860 and early 1861, before Lincoln could even be inaugurated, South Carolina, Mississippi, Florida, Alabama, Georgia, Louisiana, and Texas all seceded from the Union. As they began to form the Confederate States of America (CSA), women across the nation, of all colors, braced for war.

Bibliography

Field, Corinne T. *The Struggle for Equal Adulthood: Gender, Race, Age, and the Fight for Citizenship in Antebellum America*. 1st edition. Chapel Hill: The University of North Carolina Press, 2014.

Hunter, Tera W. *Bound in Wedlock: Slave and Free Black Marriage in the Nineteenth Century*. Reprint edition. Cambridge, MA: Belknap Press: An Imprint of Harvard University Press, 2019.

Isenberg, Nancy. *Sex & Citizenship in Antebellum America*. New edition. Chapel Hill, NC: University of North Carolina Press, 1998.

Myers, Amrita Chakrabarti. *Forging Freedom: Black Women and the Pursuit of Liberty in Antebellum Charleston*. Reprint edition. The University of North Carolina Press, 2014.

Nunley, Tamika Y. *At the Threshold of Liberty: Women, Slavery, and Shifting Identities in Washington, D.C.* Chapel Hill: The University of North Carolina Press, 2021.

Oertel, Kristen Tegtmeier. *Bleeding Borders: Race, Gender, and Violence in Pre-Civil War Kansas*. Illustrated edition. Baton Rouge: LSU Press, 2013.

Varon, Elizabeth R. *We Mean to Be Counted: White Women and Politics in Antebellum Virginia*. 1st edition. Chapel Hill: The University of North Carolina Press, 1998.

Wellman, Judith. *The Road to Seneca Falls: Elizabeth Cady Stanton and the First Woman's Rights Convention*. Illustrated edition. University of Illinois Press, 2010.

Yellin, Jean Fagan, and John C van Horne, eds. *The Abolitionist Sisterhood: Women's Political Culture in Antebellum America*. Illustrated edition. Ithaca: Cornell University Press, 1994.

CHAPTER 9

The Civil War: Women's Homefronts and Battlefields

Historical timelines are punctuated by wars because as social, political, and martial events, wars often bring with them significant social, political, technological, medical, and economic change. In the chaos of troop movements, the destruction of artillery, and shifting battle lines, civilians face daily choices of who to support, who to hinder, and when to simply get out of the way. Much of the American Civil War was fought in the American South with a few notable exceptions in the West and in the North. Women of all classes, races, and regions were impacted by the war's destruction: some on the Civil War's home fronts, others in military encampments, and even a few among the troops fighting the war's battles. New more efficient weapons made for bloody battles with high casualty counts unlike any other in American history. The destruction of property and agricultural products accords the American South visited unimaginable hardship upon the region's civilian population. The large-scale flight of Black Southerners from their enslavers to Union Army camps pressed a previously small federal government to rethink its role in the daily lives of its citizens and its reach to govern what were previously seen as state-specific issues. In all of this, women were present: on the battlefield, on the home front, within newly organized sanitary and medical units, and at the vanguard of finding new ways to grieve loss.

Harriet Tubman: Foot Soldier of Emancipation and War Veteran

As the turn of the twentieth century neared, Harriet Tubman, the Moses of her people, struggled to make ends meet. From 1849, her life had been spent on the frontlines of the fight for emancipation and freedom. She liberated herself and then personally

American Women's History: A New Narrative History, First Edition. Melissa E. Blair, Vanessa M. Holden, and Maeve Kane.

shepherded African Americans from her native Eastern Shore of Maryland north to freedom in New York and Canada. When the Civil War came, Tubman traveled to Port Royal, South Carolina, where the Union Army had a stronghold and recently emancipated people and soldiers needed care. There she worked for the US Army as a cook and a nurse. Famously, she also worked as a spy and lead of the Combahee River Raid in June 1863, freeing hundreds of enslaved people and destroying the estates where enslavers once held them in bondage.

After the war and after her first husband's death, Tuman married for a second time and continued to work to improve the prospects of the African American community in New York State. She eventually founded the nation's first convalescent home for African Americans, the Tubman Home for Aged and Indigent Negroes. The Civil War Era and the Era of Emancipation held great promise for Harriet Tubman, and the thousands of African Americans across the United States and its territories that hoped the bloody conflict would bring freedom and equality. But the government and the President's path to abolition was far slower than enslaved people's feet that carried them to Union Army camps. The federal government, US Army, and government officials would take four blood-soaked years to realize what Black Americans and their allies had long known: the time for abolition had come and slavery's days were numbered.

Even after the war, the issue of political, social, and economic racial equality would persist. During the war, Harriet Tubman only received $200 for three years of labor. At war's end, the government did not deem her service as a cook, a spy, and a nurse worthy of a government pension. Her work orchestrating the Combahee River Raid, a combat mission, did not make her eligible for a pension like the thousands of Black men who served. She did receive a widow's pension in recognition of her husband's service after his passing. But like many women in her generation, the government only recognized her service to the United States as a wife and not as solider and spy. Her eight dollar a month widow's pension payment was her only steady means of support.

Harriet Tubman, perhaps the most famous Black woman of her generation, renowned for her work on behalf of enslaved people and free people of color, navigated a post-Civil War America that had finally conquered the national sin of slavery but failed to leave behind racism and gender discrimination. Like many elderly people at the time, without savings or the ability to work, Tubman faced poverty in her final years. In the 1890s, with the help of white friends, Tubman sought an increase to her pension in recognition of her service. In 1899, after years of navigating bureaucracy, President McKinley approved Congress's increase of Tubman's pension from $8 to $20 a month. Officially, Congress awarded the increased pension in recognition of her husband's service. Congress was only willing to tacitly acknowledging what many knew: American women had served during the Civil War, and their underpaid and unpaid labor bolstered the Union's victory but offering them pensions for their service was not economically prudent.

1861: The Beginning

The American Civil War was supposed to be short and swift. Many, including newly elected President Lincoln, hoped it would not be a war at all. Before he could even take office a handful of Southern states lead by South Carolina seceded from the

United States. Still, the tone of the new President at his inauguration on 4 March 1861 was conciliatory yet firm. He ended his first inaugural address with the plea, "We are not enemies, but friends. We must not be enemies." Lincoln wanted to bring South Carolina, Georgia, Florida, Alabama, Mississippi, Louisiana, and Texas back into the Union without bloodshed.

In April 1861, cadets from the Citadel in Charleston, SC, fired on the US Army Fort, Ft. Sumter. Capturing the fort made negotiation without a show of force untenable for President Lincoln. Instead, he needed to send Federal troops to South Carolina to bring the states in open rebellion to heel. His call for military action led other states to secession. Virginia, North Carolina, Tennessee, and Arkansas left the union between April and June 1861. Delaware, Maryland, Kentucky, and Missouri, all slave states, remained in the Union but only tenuously. Civil War, a conflict avoided so many times in the nation's young history, had arrived. Patriotic fervor on both sides of the conflict held that victory was but one decisive battle away – that sacrifices would be necessary but that it would not last the year. Instead, Americans faced loss beyond their imagining and rates of attrition in battle previously unknown.

In the South, Euro-American women braced themselves for life without the male kin who would be called up to fight and for the potential arrival of federal troops. Black women, enslaved and free, saw the war as an opportunity to assert their freedom. Particularly in states closer to those that remained in the Union, along the coasts, and in major cities, African Americans saw the war as a war to free them from slavery from its beginning. Washington politicians and the President may have made overtures toward reunion without abolition, but enslaved and free people knew that they did not plan to remain enslaved.

Federal and military officials made no initial provisions for self-emancipated people arriving at US Army camps. Their strategy focused on encircling the South with US Naval vessels to cut them off from shipping lanes, attempting to command the Mississippi River to cut the heart of the CSA off from overland supply, and to slowly constrict until the CSA relented. Most hoped that the war would not even require the completion of the strategy. With a superior naval force, the United States quickly found success in major Southern ports and set up a formidable blockade. The Confederates, most Americans hoped, would come to their senses after a few key shows of force. But the first Bull Run, just outside of Washington, D.C. near Manassas, Virginia, demonstrated that the Union Army was not going to easily overtake the southern rebellion. The question of what to do with the thousands of Black men, women, and children who fled to early Union strongholds in coastal Virginia, South Carolina, and Louisiana remained. Were they slaves? Were they free? Would allowing them to stay with the Union Army encourage others to flee? What was the best way to keep states like Kentucky and Missouri in the Union?

Self-emancipated people did not care. And their insistence that they were free, particularly the insistence of Black women, forced the President, the Federal Government, and the US military to face the question of slavery whether they wanted to or not. Congress, now without firebrand Southern representatives to negotiate with, quickly began to enact policies that would have been impossible before. In December 1861, the House of Representatives passed legislation to abolish slavery in the District of Columbia. By April 1862, a year after Fort Sumner, the bill was law. All the while, the Black population of the Washington DC swelled with refugees from Virginia and Maryland. In this way, Southern Black women, without the vote or even legal ownership of themselves, defied law and custom to insist upon freedom for themselves and their kin.

Bloody Realities

At the start of armed conflict, most American women could not have predicted the large-scale suffering the war would bring. Antebellum Americans practiced a range of cultural rituals to grieve the passing of loved ones. White middle- and upper-class Americans, some of whom had access to embalming practices, marked the passing of loved ones in the way that they dressed. Women, in particular, were responsible for caring for the remains of the deceased, washing, and clothing the corpse. Family members took turns sitting with the body and neighbors and kin visited. Popular depictions of "good" deaths, a feature in melodrama and visual culture, included family gathered to sooth ailing loved ones as they ended their time on Earth peacefully. Ideally, the deceased's family laid them to rest in a local churchyard, cemetery, or family plot where their grave could be looked after by women in the family and their memory could be preserved with dignity. As time passed, family and descendants could visit the resting place of their ancestors and kin. This was not the reality for Americans who did not have the wealth needed to achieve this ideal. But "good" deaths were culturally significant at a time where death from illness, accidents, in childbirth, and in childhood were common. The Civil War upended cultural expectations for "good" deaths and women's roles in seeing to the remains of loved ones. Women's roles tending to the memory of lost loved ones shifted.

Neither Army was truly prepared for the volume of human remains left on battlefields because of increasingly efficient weapons. Estimates that account only for battlefield casualties place the number of American casualties during the American Civil War at 620000. Of course, soldiers were not the only people suffer death and injury during the war and some historians estimate a number closer to 800,000 total casualties to account for the loss of civilian life during the war. Casualty rates outpaced American's expectations at each engagement. During the Mexican War, a generation before, the United States lost just over 13,000 troops in battle. At Gettysburg, more than three times that number died. The 51,000 dead at Gettysburg outpaced the total casualties for the Revolutionary War and the War of 1812 combined. Accepted tactics dictated that a singular great battle would break the will of the enemy and bring about a swift end to fighting. This did not happen and with each battel came longer and longer lists of casualties.

For much of the early war, neither army had an official means by which to notify family or next of kin. Americans waited for newspapers to post lists of casualties but often had not means of knowing if injuries were severe or if at the time of posting their loved one was already dead. Without embalming, residents near battlefields and armies often scrambled to intern human remains quickly to avoid the outbreak of disease. Cannon fire had the ability to destroy soldiers' bodies and, even if they could have traveled to battlegrounds, families would not have found any of their loved one's remains left to bury.

Army camps were notoriously disease ridden. Large encampments of men with poor sanitation and close quarters bred epidemic disease quickly. Encampments became health hazards even more rapidly with the addition of hundreds or even thousands of African Americans fleeing bondage. Officials had only rudimentary understandings of contagion. Germ theory, pioneered in Europe, was in its infancy in the early 1860s and still many years away from wide acceptance. Together with battlefield casualties, disease posed a significant threat to the lives of soldiers on both sides and quartermasters remained ill equipped to combat outbreaks.

American women, of all classes, did the overwhelmingly unpaid labor of nursing, cleaning, and seeing to the health of their family members. From laundry to properly preserving and cooking foodstuffs, women's skilled labor kept men and children healthier. Whether that labor was done by an enslaved woman, a hired domestic worker, or the women of a household themselves, it was critical to the health and safety of American families. Wartime conditions took men far away from home and away from the work women had done for them their entire lives. Army camps did employ women as washers and the Army did consider how best to supply troops with very basic subsistence. Armies had always attracted camp followers, some the wives and families of soldiers, other women who engaged in both domestic and sex work. But more bodies often contributed to the problems of poor sanitation.

In 1861, the federal government authorized the formation of the US Sanitary Commission, a privet organization taxed with managing the high volume of dead and wounded soldiers. Women were on the frontlines of the push for better camp conditions and increased resources for sanitation. After the first Battle of Bull Run on 21 July 1861, members of the Women's Central Association for Relief (WCAR) based in New York were shocked to learn of the lack of medical supplies and sanitary precautions taken for the health of the wounded. Formed in April 1861 to organize women's efforts to send bandages, clothes, and even nurses to bolster the Union Army, the WCAR was like many women's organizations. With years of experience in reform movements, Northern middle-class women were quick to act in support of the war effort. Like many moderate organizations, the WCAR had a male president, Henry W. Bellows. Bellows personally traveled to Washington, D.C., to advocate for an organization that could take up large-scale sanitary efforts. In June 1861, the United States Sanitary Commission (USSC) gained the President's approval.

The USSC served as a central coordinating hub for relief organizations, with significant female membership, across the country. While not all relief organizations agreed to fall under the USSC's umbrella, the USSC did harness the volunteer labor of countless Northern women to supply the US Army with much needed medical supplies US Sanitary Commission volunteers and workers also played a pivotal role in advocacy in Army camps.

The same year that women's more traditional organizing pressured the Federal Government to fund the US Sanitary Commission, a much less traditional woman arrived in Washington, D.C. Dr. Mary E. Walker, a graduate of Syracuse Medical College in 1855, applied for an appointment as an Army surgeon. At the time, US officials were staunchly against women's official participation in the war as Army personnel. Walker famously wore bloomers, billowing pants, rather than a skirt marking her as a radical feminist who believed in dress reform – a movement to change women's clothing to suit their active lives and mitigate the danger of the large skirts in fashion at the time. Her application met staunch resistance, and the only option open to her was work on a volunteer basis in the many army camps in and around the city. While women's work supplying domestic goods, organizing sewing circles, and venturing into volunteer nursing would eventually transform nursing into a feminized profession, for women like Dr. Walker, the war would only provide the most meager of opportunities.

1862: A War for Emancipation

The question of what the government's responsibility to self-emancipated African Americans who continued to flee slavery was imperative as more and more Black refugees flooded Washington, D.C. The nation's capital city, once a hub of the internal slave trade from the upper to the lower South, swelled as African American's arrived determined to live free. Often destitute but determined, this growing population's defiance stood as a daily reminder that the question of slavery could not be ignored.

Congress and President Lincoln took steps toward abolition in 1862. Those first steps were the result of African Americans' long fight for freedom, abolitionists' advocacy, and the bravery of self-emancipated people. Congress decided first that fugitives from slavery would be labeled Contrabands of War, akin to the cannons and supplies commandeered by conquering armies. Congress argued that Confederate leaders benefited from the labor of enslaved people just as they had before the war. Military officials were not wrong in asserting that allowing fugitives from slavery to deprive their enslavers of their valuable labor was an important strategic move. But the government's insistence that self-emancipated people were still contraband property denied the reality evident when fugitives from slavery arrived in Union Army camps: Black people wanted freedom. At the start of the war Black men were not eligible to fight, but they did the hard the US Army needed to stay battle ready. They cleared land, dug ditches, built fortifications, and dug graves. Black women also found themselves in service of the US Army doing laundry and other domestic work as well as working land that the Army confiscated. African Americans were ready for freedom and acted accordingly, even if the Army and the Federal Government were not.

Hopes that the Civil War would be a short and swift conflict began to evaporate by 1862. And new weapons made the business of death far more efficient on both sides of the battle line with devastating consequences. The South, though outnumbered, out armed, and cut off from important global trade networks, held its own against the US Army. In the fall of 1862, Robert E. Lee executed an invasion on Union soil in Maryland, in hopes of mitigating destruction in the South and forcing negotiations between the United States and the Confederate States. When, after some initial engagements, the opposing armies met at Antietam, the resulting casualties stunned both sides. By the Battle of Antietam's end, an estimated 22,717 casualties overwhelmed the medical capabilities of both armies. The Confederates were forced into retreat. Union Commander George B. McLellan refused to pursue.

At the end of 1862, claiming Antietam as a victory, President Lincoln took a significant step toward realizing what enslaved people had already put into motion: he issued the Emancipation Proclamation. In it, he gave states in open rebellion against the United States until 1 January 1863, to return to the Union. If they failed to do so, the proclamation would emancipate all the enslaved people who remained in rebellion. Effectively, because of the Emancipation Proclamation, the Union Army arrived as an army of liberation. Additionally, the Emancipation Proclamation allowed the Union Army to recruit, train, and deploy Black men in segregated units lead by white officers. For white Americans, this transformed the war into the conflict that African Americans had long known it to be, a war for Emancipation.

Escalating Casualties and Advances in Sanitation

The volume at which soldiers were wounded, maimed, and killed influenced a significant cultural shift. Neither fighting force had standard procedures for informing family and kin of battlefield deaths. For those wounded but not killed immediately, filthy conditions in field hospitals often meant a slower more painful death from infection and disease. Neither army had well-organized systems for handling the volume of corpses left on battlefields, creating another sanitation hazard. Antebellum Americans expected that surviving family members would care for the remains of the deceased in normal circumstances. Only the poorest families relied on local municipalities to bury their dead. Wartime forced Americans to reconsider their definitions of a "good" death and respectful burial.

Across the nation, on both sides of the conflict, women volunteered their time to support the war effort. Some tapped into reform networks, others relied on connections through churches, and some made individual efforts to supply the army with bandages, blankets, fresh shirts, and socks. The 1861 founding of the US Sanitary Commission was one of many steps taken by the United States to mitigate the danger of untended dead. As the war dragged on, women played an increasingly important role in the fight against unsanitary conditions and epidemic diseases in Army camps and contraband camps. Women in the North volunteered as nurses, a profession dominated by men until then, by the thousands. Their work with the US Sanitary Commission would save lives and influence the institutional practices of battlefield interment.

Reformers and activists who championed the cause of abolition viewed the war as an opportunity to increase pressure on Congress and the President to abolish slavery. For some women's rights activists, the cause of abolition coupled with the war effort took precedence. Prominent women's rights leaders hoped that, after the war, their loyal service could be leveraged to meet other their other political goals. For example, Elizabeth Cady Stanton and Susan B. Anthony used their reform networks to put pressure on political leaders during the war. Both long-time anti-slavery advocates, the two set aside their women's rights work. Anthony faced mobs who threw things at her and threatened her with violence during her anti-slavery work as an agent for the American Anti-Slavery Society. Once, pro-slavery opponents burnt her image in effigy. Staying silent while Congress and the President took their time simply would not do for either activist. Elizabeth Cady Stanton and Susan B. Anthony founded the Women's National Loyal League in May 1863 with the goal of pressuring political officials to abolish slavery by constitutional amendment. They were aware that the Emancipation Proclamation emancipated some but not all people held in bondage. They began collecting the signatures of men and women in support of abolition on thousands of petitions. Their call for a constitutional amendment directly inserting women in the political arguments of the early war year and influenced the course of Reconstruction after the war's end.

On the ground, women pushed boundaries as the Army's needs grew. Nursing, once a job for men, became a more accepted occupation for women. By war's end, women were the overwhelming number of military nurses. Clara Barton nicknamed the "Angel of the Battlefield," worked tirelessly to not only collect but also deliver much needed supplies to soldiers in battle beginning in 1862. In November o1862, Dr. Mary E. Walker traveled from Washington, D.C., and volunteered to help troops under the command of General Ambrose Burnside. She served at Warrington and Fredericksburg that winter as a field surgeon. Her battlefield career had begun despite the detraction and abuse of her male colleagues.

1863: Battlefields and Homefronts

Wars are often accounted for with the number of battlefield deaths and casualties. But the American Civil War visited devastation upon civilian populations with as shocking an effect as more efficient weapons on the battlefield visited death upon rising numbers of soldiers. Most Northern women experienced the war at a distance unless they volunteered to serve relief organizations or as nurses. But Southern women, Black and white, experienced the war as it arrived on their doorstep. They competed with both for survival. 1863 marked a distinct change in Union leadership and military strategy. By the end of the year, with Ulysses S. Grant in command, the war for emancipation would arrive deeper and deeper South as he and William T. Sherman implemented a policy of hard war, also called total war.

In the summer of 1863, two battles, the Battle of Gettysburg and the Battle of Vicksburg, altered the course of the war. A part of longer campaigns, both battles marked a shift in strategy that would win the war for the Union and bring utter destruction to the South. In the war's western theater, U.S. Grant had tried with persistence to finally conquer the Mississippi River for the Union. To command the Mississippi would be to cut the South off from western supplies and to complete the blockade that the US Navy had already successfully held together along the South's Atlantic and Gulf Coasts. The campaign a fight against the Southern environment with its swamps, channels, and well-fortified outposts on the Mississippi River and against Confederate forces. After a siege that forced troops and civilians, including the city's women, to live in dugout caves as the US Army shelled the city, ended in Confederate surrender on 4 July 1863.

Meanwhile, in Pennsylvania, Robert E. Lee tried again to shift the battle to northern soil. When Union and Confederate troops clashed at Gettysburg from 1–3 July 1863, the cost of another Union victory was 51,000 lives. Federal troops drove Lee's army from the North but stopped short of pursuing them and decisively defeating them. Lincoln, again disappointed that his generals did not pursue the Confederates, knew that the war would drag on without decisive leadership.

In New York City, from 13–16 July 1863, riots broke out. There the fight was not over slavery and freedom, but over racially informed class conflict. New York exploded with the fury of poor and working-class, often white ethnic immigrant, violence because of unfair recruitment and draft practices. While wealthy white New Yorkers could pay for substitutes to take their place in the draft and could avoid service in the Army, poor and working-class men, many of them recent immigrants, could not afford to avoid conscription. Most were incensed by this inherent inequality in the draft system. Few understood why they should be subject to compulsory participation in a war to free enslaved people, people they saw as labor competition. While white Americans disagreed about the morality of slavery, they still overwhelmingly agreed that racial equality was both unnatural and impossible. The riot foreshadowed deep fissures along racial lines that would haunt the nation in the post-war period.

By year's end, US Grant took the helm of the US Army and William T. Sherman had orders to help him to carry out a new strategy: Hard War. The strategy held that if Confederate troops could not be bested quickly enough, civilians could be made to suffer enough to break the morale and will of the Southern populous. Sherman's March to the Sea spared no one in his army's path from the middle south down through Georgia. For southern women, Black and white, arriving federal troops meant the destruction of their subsistence. Armies for both sides brought with them the need for provisions and supplies, often raiding local larders, gardens, pantries, smokehouses, and orchards to make do. While federal troops now brought freedom with them, thanks to the Emancipation Proclamation, freedom alone did not mitigate poverty. The terms of newfound freedom were contingent upon the martial presence to defend it. Women all over the South were left to pick up the pieces, negotiate the new reality of emancipation, and survive deprivation in the war's wake. Some endured and others perished.

Americans began the work of remembering the war and the war dead as it happened. In November 1863, President Lincoln visited Gettysburg, PA, and delivered one of his most famous pieces of oratory: the Gettysburg Address. His concise address marked the dedication of the Soldier's National Cemetery, now the Gettysburg National Cemetery. Earlier in the war, the US Government authorized the President to purchase land for the burial of Union war dead. In the past, the Army's Office of the Quartermaster General handled soldier's remains. Local churchyards, post cemeteries connected to Army forts, and family burial grounds were the final resting place of war dead. But the volume of soldiers killed in individual battles was often far greater than local cemeteries could absorb.

The impact of high casualty rates was compounded by Army mustering practices. Recruiting practices at the time placed soldiers into units with other men from their local area. Soldiers were mustered by state, often fighting alongside neighbors, friends, and kin. If a unit saw hard fighting, an entire small town's population of men of fighting age could disappear with a well-placed artillery barrage or an unsuccessful charge. Local municipalities, the Federal government, and workers with the sanitation commission tended to the dead and wounded, and women worked on processing the grief and loss of the nation in new ways.

In Gettysburg, first locals and later the state of Pennsylvania, tackled the labor of burying Union soldiers both out of respect and out of fear of the epidemic diseases that unburied corpses could visit on their community. With kin often very far from a deceased soldier's remains, families had to rely on a new system of burial and grief. As a sanitary, social, and moral concern, the proper handling of soldier's remains required new cultural inventions. At the war's start, there was no system for alerting families of a soldier's death or wounding. There was no system of uniform burial for war dead. This meant that there was no provision for the respectful interment of what would eventually amount to more than 600,000 fallen soldiers. In a practical sense, rotting corpses and human remains were a significant health hazard. Battles resulted in massive deaths at a rate at which armies could not spare personnel to properly bury them. Opposing sides were far less concerned with each other's war dead. Local solutions were limited in their funds, and the realities of modern warfare pushed the Federal government to get involved it what was once considered deeply personal: burial of lost loved ones.

Joining the Fight: Soldiers with Female Bodies

Among the war dead that a burial detail encountered in the aftermath of the Battle of Gettysburg was the body of a female bodied soldier in a Confederate uniform. Women participated in the war effort in visible and increasingly public and political ways over the course of the war. And while women like Clara Barton and Dr. Mary E. Walker pushed boundaries, other people with female bodies took another path: they passed as men and joined the armies of both sides of the conflict.

The US Army had a policy of immediately discharging soldiers it identified as women. While tending the wounded at Antietam, Clara Barton discovered Mary

Galloway's sex while treating a chest wound sustained in battle. Often discovered at field hospitals as the result of wounds or illness, some female bodied soldiers may or may not have identified as women.

Not every female bodied soldier was discovered during their service. Cathay Williams, born enslaved in Missouri, worked as a cook and washwoman in a Union Army camp. In that role, she traveled with the Union Army from Missouri. But, after the war's end, Williams was not ready to leave army life behind. She enlisted under the name William Cathay in the winter of 1866 and served in the far West living as a man for two years undetected despite hospitalizations. Private Lyons Wakeman, named Sarah Rosetta Wakeman at birth, served, died, and was buried as a man under their chosen name. Wakeman's sex at birth was only discovered when their letters home surfaced over a century after their death in New Orleans of dysentery. Historians estimate that the number of soldiers with female bodies may have numbered in the hundreds, though accurate counts are had to make.

1864: Women Face Hard War

In 1864, the Union executed its strategy of total or "hard" war and began to bring about the war's end. Another shift involved the internal policies of the US Army. As soon as they could, African American men joined the US Army to fight for an end to slavery. Even in the border states, where the Emancipation Proclamation did not apply, between 25 and 60% of military aged Black men found their way to US Army camps to join up. Hundreds of thousands would serve by war's end in the US Army and Navy. But their service was not without its insults. The Army relegated Black troops to menial labor and segregated army camps and units. The Army also paid Black soldiers lower wages than white troops. In early winter, 1864, Black troops protested and mutinied against this outrage and inequality. For them, the fight for emancipation and equality were linked. By summer 1864, they won equal wages.

In that same year, General Philip Sheridan launched a devastating campaign in Virginia's Shenandoah River Valley while William T. Sherman tore through the Southern interior and reduced Atlanta, Georgia, to ashes. By the fall, Sherman turned north on a route that took him through the Carolinas that became known as Sherman's March to the Sea. The Union Army burned homes, barns, and cities. They confiscated food, livestock, and horses. Enslaved people were sometimes also victims the US Army. Their meager possessions were also confiscated, and African American women were vulnerable to sexual violence.

The US Army had long practiced hard war on Indigenous groups. In turn, tactics and weapons that the US Army honed on the Civil War's battlefields would be visited Indigenous groups in the Far West. The Civil War also led to an expansion of the US Army. Increased migration during the war signaled that no amount of strife within the nation would curb America's imperial ambitions. The Homestead Act (1862) encouraged thousands of Americans to pour into the West, even as the Civil War raged.

Over the course of 1864, tension mounted between Indigenous people and Euro-Americans in Colorado. After being forced from their land a decade earlier, they were promised refuge at Sand Creek, Colorado. It was there on 29 November 1864, the US troops massacred over 230 Cheyenne and Arapaho men, women, and children. In the Southwest, Navajo that had endured fighting between Union and Confederate forces on their lands and were forced onto a reservation in New Mexico. While the Civil War was not yet over, many Union Army officials had not forgotten the West, US Imperial goals, and the potential for victory over Indigenous groups that an expanded army promised.

1865: Emancipation, Lincoln's Assassination, and Reunion

No place was untouched by the war's destruction. With troops closing in from all directions, Richmond in flames as Confederate's retreated, and the South smoldering from Sherman and Sheridan's Marches, Union victory was at hand. When, in April 1865, Robert E. Lee surrendered at Appomattox Court House, very little was settled. This famous surrender marked the end of the war, but combat would continue as word of the surrender spread. Federal Troops occupied Southern cities and states, governing conquered territory according to military districts. African Americans, some in Army camps, others on the road, and still others at the sites of their enslavement, faced an uncertain federal government's developing policy toward them. Some enslaved people would remain enslaved for months and years after war's end waiting for federal troops to arrive and enforce the Emancipation Proclamation, and later, the 13th Amendment to the Constitution. Lincoln's administration had worked to pass the 13th amendment in Congress, abolishing slavery in all US states and territories, but it was up to three-quarters of the states to officially amend the US Constitution and formally abolish slavery everywhere.

Black people had a vision for social, political, and economic equality and full citizenship. Generation's worth of American law and custom controlled by Euro-Americans made realizing African American's hopes for emancipation slow and uneven. Radical white women who had hoped their service to their country during the war and their long commitment to abolition would result in women's suffrage faced disappointment. Women's rights were overshadowed by the violence and political turmoil of Reconstruction.

In Contraband Camps and small communities of free people of color, African Americans began to carve out freedom. Even before war's end, Black women sought out legal marriages, helped to build schools and churches, formed mutual aid societies, and worked to help their communities. What many white Americans took for granted as features of everyday life often symbolized strides toward freedom for African Americans. Black women prioritized their own family and kin, sought ways to avoid field labor, and worked to support the US Army by cooking, washing, and doing domestic work. They pushed for their children's access to education and sought out basic literacy for themselves.

In Congress and the White House, political leaders focused on legal emancipation and the potential to expand the political rights of freedmen, as all emancipated people were called at the time. But Black women made clear that they also wanted social equality, protection from sexual violence, and the ability to profit from their own labor. Male officials often focused on Black men's rights, their ability to head traditional patriarchal households, and their political contribution to the survival of the Republican Party. True social and economic equality between the races were only considered by the most radical white abolitionists. Affording Black women rights threatened long held gender hierarchies.

On 3 March 1865, Congress established the Bureau of Refugees, Freedmen, and Abandoned Lands, in the War Department. Congress established the Freedmen's Bureau, as it was popularly known, to oversee all matters having to do with war refugees, recently emancipated African Americans, and land in the South that was under military jurisdiction. Over time, the bureau became more associated in with its role aiding freedmen, the term for recently emancipated people at the time. The bureau distributed rations, clothing, and necessities in contraband camps and refugee camps. After the war's end, bureau agents also intervened in labor contract and apprenticeship disputes between newly emancipated people and landowners. Some white Americans resented the Freedman's Bureau because it used Federal funds to support African Americans. The bureau never had enough staff or funding to fully mitigate the poverty of African Americans in the South or to offer adequate reparation for their generations of unpaid labor during slavery. But, nonetheless, opponents of Black equality and white leaders with an interest in ensuring African Americans remained an impoverished source of labor, used the bureau to build coalition among white male voters.

Conclusion

When John Wilkes Booth assassinated Abraham Lincoln on 15 April 1865, power to guide Reconstruction fell to his Vice President, Andrew Johnson. A southerner, Johnson's vision for bringing Southern states back into the Union imposed minimal consequences on states formerly in rebellion. Challenging racial order was not part of Johnson's plan for reuniting the nation. Much to the anger of other Republicans, Johnson sympathized with Southern states and felt no responsibility to African Americans. In fact, he attempted to dismantle the Freedman's Bureau.

Slavery ended eight months after Lincoln died. In December 1865, enough states ratified the 13th Amendment to make it officially a part of the US Constitution. Battlefields had quieted but Federal troops remained in the South. The work of resolving the conflicts that ignited the bloody conflict remained at the local level, the state level, and the federal level. American women in all regions did not sit back and watch Reconstruction happen. Their activism, organizing, and community work would leave their mark on the Era of Emancipation and Reconstruction.

Bibliography

American Battlefield Trust. "American Battlefield Trust." Accessed January 11, 2023. **https://www.battlefields.org/home**.

Blanton, De Anne, and Lauren M Cook. *They Fought Like Demons: Women Soldiers in the Civil War*. Illustrated edition. New York, NY: Vintage, 2003.

Clinton, Catherine, and Nina Silber, eds. *Battle Scars: Gender and Sexuality in the American Civil War*. Illustrated edition. Oxford; New York: Oxford University Press, 2006.

Edwards, Laura F. *Scarlett Does not Live Here Anymore: Southern Women in the Civil War Era*. Reprint edition. Urbana, IL: University of Illinois Press, 2004.

Faust, Drew Gilpin. *This Republic of Suffering: Death and the American Civil War*. Illustrated edition. New York: Vintage, 2009.

Giesberg, Judith Ann. *Civil War Sisterhood: The U.S. Sanitary Commission and Women's Politics in Transition*. Revised edition. Boston: Northeastern University Press, 2006.

Glymph, Thavolia. *The Women's Fight: The Civil War's Battles for Home, Freedom, and Nation*. 1st edition. Chapel Hill: University of North Carolina Press, 1920.

Hilde, Libra R. *Worth a Dozen Men: Women and Nursing in the Civil War South*. Charlottesville: University of Virginia Press, 2012.

Leonard, Elizabeth D. *Yankee Women: Gender Battles in the Civil War*. Reprint edition. New York: W. W. Norton & Company, 1995.

Nelson, Megan Kate. *The Three-Cornered War: The Union, the Confederacy, and Native Peoples in the Fight for the West*. New York: Scribner, 2021.

Taylor, Amy Murrell. *Embattled Freedom: Journeys Through the Civil War's Slave Refugee Camps*. Illustrated edition. The University of North Carolina Press, 2020.

Williams, Heather Andrea. *Self-Taught: African American Education in Slavery and Freedom*. The University of North Carolina Press, 2007.

"Women's Stories of. . . - Women's History (U.S. National Park Service)." Accessed January 11, 2023. **https://www.nps.gov/subjects/womenshistory/women-s-stories-of.htm**.

CHAPTER 10

Reconstruction and the Rise of Jane Crow

Westward expansion was a key feature of the Era of Emancipation. Political Reconstruction offered a glimmer of hope for some American women that they might just be included in the nation's political life. For others, Reconstruction equated with a world turned upside down, a loss in social status, and an uncertain future for the white supremacy. For Indigenous women, the steady flow of American settlers turned to a deluge, and old battles rekindled as they strategized to survive America's genocidal Indian Wars in the Far West. Americans remained on the move. Mobility for formerly enslaved women was an important feature of freedom. They demonstrated the value of mobility by moving to the West, to the urban South and the North, and leaving former sites of enslavement behind. Euro-Americans and recent immigrants to the United States hoped that migration could be their route to prosperity. Northerners moved South to grasp at the money to be made rebuilding the South. Easterners moved West looking for land of their own. Expansion and economic renewal were so important to Americans and American leaders that they often overshadowed the radical values that propelled the United States to victory in the Civil War.

In 1862, Abraham Lincoln had a war on his hands. Wars are expensive endeavors. They cost lives, matériel, and impact the economic production of belligerent nations. Wars are won on fields of battel, with the endurance of civilian resolve, and in the checks and balances of quartermasters' account books. The West, the land that the Federal Government still controlled, presented a hopeful solution to the United States' woes once again. Lincoln signed the Homestead Act on 20 May 1862. The act promised citizens and future citizens of the United States 160 acers of public land. In exchange, citizens were expected to live on the land for at least five years and "improve" it by farming it, adding small structures, or making other small changes. Claimants could then pay a small fee and hold title to the land free and clear. Another option was to live on the land for six months and pay the government $1.25 an acre. Union soldiers were offered the option to deduct time they served in the army toward their residency.

The act incentivized army service, and it established a stream of revenue for the US Government and pushed Americans of limited means to consider populating

American Women's History: A New Narrative History, First Edition. Melissa E. Blair, Vanessa M. Holden, and Maeve Kane.
© 2024 John Wiley & Sons, Inc. Published 2024 by John Wiley & Sons, Inc.

America's vast territories in the West. During the Civil War, the West had served as a theater of war. Confederates eager to establish empire pushed into the Arizona Territory in hopes of establishing control of land to the Pacific Coast. Federal troops drove Confederates back into West Texas over the course of an arduous campaign waged in the high desert. All the while, both forces contended with local Indigenous groups with generations of experiences fighting off invaders: the Spanish, the Mexicans, and the Americans in turn. Even with a destructive war raging, the West remained in the minds of both Confederate and Union leaders. The desire for empire, for the competing visions of expansion that had precipitated the Civil War, did not fade even as cannon fire blasted away.

Slavery ended with the ratification of the Thirteenth Amendment to the Constitution in the winter of 1865. Abolition, the goal of so many women's organizing and activism, had finally been won. African American men had served bravely in the US Army and Navy. African American women had contributed labor and kin directly to the war effort. Northern white women had transformed sanitation practices, set up effective systems for respectful burial of fallen soldiers, and participated in the political push for abolition. They had sacrificed kin, hours of labor, and lonely months on the Homefront shouldering missing men's labor along with their own.

Southern white women endured the deprivation of the late war and faced their world upturned. They had patriotically supported secession. They had also organized for the war effort in urban centers and individually contributed to supplying soldiers as well. But at war's end, slavery, and the racial hierarchy carefully maintained to support it, no longer ordered society. Any departure from the old racial order, even something as simple as newly emancipated people refusing to work without pay, felt to them like an affront to their very personhood. Confederate troops had a higher rate of attrition than their Union counterparts. The war, particularly in its later years, destroyed cities, towns, and individual plantations in the name of total war. Just as before the Civil War, women from different classes, races, and regions had competing visions of what it meant to be a woman and what it meant to be an American.

The Emancipation Generation

A little over two months after Lincoln signed the Homestead Act, a girl was born into slavery in Holly Springs, Mississippi. Just northeast of the state's Mississippi Delta region, almost on the border of southeastern Tennessee, the countryside surrounding Holly Springs was known for cotton production. Only a few months after the arrival of James and Lizzie Wells's oldest daughter, General Ulysses S. Gant camped his army in Holly Springs drawing Confederate raiders to the area. Grant's campaign to capture Vicksburg, MS, launched successfully despite Confederate resistance. Young Ida Bell was only approaching three years old when the Civil War ended, and emancipation came to Holly Springs. Her parents were active politically in the local Republican party and organizations that served freedmen, as emancipated people were called at the time.

A true child of the Era of Emancipation, Ida B. Wells took her education seriously and attended Rust College. The school was founded by the Freedman's Aid Society of the Methodist Episcopal Church in 1866. In its early days, the school accepted both adults and children as students for basic instruction in literacy and arithmetic later adding high school and college courses. At only 16, Wells lost a sibling and both of her parents to a yellow fever outbreak, leaving her to support her remaining siblings by landing a teaching job. In 1882, like many other African Americans searching for greater opportunity and respite from agricultural labor, she moved to the urban South. Wells and her sisters arrived in Memphis, Tennessee, in 1882.

At the time, political Reconstruction had ended. The Thirteenth Amendment abolished slavery in 1865. Freedmen and women were granted citizenship by the Fourteenth Amendment in 1868. Black men had secured the constitutional right to vote with the Fifteenth Amendment in 1870. Federal troops had long withdrawn from the region and the South was no longer sectioned into military districts. These incredible leaps in civil rights that were unthinkable the year Ida B. Wells was born, were ratified, and codified in the US Constitution when she migrated to Memphis. By the time she traveled by train between Memphis and Nashville, TN, in 1884, emancipation was almost twenty years old. But on that train ride she directly confronted another reality of life in the so-called "New South": the persistence of anti-Black racism and open discrimination.

Wells purchased a first-class ticket, but conductors attempted to force her to ride in a segregated railcar for African Americans. She refused to move, and conductors physically removed her from the train. She fought back by biting a crew member during the altercation and then by taking the railroad company to court. While she initially won a settlement of $500, the Tennessee Supreme Court later overturned the lower court's decision. Wells's experience radicalized her. Black women of her generation took up the struggle that their mothers and grandmothers had once shouldered: the fight for freedom *and* equality.

Fighting for Freedom: An Era of Hope and Promise

Reconstruction and the Era of Emancipation held great promise for some Americans. During the war years, Congress outlawed slavery in Washington, D.C., prohibited slavery in US Territories, and passed the 13th Amendment to the US Constitution accomplishing what had been truly unthinkable before the Civil War. They abolished slavery. Before the war, Americans had spent decades fighting over whether the US Government even had the power to make such a sweeping change. The thought of curbing the spread of slavery to western territories had ignited the furor of secessionists even before Abraham Lincoln could officially take office. But the story of the Era of Emancipation and Reconstruction is more than the story of groundbreaking amendments and political maneuvering. The era was marked by violence, conflict, and clashes between groups that had very different definitions of freedom.

Recently defeated southerners, even those who had never had the wealth to thwart changes to the racial hierarchy that slavery had helped to enforce. Poor and middling white Southerners deeply valued white supremacy. White Southerners outside of the region's class of powerful class of wealthy elites were barred from holding power in the region. For them, identifying as white, aspiring to hold slaves, and exercising privileges denied to Black people like voting, solidified their alliance with wealthier landowners and powerbrokers. After the war, white Southerners across classes resisted radical social change whenever possible.

Northern whites held out hope that by enacting abolition and bestowing basic civil rights on newly freed African Americans they could absolve the government from further interference in the daily lives of Americans. With citizenship and the vote, many reasoned that freedmen and women could look after themselves. Bringing rebellious states back into the union was one goal of Reconstruction and putting Black people to work remained central to Federal policy. The United States benefited from the economic juggernaut of the American South. Getting the economy of the South up and running was a national imperative. African Americans wanted control over their working lives, their privet lives, and their own property. But most white Americans, North and South, simply did not believe that Black people could be productive workers without white supervision.

Black women had never ceased laboring. During the war, their work in Army camps, on farms and plantations, and in their communities was critical to African American survival. In the immediate aftermath of the war, many Black women still could not escape arduous field labor producing cash crops. In some cases, the Union Army had forced women into the fields to support the war effort and to teach African American women how to be free. During the war, the Federal Plantation System began leasing confiscated plantations to northerners and staffed the agricultural operations with African Americans, often women and children. While they earned a wage, the government taxed their pay and used the revenue to cover their room and board, basic rations, and the care of indigent and elderly freed people. For many recently emancipated women, even in freedom, choice over how they labored and for whom was carefully prescribed by more powerful men.

Formerly enslaved people generated revenue on lands that white landowners fled in South Carolina's Sea Islands. Occupied by the Union early in the war, the Sea Islands became the site of early relief efforts for emancipated people. White northern philanthropists and reformers sent resources and personnel to the region to educate and tend to the basic needs of formerly enslaved people. When President Lincoln allowed for the sale of abandoned lands in the area, a federal program known as the Sea Island Experiment briefly made it possible for formerly enslaved people to purchase land at the rate of $1.25 an acre, just like the Homestead Act provided for the purchase of land in the Far West. While white northerners took advantage of the opportunity to purchase rich plantation land, some African Americans managed to purchase land and quickly turned a profit from their own labor. Their success sharply contrasted with popular racist ideas about African Americans' work ethic. Unlike racist depictions of Black people as lazy and in need of white supervision, freedmen and women demonstrated that they could manage themselves.

The Army, burdened by swelling refugee camps, and only envisioned labor for Black people. Many, even ardent abolitionists, still believed that Black people were intellectually inferior to whites and were only suited for hard labor, that they needed white people to condition them for freedom. They believed that white people were the rightful authority over Black people and that white supervision was needed to force Black people to labor.

Black women knew what freedom meant to them. Many white Americans assumed that in freedom Black women would simply continue laboring under the supervision of white landowners, just as they had as enslaved women. The only change many white Americans accepted was that Black people would work for wages. But African American women and men wanted the land they'd made profitable as enslaved people. They wanted access to education, political rights, and social equality.

Many newly freed people asserted that their labor built the South and that they were the rightful proprietors of plantations. After generations of laboring without compensation, coerced by violence and abuse, and treated as animals, the newly emancipated believed their vision for freedom to be more than fair. But even in Port Royal, where African Americans thrived without enslavers managing them, northern philanthropists lost enthusiasm for land redistribution because the thought of redistributing white people's land to formerly enslaved people flew in the face of accepted racial hierarchy.

Like Ida B. Wells' parents, many African Americans quickly worked to build community institutions, organize mutual aid, and ensure their own survival. African American women knew that their labor was essential to rebuilding the South. Their agricultural knowledge, domestic expertise, and care work made the South economically successful for generations. Politicians and government officials tried at every turn to relegate Black women to subordinate social roles and put them back to work for white landowners and in white women's households. Only Black men were eligible to serve on juries, hold office, and exercise the franchise.

Black women demonstrated in their actions and their writing that freedom meant a host of tangible and intangible things. For some, access to legal marriage, a privilege denied to enslaved people, allowed them establish families and rely on the protection that married status could afford them. For many Black people who had suffered family separation in slavery, living with family and kin in arrangements they defined made family making a powerful symbol of freedom. For some, married status was a way to grasp at respectability and the protection of traditional gender roles. Marriage was only one strategy.

Black women were determined to work for themselves. When the Congress chartered the Freedmen's Bureau in 1865, they also chartered the Freedmen's Savings and Trust Company, often called the Freedmen's Bank. Well-meaning northern philanthropists originally conceived the bank to help protect Black soldiers from being swindled and to provide them with a safe institution to teacher them to manage wages and make financial decisions. Though chartered as an institution for freedmen, both men and women used the bank as a repository for their savings. Most deposits were small but Black women were proud to finally benefit from their own labor. As historian Shannette Garrett-Scott has shown, Black women invested in their communities, Black institutions like churches, and founded mutual aid organizations. Banking with the Freedmen's Bank was one of many ways Black women demonstrated their command over their own labor, their wages, and their futures.

Beyond organizing in secret societies, mutual aid organizations, and churches, Black women participated in labor organizing. They organized around the feminine labor of domestic work and laundering. They fought to "live out," not in their employer's houses, to thwart sexual violence and constant surveillance. Some chose to do domestic work for their own families or joined their male kin in the fields rather than serve in white households. In July 1881, 20 laundresses established the Washington Society in Atlanta, Georgia. As the historian Tera Hunter has shown, these women set a standard rate for their services ($1 per 12 lbs of wash) and recruited others to increase their membership. They grew an interracial coalition of laundresses from 20 to 3000, struck for fair pay for over a month, and won.

Black women, though explicitly excluded from the Fifteenth Amendment's extension of the franchise, were not excluded from Black politics. Black women were active members of the abolitionist movement. But even before the Civil War ended, Black women also participated in activism aimed at winning Black social equality. In April 1863, Charlotte Brown suffered the same indignity that Ida B. Wells experienced decades later, a conductor ejected her from a streetcar in San Francisco, CA. Rules around segregation in California were haphazard and there was no set standard for streetcars in the city. Brown brought legal suits against the streetcar company three times. Her cases paved the way for the businesswoman and anti-slavery advocate, Mary Ellen Pleasant to defeat segregation on San Francisco's streetcars when she was ejected from one in 1866 and won the ensuing court battle.

Black women attended political meetings and, on election days, marched with Black men, armed, if need be, to the polls. Black women fought to provide their children with basic education in schools built by their communities. In a region where Black literacy had been a crime for generations, even attaining a basic education in the South was a defiant political act. Before the American Civil War, the Colored Conventions movement included multiple gatherings of free Black people organize for abolition and equality. Held in northern cities and towns with free Black populations, the conventions were powerful sites of coalition building across states. After the war, the movement continued, and organizers held conventions in the South. Some were aimed at freedmen, but Black women attended and participated. Local Sunday school meetings, benevolent society meetings, and church services were also sites of political organizing. African Americans cared about determining their own futures in freedom and did not want to depend upon the whims of white philanthropists.

In 1868, the states ratified 14th Amendment to the US Constitution. The 14th amendment guaranteed citizenship to formerly enslaved people. Black women played a critical role in forcing both the President and Congress to enforce this important amendment. Black women's testimonies about violence and sexual violence directly influenced leaders in congress to pass the Ku Klux Klan Act in 1871. With the radical change of emancipation came violent reprisal from whites in the South who were anxious to reestablish dominance. Along with physical and economic violence, Black women and girls were vulnerable to sexual violence. Even with the presence of Federal troops in the South, violence was rampant despite early congress's vision of a newer, more equal, nation. Newly elected Black representatives and white Radical Republicans pushed for laws to prohibit and punish vigilantly groups like the Red Shirts and the Ku Klux Klan. Women's testimonies about violence helped leaders to see the need for legislation. President Grant also created the Department of Justice to help enforce the law and uphold the US Constitution. Black women contributed to the creation of the Federal institution that would come to the aid of future generations of freedom fighters.

Black women used their new mobility and their right to manage their own time to piece back together their families. Black women, like Ida B. Wells and the laundresses who struck for higher pay in Atlanta, moved from the rural South to the urban South in search of better paying work, education, and opportunity. Black women searched for kin lost to sale in the internal slave trade. In African American newspapers and religious newspapers, African Americans placed "Lost Friends" and "Information Wanted" ads seeking information about family and friends that white enslavers had separated them from during slavery. Some even took to the road to seek out lost kin or went back to their state of birth in hopes of reuniting with family.

Some African Americans decided to move out of the South to find better economic opportunities, safety from racial violence, and land of their own. Born in Virginia and sold to a slave trader in Kentucky as a young girl, Eliza Carpenter ended up enslaved on a Missouri planter's land. After emancipation, Carpenter returned to Kentucky where she became and accomplished horsewoman learning to trade, breed, and jockey racehorses. She brought her horse knowledge and skill with her to Kansas, where she established a successful herd of horses. Local legend in what is now Ponca City, Oklahoma, claims she participated in local land races and won her land claim. The federal government hosted horse races for land claims to distribute Indigenous people's lands to settlers. Whether the legend is true or not, Carpenter was a successful jockey, breeder, and businesswoman.

Many African American women moved to Black communities in the Midwest, West, and Far West just like Eliza Carpenter and participated in settling land that Indigenous groups were once promised by the Federal government. Calling themselves Exodusters, African Americans from all over the South set off in community groups to western states like Kansas, Nebraska, and Oklahoma where they hoped to settle. One poster encouraging African Americans in central Kentucky to leave for Kansas touted Black elected officials and an armed militia. There were also women who were both Black and Indigenous who lived at the intersection of Black claims for freedom and Indigenous people's struggles to maintain their culture, stave of incursion, and survive. The West and the Far West held both promise and hardship for Black women. After the Civil War, leaving the South, their former enslavers, and violence behind for the West was a significant assertion of freedom for Black women and their families.

The land the Eliza Carpenter raced for at the end of the nineteenth century was once considered Indian Territory. African Americans' entree into the West was made possible by the violent expulsion of Indigenous people from their lands. The Era of Emancipation held hope for some but for others it signaled a new beginning to violence, dispossession, and genocide. Racialized violence that had huge implications for women's lives did not fade away. It intensified throughout Reconstruction and culminated in the invention of new forms of racial discrimination.

Reform and Reconstruction: Women's Rights and African American Civil Rights Clash

Reconstruction was an era of radical possibility and activist women in the North felt that they should be a part of rebuilding the nation. Some returned to social causes in line with the abolitionist leanings. They volunteered with the Freedman's Bureau, worked as teachers or nurses in Freedman's camps, or advocated for the fair treatment of recently freed people. Others turned to causes they had laid aside during the war like women's rights and women's Women had worked among the wounded, struck out to teach in squalid Freedman's camps, and endured the grievous loss of male kin. Some women felt that their service during the war, their sacrifice, and their demonstrations of patriotism and loyalty should win them the right to political equality. Others, who were less radical, returned to causes like temperance, prison reform, work among the poor, and other charitable causes that did not challenge gender hierarchy. Northern white women's activism, particularly among middleclass and upper-class women, did not fade away after the Civil War. Wartime necessity emboldened women to take on public work and articulate political demands.

Congress and national political leaders, mainly Radical Republicans, saw the benefit in enfranchising freedmen who they assumed were destined to become

Republican voters. But they did not think that upending patriarchal power by affording women political equality made much sense. Most did not want women to run for political office, hold positions of authority over men, or have the right to vote. They knew that political equality could lead to social equality and a reorganization of accepted gender norms. At the time, popular gender ideology held that men and women were biologically different, and that God specifically designed men for public life, to head households, and to protect their wives and children. Even many women reformers blanched at the idea of women's suffrage. Many women did not see political and social equality as congruent with their beliefs about women's proper place in society as wives, mothers, and moral authorities. Women's rights, including economic and political rights, conflicted with their own sense of respectable womanhood. Advocating against the consumption of alcohol was one thing, demanding a say in American political life was another.

Nonetheless, women's rights activists like Elizabeth Cady Stanton and Susan B. Anthony had hope that the post-war expansion of civil rights and radical social change could and should include women. They had successfully campaigned for the 13th Amendment during the war. In the spring of 1866, a little more than one year after the end of the Civil War, Stanton and Anthony founded the American Equal Rights Association (AERA). Their stated goal was to pursue equality for Americans of all races, religions, and genders. They built a broad coalition of members of both Black and white men and women. Prominent African Americans like Frederick Douglass, Sojourner Truth, and Harriet Forten Purvis joined with longtime white activists like Lucretia Mott, and Lucy Stone to pursue voting rights.

Over the next three years, activists in favor of women's suffrage faced very few wins. In Wyoming, still a territory at the time, women did gain the right to vote. But in each state that held a referendum on women's right to vote, they failed. Activists hoped that Federal law or a constitutional amendment might be the path to suffrage for African Americans and women. But women's hopes faded when, in 1868, language in the 14th Amendment made it clear that lawmakers only saw men as voters. When congressmen began to discuss a 15th Amendment that would prohibit discrimination against voters based on color, it became clear that the voters they planned to protect would be men. Ulysses S. Grant campaigned in favor of the 15th Amendment and made no indication that Women's suffrage would be a priority for him.

This caused deep rifts in the activist community and the AERA's descent into conflict illustrated deep fissures. Some members saw a path to women's suffrage *after* Black men gained the vote. They argued that the AERA could pursue women's suffrage once the 15th amendment passed. Some even stated plainly that they thought Black men's voting rights *should* come first. Other members, most famously Elizabeth Cady Stanton, were appalled. She explicitly argued that Black men were less qualified for the franchise and that Black people were not prepared to participate in political life. Both she and Anthony believed that a constitutional amendment that ignored women's right to the franchise was objectionable. At the 1869 annual meeting of the AERA, Frederick Douglass took Elizabeth Cady Stanton and those who agreed with her to task for her racism then stated his case. Black men, he argued, deserved the franchise and women could wait their turn. Black women like Sojourner Truth and Francis Ellen Watkins Harper were not silent. Instead, they noted how both factions, Black men and white women simply overlooked them in their squabble over who deserved which rights and in what order.

In the end, the argument that put Douglass on one side and Stanton and Anthony on the other resulted in the dissolution of the AERA. The 15th Amendment, passed by congress in February of 1869 and ratified by the states in February of 1870, explicitly identified voters as men. This slammed the door shut on women's activists who had hoped to benefit from the radical political moment and made them reassess their strategy. Stanton and Anthony founded a new organization, the National Woman Suffrage Association (NWSA), with the goal of advocating for a women's suffrage amendment to the constitution and other women's rights. Lucy Stone and Julia Ward Howe founded the American Woman Suffrage Association (AWSA) and focused on state laws avoiding other causes like divorce law and women's property rights. The movement for women's suffrage and other women's rights continued to grapple with racism. As Black women activists pointed out early on, the white women in leadership of prominent organizations for women's rights often ignored Black women and explicitly excluded them.

Creating an Old South to Build a New South: Southern Women

In the South, white women of all classes sifted through the rubble to make sense of what Reconstruction would mean for them. In some cases, the rubble was literal. Many of the region's major cities had been reduced to ashes during the Civil War: Richmond, Virginia; Atlanta, Georgia; Vicksburg, Mississippi; and Columbia, South Carolina all lie in ruin after the war. In the middle of the war, with the inflation of Confederate Currency out of control, women had rioted for food and subsistence goods in the region. In Richmond, VA, capitol of the Confederacy, officials had threatened the rioters with violence to disperse the mobs attempting to ransack stores. Deprivation only got worse as the South gradually felt the strain of wartime on agricultural production and lived under a Union blockade that kept foreign trade restricted. White women's suffering and sharp loss of morale contributed to the region's inability to continue the rebellion against the United States.

After the war, sweeping change destabilized old hierarchies and left white women wondering what the destruction of slavery would mean for their place in society. On a practical level, wealthy and middleclass Southerners relied on slavery, and the monetary value of enslaved people, to stay solvent. In the antebellum period, enslaved people were often worth more than the land they worked in the Upper South. In the cotton South, large landowners often borrowed against the value of enslaved people to float their agricultural operations. Both the produce of enslaved people's labor *and* the lucrative trade in Black people between regions bolstered the entire region's economy. The Thirteenth Amendment did not stipulate a program of compensation for enslavers. The wealth they built in human property simply ceased to exist.

During slavery, white people of all social classes enjoyed privileges that African Americans, even free people of color, could not access. African Americans could not testify against whites in court. They could not resist capture by local slave patrols. White people could never be held in bondage and traded as chattels. For free people of color, bondage was one bad debt or kidnapping away. Cultural ideals held that white women occupied a superior moral and genteel place in social hierarchy. Modeled after the wealthiest female enslavers, this ideal made white women the model for moral purity and Christian values. While many white women all over the South never enjoyed the level of wealth that would allow them to escape all domestic labor, white women actively participated in enslaving African Americans. They relished their privileged position in society and demanded that white men protect it and them.

If the Civil War featured unimaginable violence and destruction, white southerners in the Reconstruction South visited that violence on Black communities with swiftness and vigor. Freedmen and women were targets for extralegal violence. In more than one Southern state, political leaders quickly instituted Black Codes that simply subbed the term "freedman" for "slave" and used slave laws verbatim. Lead by Confederate veterans, rifle clubs and secret vigilantly groups like the Ku Klux Klan burned Black churches and schools, murdered freed people, and engaged in a violent campaign of intimidation targeting Black politicians and community leaders.

White women supported the violent effort to subjugate the African American population of the region while working actively to bolster white supremacy in other ways. They were ideological foot soldiers in the battel over Civil War memory. White women of all classes lost family and friends during the Civil War. While their northern counterparts worked to revolutionize sanitation and burial practices, a similar widely organized effort did not exist in the South. Operating in an acceptable public venue for women, particularly those who were widowed by the war, Southern women set about establishing sites of memorial and remembrance even as the war raged on. Initially organized around commemorating specific groups of war dead, the movement to memorialize soldiers lost in battle transitioned into reshaping the memory of slavery and what they termed the "Lost Cause" of the Confederacy.

Later in the nineteenth century, Southern white women of Ida B. Wells's generation would come together to rewrite the history of the Civil War. Much like their mothers and grandmothers who organized and participated in reform at a far lower rate than Northern women, Southern women post-Civil War rallied around the cause of white supremacy. In 1894 in Nashville, the city Ida B. Wells was attempting to travel to a decade earlier, a group of white women founded the United Daughters of the Confederacy. The group would eventually publish textbooks, raise funds to erect elaborate monuments, and found a children's auxiliary to educate children directly about their version of Southern history. Wealthy women and middle-class women worked to depict slavery as pastoral and benign, enslavers as kindly and honorable, and the men who went to war as gallant and genteel. They emphasized the Confederacy's legitimacy as a nation state, preferring the term "the War Between the States" to the Civil War. Significantly, their education and public monument campaigns sought to legitimate a new manifestation of white supremacist social hierarchy: Jim Crow. Early southern women's associations aimed at helping war widows, rebuilding agricultural operations and cities, and surviving post-war deprivation influenced the next generation of white women's practices of memorialization.

New Waves of Immigration: New Americans, Old Prejudices, and the Era of Chinese Exclusion

Urbanization and industrialization began to change American life before the Civil War. In the American North, textile mills presented an early indicator of just how important industrialization would become for the region. Those early mills used the labor of women and girls to run the industrial looms that turned Southern cotton into finished cloth. Initially, mills employed white women from the surrounding countryside outside of mill towns. But, with the influxes of Irish women in the antebellum period, mill owners shifted to immigrant laborers who could be hired for cheaper. Abusive labor practices that exploited underpaid immigrants, women, and children fueled the rapidly expanding industrial economy.

After the Civil War, immigration from Europe to the United States began to shift demographically. While immigrants from the British Isles and Central and Northern Europe still came to America, immigrants from Southern and Eastern Europe also began to arrive in larger numbers by the 1880s. Women often came with family groups and settled in America's urban centers. Immigrants, including women and children, posed the threat of labor competition to American-born whites and immigrant groups who established themselves before the war. This crowding in American cities was good for bosses and factory owners but bad for workers who lived in cramped squalid conditions making wages far too low to sustain them.

The rising numbers of Catholic and later Jewish immigrants rekindled anti-Catholic and antisemitic sentiments among protestant Americans. But even rampant prejudice did not diminish the economic importance of a cheap, renewable, and vulnerable labor force to business interests. American factories, particularly in American urban centers, would come to attract and depend on immigrant laborers in greater and greater numbers through the end of the nineteenth century. Immigrant women, whether on factory floors or doing piece work in their homes, would be a critical part of American economic success.

The North was not the only region to grapple with the influx of immigrants. In the West, immigrants from east Asia, particularly China, had long concerned Euro-Americans and been the target of anti-Asian racism. Chinese laborers played a significant role in California's antebellum gold rush, the expansion of American railroads, and agricultural operations on America's west coast. This labor competition and the measured success of Chinese entrepreneurs threatened racial hierarchy for white Californians, for example. Many wanted a state where free white men, particularly those of middling status, could carve out a livelihood. African Americans, including some enslaved people before statehood, Chinese immigrants, laborers from South America, Californios (Mexican ranchers), and especially Indigenous Californians did not figure into their dreams of American Empire in the Far West. White Californians were not alone in their exclusionary sentiments. While still a US Territory, Oregon's white residents enacted a series of laws to exclude African Americans from migrating to its borders. When Oregon entered the Union as a free state on the eve of the Civil War in 1859, its constitution included a clause that excluded African Americans from settling there.

Mary Tape arrived in the California from China in 1868 as an 11-year-old girl. The Ladies' Protection and Relief Society, a local white women's reform organization, took her in and gave her shelter. Like "civilizing" missions among Indigenous people and women's relief organizations in the East, Tape's life at the relief society included learning English and assimilating into American gender and cultural norms. She also took an anglicized name, Mary McGladery. Upon her marriage to Jeu Tape, who worked as a domestic servant like many Asian men in the region, her name became Mary Tape. They built a life together and endured the racism of the law and their white neighbors.

In the Civil War era, right before Mary Tape arrived in the United States, California passed a series of restrictive laws limiting Chinese immigrants' ability to run businesses and prevented them from becoming naturalized citizens during the Civil War Era. While the US Government invalidated these state laws to uphold treaty agreements with China, racist anti-immigrant sentiment remained potent in the region. White Californians wanted to stop Chinese immigration and used arguments about the morality of Chinese women to do so. Traffickers engaged in a range of abusive labor practices in the region that targeted both Chinese men and women. Women and girls were particularly vulnerable to sex trafficking. But social norms blamed women who engaged in sex work, whether trafficked or by choice, and assumed that their own immorality was to blame for the proliferation of brothels. Organizations like the Ladies' Protection and Relief Society that took Mary Tape in as a girl offered protection from traffickers and an alternative to sex work, often one of the few types of work girls and women could get.

In the 1870s, on the heels of groundbreaking constitutional amendments that expanded American citizenship and the franchise, President Ulysses S. Grant considered and approved restrictive legislation that effectively banned Asian women from immigrating to the United States. Parallel with the violence against African Americans in the wake of emancipation, anti-Chinese campaigns and violence against Chinese communities were a regular feature in the West. White leaders who argued against Chinese immigration held that Chinese migrants were really bound unfree laborers, that they were racially inferior and naturally immoral, and that as non-Christians their integration into American society was impossible. Anti-Chinese leaders and campaigns appropriated the language of abolition and reform to further their cause. Politicians then turned racist anti-Chinese sentiment into policy. The Page Act, signed into law in 1875, established a policy of questioning "any subject of China, Japan, or any Oriental country" to determine if they were either bound as indentured servants or intending to do sex work. Claiming to want to protect women from trafficking and preserve the moral character of white communities, anti-Chinese leaders targeted Chinese women. They assumed all East Asian women were sex workers, and racist officials effectively excluded all Asian women from entering US ports.

In 1882, the year that Ida B. Wells and her sisters moved to Memphis, President Chester A. Arthur signed the Chinese Exclusion Act into law. The legislation prohibited all Chinese immigration for a decade, prohibited the reentry of Chinese immigrants if they left the US, and no longer allowed federal or state courts to grant citizenship to Chinese immigrants. In coming decades, the US Government would renew the policy and continue to prohibit immigrants from East Asia. But in an echo of the struggles Well's faced on her journey from Memphis to Nashville, Mary Tape also faced down segregation.

In 1884, Tape attempted to enroll her daughter in an all-white school. There was no law mandating segregation in San Francisco's public schools and California law guaranteed children the right to public education. Local officials were not keen to have Chinese and Chinese American children attend school alongside white children. They also knew that educating Chinese and Chinese American children would counter Chinese exclusion. Tape and her husband sued the San Francisco Board of Education and school board officials for the right to enroll their daughter in their local public school. They won their case when California's Supreme court ruled in their favor citing the 14th amendments equal protection clause, linking civil rights gains for African Americans with Asian Americans' battles for civil rights explicitly. Quickly, California's legislature acted to amend state law with the U.S. Constitution in mind that foreshadowed future white supremacist strategies. They created segregated schools for children of Asian and Chinese descent. The US Supreme Court would not rule in favor of "separate but equal" public accommodations until the 1890s. But struggles against white supremacist laws and ideology were linked across regions and racial groups. Like African Americans, the Tapes fought to provide equal treatment for their children. Similarly, they faced intrenched racism and a far longer fight that she never saw finish in her lifetime.

Even amidst repression and racist national immigration policy, the era of exclusion also produced another one of Chinese immigrant women's greatest champions: Mabel Ping-Hua Lee. She took up the fight of women in Mary Tape's generation. Born in 1896, Lee immigrated with her family from China to New York City in 1900. Her parents' occupation as teachers in a Baptist school allowed them to skirt US regulations. She arrived in a United States that refused her a pathway to citizenship and denied her voting rights. As a young woman Lee actively participated in New York City's movement for women's suffrage, became the first Chinese woman in the United States to earn a doctoral degree, and worked in her community in New York's Chinatown neighborhood. The US government did not repeal the Chinese Exclusion Act until 1943.

Conclusion: Freedom Dream Deferred and the Gradual Arrival of Jane Crow

The event in 1884 that radicalized Ida B. Wells, her expulsion from a first-class rail car because of her race, was characteristic of another gradual change in US society after the Era of Emancipation. Like others of her generation, Wells faced discrimination in public accommodation and violence that a white woman would never have endured at the hands of railroad personnel. Congress had acted before to thwart Southern whites' attempts to instituted Black Codes that repurposed restrictive slave codes for the surveillance and criminalization of freed people. But two decades after the end of the Civil War and a decade after Black men gained the right to vote, Southern whites began to enact new racist policies. Initially, it had not made much sense to white Southerners to segregate neighborhoods, public places, and transportation. After all, proximity to African Americans was part of many Southerners' upbringings. During slavery, most enslavers kept enslaved people close by so that they could work for them. After Emancipation, Black women and men could often only find work in service professions or as agricultural laborers.

The change was slow and evolved over decades, but even before the Supreme Court endorsed the tenet of "separate but equal," African Americans began to endure the rise of Jim Crow Laws alongside continued white violence. Steadily, white workers pushed skilled Black laborers out of trades that commanded higher pay than unskilled laborers. Black women endured lasting gender and race discrimination. Field labor, domestic work, and laundry work were the only jobs open to them. Sexual violence was a tool of domination during slavery. White men used racial stereotypes of Black women as immoral and hypersexual to explain why they perpetrated rampant sexual violence against African American women. Physical violence, discriminatory laws, criminalization, and sexual violence defined the rise of Jim Crow, or Jane Crow, for Black women. De facto discrimination based on custom and upheld by extralegal violence made way for du jour discrimination and segregation mandated by law and upheld by the judicial system.

Euro-Americans began to pass laws excluding African Americans from the use of public spaces like parks, water fronts, and sites of leisure. Cities instituted segregated seating on public transportation. Businesses refused service to African Americans or required separate entrances. Shopkeepers refused to serve Black patrons until after whites had been served. Restaurants refused to serve Black people or required them to dine outside at restaurants. Slowly, municipalities excluded Black men from juries and violence and voter suppression efforts made it impossible for Black officials to win elections. Courts and law enforcement upheld the rising system of discrimination and racial violence enforced it. Sexual and physical violence remained ever-looming threats to Black women.

Ida B. Wells's home state of Mississippi did not ratify the 13th Amendment at the end of the Civil War. Mississippi continued to decline to do so officially until the paperwork finally made its way to Washington, D.C., in 2013. Reconstruction and the Era of Emancipation were full of radical change and an unprecedented expansion of citizenship and civil rights. But those rights were often explicitly expanded for men. Once established, Euro-American leaders, politicians, and officials chipped away at hard-fought freedoms and political agency. While congress strove to guarantee Black men a place in US society, that same promise of citizenship evaporated for East Asian Immigrants. Indigenous people faced the full force of America's imperial project to displace them from their lands. Slavery had ended but racism had not. For the generation of women born during and just after the Civil War, defining freedom and citizenship relied on the advancement of education, labor organizing, and increasing political activism. Their daughters and granddaughters did not give up the fight for hard-fought gains. Women's activism continued in the new century and relied on the lessons learned by generations past. The fight for equality, safety, and the new civil rights that radical constitutional amendments guaranteed at the end of the Civil War would remain an enduring struggle in all regions.

Bibliography

Cox, Karen L. *Dixie's Daughters: The United Daughters of the Confederacy and the Preservation of Confederate Culture. With a new preface edition.* Gainesville: University Press of Florida, 2019.

Foner, Eric. *The Second Founding: How the Civil War and Reconstruction Remade the Constitution.* 1st edition. New York: W. W. Norton & Company, 2020.

Foreman, P Gabrielle, Jim Casey, and Sarah Lynn Patterson, eds. *The Colored Conventions Movement: Black Organizing in the Nineteenth Century.* Chapel Hill: University of North Carolina Press, 2021.

Garrett-Scott, Shennette. *Banking on Freedom: Black Women in U.S. Finance Before the New Deal.* New York: Columbia University Press, 2019.

Giddings, Paula J. *Ida: A Sword Among Lions: Ida B. Wells and the Campaign Against Lynching.* Reprint edition. New York: Amistad, 2009.

Hunter, Tera W. *To 'Joy My Freedom: Southern Black Women's Lives and Labors After the Civil War.* Reprint edition. Cambridge, MA: Harvard University Press, 1998.

Peffer, George. *If They Don't Bring Their Women Here: Chinese Female Immigration Before Exclusion.* Urbana: University of Illinois Press, 1999.

Rosen, Hannah. *Terror in the Heart of Freedom: Citizenship, Sexual Violence, and the Meaning of Race in the Postemancipation South.* New edition. Chapel Hill: The University of North Carolina Press, 2009.

Smith, Stacey L. *Freedom's Frontier: California and the Struggle over Unfree Labor, Emancipation, and Reconstruction.* Reprint edition. Chapel Hill, NC: The University of North Carolina Press, 2015.

Tetrault, Lisa. *The Myth of Seneca Falls: Memory and the Women's Suffrage Movement, 1848–1898.* Reprint edition. Chapel Hill: The University of North Carolina Press, 2017.

Tong, Benson. *Unsubmissive Women: Chinese Prostitutes in Nineteenth-Century San Francisco.* Norman: University of Oklahoma Press, 2000.

Williams, Heather Andrea. *Help Me to Find My People: The African American Search for Family Lost in Slavery.* The University of North Carolina Press, 2012.

"Women's Stories of. . . - Women's History (U.S. National Park Service)." Accessed January 11, 2023. **https://www.nps.gov/subjects/womenshistory/women-s-stories-of.htm**.

PART III

Melissa E. Blair

CHAPTER 11

New Women: 1890–1920

In 1905, suffragist Adella Hunt Logan wrote an article calling on men to support women's suffrage whenever it came before them on the ballot or in the legislature. As generations of suffragists had before her, Logan argued that "government of the people is but partially realized so long as woman has no vote." She spent the next 10 years traveling the country as the head of the Suffrage Department of the women's organization to which she belonged, teaching women nationwide how to organize for suffrage rights on the local and state levels, until her premature death in 1915.

Adella Hunt Logan was not a white woman from the North, but a middle-class African American woman from Tuskegee, Alabama. The organization that sponsored her travel was not the National American Women's Suffrage Association (NAWSA) but the National Association of Colored Women (NACW). In all her articles, Logan outlined the longstanding arguments for women's suffrage but also declared that African American women in particular needed the vote. In a 1905 piece for the *Colored American Magazine* she wrote:

> *If white American women, with all their natural and acquired advantages, need the ballot, that right protective of all other rights . . . how much more do Black Americans, male and female need the strong defense of a vote to help secure them their right to life, liberty, and the pursuit of happiness?*

The vote, Logan argued, was even more important to Black women than it was to White women.

Middle-class African American women like Logan were just one of the many groups of women working to reform the United States between 1890 and 1920. As had always been true of American women's rights work, suffrage was just one component of a multifaceted agenda. And some reformers disagreed with the goal of enfranchising women. White middle-class reforming women were often referred to by the press of the era as the "New Woman," but they were just one group of "new women" pushing to change the nineteenth-century norms they inherited and create new possibilities for American women.

American Women's History: A New Narrative History, First Edition. Melissa E. Blair, Vanessa M. Holden, and Maeve Kane.
© 2024 John Wiley & Sons, Inc. Published 2024 by John Wiley & Sons, Inc.

African American Women's Activism, 1890s–1920

The NACW, the organization which sponsored Adella Logan's suffrage work, was founded in 1896 with a goal of improving communication and coordination among the hundreds of Black women's clubs that had emerged throughout the country since the late 1880s (see Chapter 10). The NACW brought those clubs under a single umbrella, but its leaders – mostly elite Northern Black women including Mary Church Terrell and Josephine St. Pierre Ruffin – did not mandate a uniform agenda. Local clubs remained free to prioritize projects that met the needs of their members and community residents. For example, the Mount Meigs Institute of Waugh, Alabama, a small town outside of Montgomery, taught sewing classes to young women and displayed their work at an NACW national convention. Clubs in larger cities throughout the country established day nurseries where working mothers could leave their small children during the day. As the twentieth century dawned and the club movement grew, NACW-affiliated clubs began to open libraries, parks, and health care clinics, as well as boarding houses for young, single women who were moving to cities to find work. These Working Girls' Homes, along with housing offered by "colored" branches of local YWCAs, were critically important during the Great Migration that began in 1915. As steadily increasing numbers of young African American women moved north to find more stable and better-paying employment, it was difficult for them to find housing in segregated Northern cities. Privately owned apartments that would rent to African American tenants charged disproportionately high rents, knowing that the tenants had few other options. The boardinghouses run by women's clubs and organizations were therefore vital in enabling many young women to make a start in their new homes.

NACW-affiliated clubs were not the only avenue through which Black women pursued this kind of community work. The Young Women's Christian Association (YWCA) was organized in the United States in 1858. In 1889, at the same time that many independent African American women's clubs were founded, the first black "branch" YWCA was organized in Dayton, Ohio. Segregated Y branches provided a range of services to African American women, from boardinghouses and cafeterias to reading groups, study clubs, and exercises programs. While the white leadership of a city's YWCA usually had final say on any large new projects undertaken by their city's branch – buying a new building, for example – the day-to-day operation of branch YWCAs was left to the African American women who made up the branch's Board of Directors.

Regardless of the organization or particular target of activism, the middle-class African American women who undertook reform work were united by several common motivations. First, the rising tide of African American women's public activism coincided with the push to legally exclude African American men from politics and public life through the passage of Jim Crow laws. While discrimination and segregation had been in place through custom and intimidation since the end of the Civil War, it was in the 1890s that disfranchisement and segregation were written into Southern states' laws. At precisely the moment that African American men were being pushed out, women stepped forward. For many of them, their work also involved actively working to gain the right to vote, as it did for Adella Hunt Logan.

All of these women's groups were grounded in a similar set of beliefs, known as the "politics of respectability." The politics of respectability, at its most basic, was an effort by African Americans (men as well as women) to live up to and urge other African Americans to live up to the stated behavioral norms of middle-class whites. They should dress modestly, abstain from alcohol, and attend church regularly. Young single women should not go out with men without adult supervision. Following these rules, Black community leaders hoped, would force white Americans to see African Americans as equals and treat them accordingly.

Women who engaged in reform work and promoted the politics of respectability were known at the time as "race women," and many of them drew direct connections between their time in women's clubs and their larger community and political work. Fannie Barrier Williams, for example, wrote in 1901 that "in all of [the women's clubs and organizations] race problems and sociological questions directly related to the condition of the Negro race in America are the principal subjects for study and discussion." Race women understood all of their work, from opening a library to promoting temperance, as connected to the broader goal of improving the lives of African Americans.

Some women drew these connections more explicitly, most famously Ida B. Wells (later Ida B. Wells-Barnett). In 1892, while she was co-owner of the Memphis newspaper the *Free Speech,* Wells wrote articles that asserted that the sexual liaisons which were frequently cited to justify lynching were not the result of rape, but rather of consensual relationships between white women and black men which were discovered, and the women then cried rape to protect themselves. Publishing this analysis led to the destruction of the *Free Speech's* office and press by a white mob and chased Wells out of the South permanently. Later that year, while living in New York, Wells published *Southern Horrors,* a pamphlet which documented her statistical analysis showing that rape was only even alleged as the crime in 30% of documented lynchings. In this work, Wells argued forcefully that the purpose of lynching was not, as white Southerners maintained, to "protect white womanhood," but to intimidate and subordinate African Americans. The rising tide of vigilante violence against black men, coinciding as it did with the creation of the legal Jim Crow regime, added even more fuel to African American women's convictions that they must be active in the public sphere not only for their own sake, but for the sake of "the race."

Many African American women who promoted the politics of respectability, such as Anna Julia Cooper, understood it as just one of many tools through which African American women could fight back against racism. Gaining education and employment were others, as was working for the right to vote. But the politics of respectability quickly grew into a concept that shaped the daily lives of African American women of all classes and ages. For African American girls, it created clear guidelines on how to be a "nice" girl. As historian LaKisha Simmons argues, the politics of respectability "dictated how young women interacted with the city, what they wore, how they carried themselves and, in turn, how they understood themselves." It also shaped African American women's political activism in fundamental ways, sometimes leading them into alliance with white women, but often working independently to meet the needs of the African American community and fight racism.

Some working-class African American women chose to reject the calls for respectability, instead shaping norms of behavior and dress that spoke to their days of hard physical work, self-ownership, and autonomy. Such choices often brought working-class women under scrutiny, as for working-class women in Atlanta who faced disapproval not only from employers but also from middle-class African Americans when they chose to use their leisure time to dance, frequent blues clubs, and wear dresses in colors and cuts that would not be acceptable in middle-class parlors. As will be discussed below, for women of color in the urban North and West, making similar decisions could land one in a women's reformatory.

Marriage, Children, and Family Life

A large majority of American women in these years married and had children. Historian Stephanie Coontz has noted that "the need for economic security and the desire for a home of her own" were important considerations for women in these years, as even college-educated single women often had difficulty supporting themselves financially. The marriage rate from the 1870s through the turn of the twentieth century was relatively stable, and the number of marriages generally increased over the first 20 years of the new century. Looking at the number of women who never married shows similar trends. While the percentage of women in their thirties who had never married continued increasing in the 1890s, reaching roughly 17% in 1900, the number then began to drop, falling to roughly 14% by 1920.

For immigrant young women in the nation's biggest cities, how they met their future spouse changed dramatically in these years. Around the turn of the century, commercialized leisure activities, such as amusement parks and dance halls, opened in cities like New York, Chicago, and Los Angeles. From Coney Island to the Long Beach pier, working-class teenagers took their half-day off work on Saturdays to socialize with their peers, away from their parents and neighbors. In earlier generations, courtship had occurred on the front stoop or in the streets, subject to the supervision of all the adult women of the neighborhood. Now, young women could meet boys from outside the neighborhood, of different ethnic and religious backgrounds. Because teenaged daughters usually surrendered most if not all of their pay to their fathers, young men would pay for their dinner or admission to the dance hall. This system was called treating, and young men usually expected a kiss or some other kind of physical repayment at the end of the night. What most scandalized parents was not this aspect of the system, however, but the fact that they were losing some of their control over the courtship system.

Most of these young women, like all women, eventually married and had children. For native-born white Protestant women, the birth rate continued its long, steady decline that had begun around 1800. But most other groups of women also saw their birth rates begin to drop in the years around the turn of the twentieth century. The number of births per one thousand people dropped from 40 in 1880 to 32 in 1900 and continued to fall, reaching only 28 per one thousand people in 1920. The declining birth rate did little, at least initially, to help the long-standing infant mortality problems. In 1900, 165 out of every one thousand babies would die in the first year of their life. While childhood diseases like scarlet fever and measles spread regardless of race or class, working-class, immigrant, and poor families bore the brunt of these high infant mortality rates.

One place where those rates were extremely high was on newly formed Indian reservations. The process of forcibly moving Native Americans to reservations largely concluded in the early 1890s. On the reservations, land was allotted to heads of households, a policy designed to force Native Americans into nuclear family arrangements and out of the networks of kin and clan that had ordered their lives for centuries. On some reservations, the Bureau of Indian Affairs (BIA) also moved in and began to provide some health care, including obstetric care, hoping to replace midwife-attended births and a system of entire kin groups raising children, what historian Brianna Theobald has called "flexible childrearing." The reason for these policies, at least for the white middle-class BIA women who developed them, was to address the high infant mortality rates. The programs focused on a style of childrearing called "scientific motherhood," which emphasized the mother as primary caregiver who kept the infant on a strict schedule of sleeping and eating. On some reservations, there were even "beautiful baby" contests sponsored by the BIA, where the mothers whose infants most closely achieved white middle-class norms were given prizes.

While BIA agents were attempting to address infant mortality through "scientific motherhood," the burgeoning birth control movement was trying to help women not have as many children in the first place. Margaret Sanger was the most visible birth control advocate in these years. Sanger worked as a public health nurse in immigrant neighborhoods in New York City at the turn of the twentieth century. As she visited the tenement districts that were home to the hundreds of thousands of working-class immigrants, she was deeply troubled. Many of the women she spoke with were unaware of the biology of their own bodies, and therefore had no idea how to pre-vent their frequent pregnancies. Doctors provide no guidance to their patients. For women who could not afford or did not want any more children, help was even less forthcoming. Many women resorted to illegal abortions to avoid unwanted pregnan-cies, and some of those women died from complications of those abortions.

Sanger began her work to change all of these circumstances with an education campaign. Both through speaking in front of groups in New York and by talking to patients door-to-door as she continued her work as a nurse, Sanger educated women about their bodies. In 1914, she began to publish a newsletter titled *The Woman Rebel,* which featured articles on birth control and women's rights. Sending the news-letter through the mail violated the federal Comstock Law, which had been in place since the early 1870s and prohibited sending anything "obscene" through the mail. All information about birth control was defined as obscene. Sanger was arrested for violating the Comstock Law a few months after the *Woman Rebel* was founded. She fled to England, where she met English sexologist Havelock Ellis, who introduced her to the diaphragm, the most effective form of artificial contraceptive then avail-able. Sanger returned to New York in 1915, and the following year she and her sister opened the country's first birth control clinic. Both women were arrested for violat-ing a New York state law which banned the distribution on contraceptives. Sanger's sister, Ethel Byrne, spent 30 days in a workhouse and went on a hunger strike while there. The sisters' arrest and trials brought national attention to the birth control movement for the first time, and gained Sanger wealthy donors who would help her expand the movement after World War I.

In giving women knowledge about their bodies and teaching them that they had the power to prevent pregnancy, Sanger was directly challenging nineteenth-century ideas about women and sexuality. And she was not the only one. The turn of the century was a high tide of sexology, a field of science that attempted to define the parameters of human sexuality. Some sexologists, such as Dr. Robert Shufeldt in New York, focused their work on trans women. Shufeldt published a study of a trans woman known as Loop-the-Loop in 1917, summarizing a decade's worth of interviews with and examinations of Loop. Like most sexologists, Shufeldt was also a eugenicist. Eugenics was cutting-edge science in these years. Its followers promoted the belief that humans could be divided along levels of "fitness," similar to Charles Darwin's work on animals in the middle of the nineteenth century. Eugenicists, therefore, tried to identify what made humans "fit" and "unfit." As scholar Hugh Ryan has argued, eugenic goals shaped Shufeldt's analysis of Loop. In his writing Shufeldt argued that Loop was trans because of problems with her body. This was an era before psychiatry had come to dominate questions of sexuality, and so Shufeldt and his peers argued that it was physical "abnormalities" that made people trans or homosexual. It would take the rise of psychiatry in the decades after World War I to challenge these understandings of homosexuality and trans identity, and in many ways the belief in underlying biological causes never completely went away.

Women and Work at the Turn of the Century

Loop-the-Loop and Sanger's patients were part of the massive working class of these years. That working class included the majority of African Americans. Black women worked as farmers, domestic workers, wives, and mothers who often struggled to make ends meet in the context of Jim Crow. Most African Americans remained in the South until the Great Migration began in the 1910s, and 80% of the South's population was rural in 1900. For working-class Black women living there, there were few options. Rural women worked on their family's land, which was usually rented on exploitative terms from white landowners. The sharecropping system was designed to keep Black families in poverty and tied to the land, and rural Black southern wives did as rural wives did everywhere, working hard at preserving produce, repairing and altering clothing and linens, and helping in the fields during planting and harvest to try and keep their families clothed and fed. Starting around 1915, tens of thousands of African-Americans began moving to cities in the North and Midwest, filling industrial jobs that had previously been taken by European immigrants. World War I drastically reduced the immigration rate from Europe, both because young men were drafted into the military there and because Atlantic crossings became very dangerous due to German submarine warfare. And so Black men and women began to be hired in Northern factories for the first time, spurring the Great Migration of African Americans out of the South.

Many African American women both urban and rural, throughout the country, were employed as domestic workers. Domestic work was physically demanding. Laundresses collected their clients' dirty clothing, carried it back to their homes or the commercial laundries where they worked, and then begin the process of washing by hand in lye soap, wringing out with a crank, and hanging on a line all the large, heavy garments of the era. Anything that required ironing presented another day's work using heavy irons heated on a fire. For those women who worked as maids, the work was more varied but still physically difficult. Maids were required to move and beat out carpets, wash windows, and scrub floors and bathtubs, often without the benefit of running water and never with hot water unless they heated it on the stove first. Maids working in private homes also had to deal with the changing moods and demands of their employers, something many of them found challenging. Maids that lived in lacked privacy, were on call 24 hours a day, and were isolated from other working-class people, preventing them from forming the kinds of work communities that other working-class women developed in these decades. Whenever any other option was available, most working-class women chose not to work as domestics. But for African American women, there were few other options.

For women who were not African American and lived in the nation's rapidly growing cities, however, the period from 1890 to 1920 was a time of expanding workplace choices. Factories began to hire increasing numbers of young women and entire new industries like retail opened up to them. Most of the women in these fields were teenagers or in their early twenties and worked as part of a family economy that also included wage-earning fathers and brothers plus mothers who may have taken in boarders or done piece work in their home. The highest paid female industrial workers earned more than any other group of urban working-class women but getting to that top pay took years of persistence. In the clothing factories like those that made women's blouses, known as shirtwaists, an apprentice worker made only $2 a week. It took several years to work up to the top pay of $7–9 per week that the most experienced women received. The average weekly wage for working women in 1900 was just over $6.

Many of the women doing this urban, industrial work were immigrants, mostly from Southern and Eastern Europe and the Russian empire. In the West, especially California, they were joined in the workplace by Mexican immigrant and Mexican American young women as well. In California, the factories were more likely to produce canned fruits and vegetables than blouses, but regardless of the product being made, work in these industries was repetitive and dangerous. None of the women in these factories had any opportunity for upward mobility at work. And most of them expected to leave the factories when they were married and had children.

For working-class mothers, there were also many similarities across region and ethnicity. Immigrants throughout the country clustered in ethnically distinct neighborhoods, from Chinatown in San Francisco to the "Bohemian" neighborhoods of Chicago to the Jewish tenements surrounding the garment factories of the Lower East Side of Manhattan. Married women who did not work in the factories but lived in these neighborhoods still worked extremely hard. They were responsible for feeding and clothing large families in apartments of two or three rooms, as well as doing any work that they could to make cash within their households, from taking in sewing to providing food, cleaning, and housing for paying boarders. They had to clean, do laundry, and cook in apartments that did not have running water – the newest tenement buildings had water pumps on each floor of the building, but women living in older buildings had to haul water up several flights of stairs from a backyard pump. For many women, shopping was their one reliable way to get out of the apartment regularly, and it was time-consuming work. Without electricity for refrigeration, groceries had to be bought almost daily, and working-class wives did their best to feed their families well on as little money as possible. Most of these women were also caring for many children since, as Sanger found, knowledge of birth control was virtually nonexistent among immigrant communities in this period. As one Chinese immigrant woman in California recalled, "We didn't know about birth control. We would become pregnant every year without realizing it." Similar statements could have been made by immigrant women of all backgrounds across the country.

For some working-class women in the factories, the difficult, dangerous work for low wages led them to organize. The most famous labor protest by working-class women occurred in New York in 1909, when some 20,000 young women, mostly Jewish and Italian immigrants, walked out of dozens of clothing factories as part of a general strike that sought shorter hours, higher pay, and safer work conditions.

The young immigrant Jewish women who led this strike – Clara Lemlich, Rose Schneiderman, Pauline Newman, and others – became professional labor organizers, traveling the country and inspiring other shirtwaist makers' strikes over the next several years. These strikers were assisted by the well-off women of the Women's Trade Union League, a group formed in 1903 by Progressive women to build bridges between working-class and well-off women. The goal of the WTUL's creators was to make an organization where working-class, middle-class, and elite women all came together to make changes in the industrial workplace. WUTL chapters eventually existed in several cities, and Uprising of the 20,000 veteran Rose Schneiderman led the New York chapter for almost 40 years.

These New York women were far from the only ones to organize to improve their working conditions, however. Two decades earlier, African American laundresses had gone on strike in Atlanta, demanding and receiving higher wages for the backbreaking work they conducted each week. In Tampa, a Puerto Rican-born labor activist and feminist named Luisa Capetillo was one of the organizers of a strike among cigar makers in 1913. Capetillo's rhetoric on the strike platform linked anti-colonial opposition to the American occupation of Puerto Rico, advocacy for greater rights for women, and improved treatment of working-class men and women. Hers was an expansive vision, not unlike that of the Atlanta washerwomen who both boycotted their clients until they agreed to pay higher fees and pushed back against middle-class African American community leaders who discouraged them from spending their evenings at blues clubs. Lemlich, Schneiderman, and their allies also had big goals, joining their calls for better working conditions with demands for educational opportunities and paid vacation time. Organizing to improve the conditions of work was often the most visible kind of activism in which working-class women engaged, but it was never the only issue.

These disparate groups of working-class women were able to create multifaceted activist agendas in part because the sex segregation of the workplace and the racial segregation of neighborhoods created spaces in which the women could come together as working women, talk about their problems, and brainstorm solutions. The Atlanta washerwomen gathered laundry from around the city and carried it back to their segregated neighborhoods, where groups of women worked together, communally using large washtubs set up in adjacent backyards. The shirtwaist workers worked in close quarters six days a week, then went home to the same tenement buildings and perhaps spent time at Coney Island together. Capetillo and her comrades in Tampa all lived in Ybor City, the majority-Cuban neighborhood that was built near the cigar factories. Working-class women at the turn of the century were able to create communities that facilitated activism to improve their lives. By the 1910s, that activism included agitating for the right to vote as well.

The Progressive Movement

Working-class labor organizers were not the only Americans who worked to solve the problems of industrial capitalism as they understood them. Many middle-class men and women became part of the Progressive movement, which tried to address similar issues of workplace safety and workers' living conditions. The solutions that these middle-class reformers promoted, however, were quite different than those that working-class women advocated for through their unions. While there was some overlap in terms of changes to working conditions, the reforms to be made outside the shop floor differed greatly. Working-class women talked about access to education, the right to their own kinds of leisure, and an overall opening up of working-class life. Middle-class reformers, in contrast, often sought to narrow the range of options working-class people had through efforts to ban alcohol, shut down dance halls, and otherwise enforce middle-class ideas of respectability on working-class communities.

Perhaps the most famous female Progressive reformer, Jane Addams' life reflects many of the movement's themes. Addams attended college and graduated from the Rockford Female Seminary in Illinois, her home state, in 1881. Struggling with back problems and lack of direction in her life, Addams battled depression for the next several years. During a trip to Europe with friends in 1888, she visited Toynbee Hall, a settlement house in the poor East End of London. Inspired, Addams returned to Illinois and, with her partner Ellen Starr, opened Hull House in Chicago in 1889.

Hull House was an old mansion located in a neighborhood that was home to a mixture of European migrants from throughout that continent. Italian, Jewish, Bohemian, Greek, and Irish immigrants all resided in the neighborhood that Addams called home for the rest of her life. Hull House was designed to provide a variety of services to these working-class people, from a health clinic and translation services and English classes to a kindergarten, a gymnasium, an art studio, and a garden. Addams and the other women who lived in the house throughout its existence were dedicated to serving their immigrant neighbors. But more important for Addams was what she called the "subjective necessity" of settlement houses. By creating a space in which women lived (between 6 and 10 middle-class women lived in the upper floors of the house), Hull House and all the settlement houses that followed it gave educated middle-class young women opportunities and connections to build careers. Addams knew that women were hungry for ways to support themselves and do meaningful work, and the settlement house network that emerged from Hull House provided exactly that. It also provided a haven for women whose lives did not conform to the gender norms of the era. Florence Kelley came to Hull House with her three children as a safe place to flee her physically abusive husband in New York. She never remarried and remained with her children at Hull House for several years. Jane Addams purchased the house with her partner Ellen Starr. That relationship ended shortly thereafter, and Addams soon began a relationship with Mary Rozet Smith which lasted until Smith's death in 1934. Many other women in the Progressive movement and who moved through Hull House, such as Sophonisba Breckenridge, were also lesbians. While these women were not publicly "out" in the modern sense, their relationships were also not secret to those who knew them.

Settlement houses were the backbone of much of the rest of women's Progressive reform. They were physical places, spaces that existed in all major northern and Midwestern cities by the early twentieth century. If you wanted to become involved in Progressive work but did not know how, you could simply go to Hull House, or the Henry Street Settlement in New York, or any other of the dozens of settlement houses, and find ways to get involved. As the movement grew, women worked on a huge range of issues. They protested the unsafe meatpacking conditions and unknown quality of food and medicines, work which led directly to the creation of the Food & Drug Administration in 1905. They lobbied to create a separate juvenile justice system. Some worked to create divisions within the federal government that would oversee efforts to improve the lives of women and children, creating the Children's Bureau in 1912 and the Women's Bureau in 1920.

One area of work that attracted many women was using the law to improve industrial working conditions. Male and female Progressives wrote state laws that established minimum wages, maximum working hours per week or times of day one could work, required breaks, or restricted child labor. As a group, the laws were known as protective labor legislation, and a number of states passed such laws in the first years of the twentieth century. In New York, the state legislature passed a law forbidding bakers from working more than 60 hours a week or 10 hours a day. A group of male bakers sued, and in 1905 the Supreme Court struck down the New York law in a case called *Lochner v. New York,* stating that the government could not interfere in an individual's right to make a free contract. Three years later, the Supreme Court heard a similar case, *Mueller v. Oregon.* Unlike the New York law, Oregon's law only applied to women, mandating that women could not work more than 10 hours per day. Progressive activists and lawyers, led by future Supreme Court justice Louis Brandeis, argued that because women were "actual and future mothers of the race," the state had an interest in protecting their health by regulating their work conditions. The Supreme Court agreed, and the Oregon law was upheld. This 1908 case let to a rapid expansion of protective labor legislation throughout the country, but that legislation could only cover women in order to be constitutional. While this approach helped improve women's work conditions in the short term, many critics claimed that it artificially restricted women's employment opportunities. It also defined women's relationship to the government primarily through their status as mothers, rather than as full and independent citizens.

While Progressive women and men brought many improvements to American life and society, their work was not without controversy. Progressive activists were middle-class people, often college educated, who sought to solve the problems of the urban working class. Rarely did they ask working-class people what they wanted or needed. This tendency to assume that they knew best led many Progressive reformers to implement programs that they believed worked quite well, but which did not actually meet the needs of the communities they were trying to help.

The story of the girls' reformatory system Progressive activists built in California, described by historian Mary Odem, provides a good example of these problems. Progressive women were dismayed by the number of teenaged girls they saw out late at night with men, dancing at public dance halls, having fun at amusement parks, or simply relaxing in parks and beaches. In both Los Angeles and Oakland, Progressive women persuaded local officials to hire female police officers who would patrol areas popular with working-class teenagers and pick up young women not behaving "respectably." Because Progressive reformers believed that the problematic behavior they saw in these young women stemmed from bad home environments, the young women would then be sent to the newly established state girls' reformatory outside Oakland for anywhere from 6 to 18 months.

Often young women were brought to the attention of the female police officers by their parents. Mexican American parents seem to have been particularly likely to use these officers to try and reign in daughters who were breaking free of the traditional system of family chaperonage that had flourished in both Mexico and California for generations. Under that system, young women would not go out in public unless accompanied by an older relative, such as an aunt or an older brother. As Mexican American teenaged girls behaved as their peers did nationwide and began to shake off that system, spending time in public with young men who were sometimes not known to their families, their parents became alarmed. Most serious of all were the cases where young women moved in with their boyfriends before marriage. Sometimes these circumstances led Mexican American parents to contact the authorities about their daughters. The parents' goals were twofold: they wanted their daughters' behavior to become "respectable" again, and they wanted their daughters to move home and continue to contribute to the family economy by giving most if not all of their pay to their father each week. Neither of those goals was achieved, however, by incarcerating the girls in northern California for months at a time, and both the girls and their parents vigorously protested those punishments.

The Mexican American young women who came to the attention of female Progressive reformers had much in common with working-class African American women in the eastern half of the country who were also rebelling against the politics of respectability in these decades. Both groups were trying to create their own rules for making their way in the world, rules that more closely matched their own personal desires and own ideas of what made up a meaningful life. Describing their efforts that way also illustrates just how similar they were to the college-educated Progressive women who chose not to marry but instead to pursue a life of career and public service. All these women were shaking off the rules of the nineteenth century and trying to create lives of purpose and meaning. They were all "New Women" of the turn of the twentieth century.

The Final Path to Women's Suffrage

In 1890, organized efforts to gain the right to vote for women were nearly 50 years old. In that year, the two national suffrage organizations that had been created in the late 1860s (see Chapter 10) consolidated into a single group, the National American Women's Suffrage Association, or NAWSA. By the turn of the twentieth century, four states – Wyoming, Idaho, Utah, and Colorado – had given women full suffrage rights. Between 1900 and the ratification of the Nineteenth Amendment in 1920, the number of suffrage activists and the diversity of their views and reasons for seeking the vote exploded. An organized anti-suffrage movement also emerged, often led by women.

One of the new trends in suffrage work in the twentieth century was the scale of African American women's participation in the movement. There had always been numerous Black suffrage activists, both male and female. But the National Association of Colored Women's Clubs adoption of suffrage as one of the group's goals gave those efforts increased visibility. Adella Hunt Logan and her peers, including Ida B. Wells-Barnett (who founded the Alpha Suffrage Club in Chicago in 1913) worked tirelessly to help Black women throughout the country fight for their political rights.

African American women were not the only group outside of NAWSA's main constituency of middle-class white women to organize for voting rights in the twentieth century. In 1907, Leonora O'Reilly, a working-class Irish American union organizer, joined with Harriot Stanton Blatch, daughter of suffrage leader Elizabeth Cady Stanton, in Blatch's new suffrage group the Equality League of Self-Supporting Women. O'Reilly and other female labor leaders increasingly engaged in suffrage work as the twentieth century progressed. For many New York working women, the tragic Triangle Shirtwaist Fire of 1911 proved a turning point. The Triangle factory had been one of the main locations of the Uprising of the 20,000 strike in 1909. Women there had been able to negotiate for better pay and hours through their strike. But they had not secured improvements to workplace safety. When a fire broke out in the factory, located on the eighth floor of a building, workers discovered that the doors to the fire escape were locked and they had no clear way out. In the birthplace of one of the most successful strikes by women workers in American history, 146 women died due to a lack of safe working conditions. For O'Reilly, Rose Schneiderman, and many others working-class women throughout the country, the need to be able to vote for politicians who would pass laws improving workplace safety, as well as the limitations of union organizing, were made horrifyingly clear. Many working-class women turned to suffrage work after the fire.

Working-class women and African American women largely organized outside of NAWSA, as did other women of color. As historian Cathleen Cahill has documented, after the turn of the twentieth-century suffrage work flourished among women of color, especially middle-class ones. Native American women such as Gertrude Simmons Bonner (Zitkala-Sa) and Marie Louise Bottineau Baldwin were college-educated professional women who saw the vote as an important tool in the fight for tribal sovereignty for Native Americans. Chinese American and Chinese immigrant women, the most famous of whom was Mabel Ping-Hua Lee, often connected their suffrage work to the Chinese Revolution of 1911, which created the Republic of China and included women's voting rights in that republic's founding constitution. Chinese American women hoped to use both the actions of the new Chinese government and their suffrage activism to fight back against the extremely discriminatory laws that shaped the Chinese experience in the United States. Just like middle-class white women who wanted the vote to pass temperance laws or protective labor legislation, then, women of color and working-class women saw the vote both as important in its own right and as a tool to use for the overall improvement of their communities.

Middle-class white women focused their suffrage activism in NAWSA. In the early years of the twentieth century, that group concentrated on growing its membership, which numbered only about 12,000 women nationwide in 1906. Aware that the group needed to grow if it was going to succeed in its goals, organizers began to recruit. They set up parlor meetings where they could explain the rationale for women's suffrage to elite women who would not go to public meetings. They also encouraged the development of a suffrage movement in the South, a region where the issue had failed to take hold among white women in the nineteenth century. In order to facilitate growth there, NAWSA's national leadership endorsed a rules change in 1903 that allowed each state's leaders to decide the qualifications for membership in that state's NAWSA affiliates. In other words, national leaders gave white Southern suffragists permission to keep the suffrage movement segregated in the South, which they did. Between 1906 and 1910, NAWSA grew rapidly in the South and elsewhere, and by 1910 there were 117,000 members nationwide, more than a ninefold increase in membership in just four years.

Not all women supported efforts to expand women's political rights. An active anti-suffrage movement emerged throughout the country as NAWSA grew, with particular hotspots in New York, Massachusetts, and the Southeast. As scholar Susan Goodier noted in her study of anti-suffrage in New York, "organized anti-suffrage women. . .sought to preserve what they perceived as the special and unique place of women in the polity. Rather than seeing this preservation as limiting women, they believed they were encouraging women to use the best of their gender's inherent talents." Anti-suffrage women had many male allies, including those in the liquor industry who believed enfranchising women would hasten the passage of a national prohibition law. There were also many men who simply believed politics was a man's game, and anti-suffrage women generally agreed. Anti-suffrage women believed that placing women within the realm of partisan politics would fundamentally alter their role in society. They saw suffrage as a challenge to their very identity as women. Conservative women would adopt similar arguments, with a remarkable degree of consistency, throughout the twentieth century.

Some anti-suffrage women articulated other, more specific objections to suffrage or the Nineteenth Amendment. Women on both sides of the debate highlighted the fact that immigrant and African American men could vote while native-born white women could not. For suffragists such as Elizabeth Cady Stanton, this was an argument for women's suffrage; she argued that native-born women should not have fewer rights than newly naturalized immigrant citizens. For anti-suffrage women, however, expanding the vote to women was seen as doubling the number of "undesirable" citizens who would have the power to vote. Some white Southern women who supported women's suffrage were opposed to achieving it through a federal, Constitutional amendment. These women argued that voting was a state right, as the Supreme Court had said in *Minor v. Happersett* in 1874. This argument was also, at its core, about race. Passage of the Nineteenth Amendment would create another opportunity to make voting a federally regulated issue, and, they feared, could negate the Jim Crow disfranchisement laws that were so effectively preventing African American men from voting.

The 1910s was the successful decade for women's suffrage, as many factors came together to push the Constitutional amendment across the finish line. One factor was a focus on that amendment, which NAWSA had largely relegated to the back burner in the 1890s and 1900s. In 1912, a young woman named Alice Paul returned from two years of graduate work in Great Britain and joined NAWSA, taking over the leadership of the Washington, D.C. chapter and the organization's largely dormant Congressional Committee. Paul was dedicated to securing women's voting rights through a constitutional amendment. She believed that only an amendment guaranteed women's rights forever. If suffrage was only secured through state laws, she argued, state lawmakers could simply choose to take the right away if they wanted to. Paul's focus on the amendment and, especially, her tactics and sympathy with the more radical British suffrage movement, made her a polarizing figure within NAWSA. Her first major event, a suffrage march that coincided with Woodrow Wilson's inauguration as president in 1913, was designed to provoke backlash and headlines. Roughly eight thousand women participated, and they were heckled, jeered, and taunted by the crowd. Some bystanders threw things, injuring a few of the marchers and gaining the suffrage campaign the headlines Paul believed necessary to spur action on the stalled amendment. NAWSA leaders disliked Paul's tactics, and she and her followers split from NAWSA in 1914 and formed the Congressional Union, which they renamed the National Women's Party (NWP) in 1916. While the NWP's tactics differed from NAWSA's, its membership did not: the group was overwhelmingly white and middle or upper class. Indeed, the support of wealthy women such as Alva Belmont, an heiress to part of the Vanderbilt fortune, was critical to the NWP getting off the ground as an independent organization.

By the time Paul split from NAWSA, that organization had a new president who was willing to devote more resources to the constitutional amendment while continuing to fight for suffrage at the state level. Carrie Chapman Catt, who had briefly held the NAWSA presidency earlier in the century before stepping down to care for her ill husband, became president again in 1915. She pursued what she called the "Winning Plan," in which NAWSA worked on both the federal and state level simultaneously. Catt believed that the two approaches in fact supported one another. She hoped that more populous states giving women the right to vote – as California did in 1911, and Illinois in 1913 – would increase the pressure on the federal government to act. She also knew that, if the constitutional amendment passed, it would have to be ratified by three-quarters of the state legislatures to become law. Keeping the state-level organizations active would be useful if and when the constitutional amendment passed.

After President Wilson was reelected president in 1916, as World War I raged in Europe, the final push began. Paul and other members of the National Women's Party began to picket the White House in 1917, displaying banners with questions like "Mr. President, How Long Must Women Wait for Liberty?" They continued to picket the White House after the United States entered World War I in April 1917, a decision which was deeply controversial. Dozens of women were arrested for obstructing traffic during the pickets and refused to pay the fines that courts levied against them. They argued that doing so would be an admission of guilt, and they chose to go serve short sentences in women's work prison in Occoquan, Virginia instead. Several women at Occoquan went on hunger strikes and were force-fed, including Alice Paul. Word of their poor treatment leaked to the press and began to turn public opinion in favor of women's suffrage.

NAWSA, as always, took a different approach. Instead of increasing its confrontations with the Wilson administration once the U.S. entered the war, NAWSA publicly dedicated itself to supporting the war effort. This was a difficult choice for many NAWSA members, including Catt, who were committed pacifists. But they believed that cooperating with the government would put them in a position of strength to negotiate for the president's endorsement of the women's suffrage amendment.

NAWSA's calculation proved to be correct. In the context of shifting public opinion and overt contributions to the war effort by suffragists, President Wilson publicly supported a constitutional amendment giving women the right to vote in September 1918. Congress ratified the Nineteenth Amendment June 1919, sending it to the states for ratification. Just over a year later, in August 1920, Tennessee became the necessary 36th state to ratify and the amendment became law.

Generations of women had fought for women's voting rights, and for many that fight persisted after 1920. The ability to vote remained elusive for Black women in the South, whom Jim Crow laws disfranchised. Most Native American women were still not citizens, but rather considered "wards" of the federal government. Immigrant women from China and Japan, and native-born women who married immigrant men from those countries, could not become citizens (or lost their citizenship) and therefore could not vote. In spite of these substantial limits on the Nineteenth Amendment's effect, its passage brought the organized women's suffrage movement to a close. The Progressive movement also ended in the late 1910s, and American women moved into the 1920s searching for new ways to be active in politics, at work, and in their families.

Bibliography

Alexander, Adele Logan. *Princess of the Hither Isles: A Black Suffragist's Story from the Jim Crow South*. Yale University Press, 2019.

Cahill, Cathleen. *Recasting the Vote: How Women of Color Transformed the Suffrage Movement*. UNC Press, 2020.

Coontz, Stephanie. *Marriage, a History*. Viking, 2005.

Cooper, Brittany. *Beyond Respectability: The Intellectual Thought of Race Women*. University of Illinois Press, 2017.

Goodier, Susan. *No Votes for Women: The New York State Anti-Suffrage Movement*. University of Illinois Press, 2013.

Gordon, Linda. *The Moral Property of Women: A History of Birth Control Politics in America*. University of Illinois Press, 2007.

Green, Elna C. *Southern Strategies: Southern Women and the Woman Suffrage Question*. UNC Press, 1997.

Hewitt, Nancy. *Southern Discomfort: Women's Activism in Tampa, Florida, 1880s–1920s*. University of Illinois Press, 2003.

Hicks, Cheryl. *Talk with You Like a Woman: African-American Women, Justice, and Reform in New York, 1890–1935*. UNC Press, 2010.

Higginbotham, Evelyn Brooks. *Righteous Discontent: The Women's Movement in the Black Baptist Church, 1880–1920*. Harvard University Press, 1993.

Hunter, Tera W. *To 'Joy My Freedom: Southern Black Women's Lives and Labors After the Civil War*. Harvard University Press, 1997.

Jones, Jacqueline. *Labor of Love, Labor of Sorrow: Black Women, Work, and the Family from Slavery to the Present*. Vintage, 1985.

McGirr, Lisa. *The War on Alcohol: Prohibition and the Rise of the American State*. Norton, 2016.

Muncy, Robyn. *Creating a Female Dominion in American Reform, 1890–1935*. Oxford University Press, 1991.

Odem, Mary E. *Delinquent Daughters: Protecting and Policing Female Adolescent Sexuality in the United States, 1885–1920*. UNC Press, 2000.

Orleck, Annelise. *Common Sense and a Little Fire: Women and Working-Class Politics in the United States, 1900–1965*. UNC Press, 1995.

Peiss, Kathy. *Cheap Amusements: Working Women and Leisure in Turn-of-the-Century New York*. Temple University Press, 1986.

Robertson, Nancy Marie. *Christian Sisterhood, Race Relations, and the YWCA, 1906–1946*. University of Illinois Press, 2010.

Ryan, Hugh. *When Brooklyn Was Queer*. St. Martin's Press, 2019.

Schecter, Patricia A. *Ida B. Wells-Barnett and American Reform, 1880-1930*. UNC Press, 2001.

Shaw, Stephanie J. *What a Woman Is and Ought to Be: Black Professional Women Workers during the Jim Crow Era*. University of Chicago Press, 1996.

Simmons, La Kisha Michelle. *Crescent City Girls: The Lives of Young Black Women in Segregated New Orleans*. UNC Press, 2015.

Sklar, Kathryn Kish. *Florence Kelley and the Nation's Work: The Rise of Women's Political Culture, 1830-1900*. Yale University Press, 1995.

Terborg-Penn, Rosalyn. *African-American Women and the Struggle for the Vote, 1850–1920*. Indiana University Press, 1998.

Tetrault, Lisa. *The Myth of Seneca Falls: Memory and the Women's Suffrage Movement, 1848–1898*. UNC Press, 2014.

Theobald, Brianna. *Reproduction on the Reservation: Pregnancy, Childbirth, and Colonialism in the Long Twentieth Century*. UNC Press, 2019.

Vapnek, Lara. *Breadwinners: Working Women and Economic Independence, 1865–1920*. University of Illinois Press, 2009.

Weiss, Elaine. *The Woman's Hour: The Great Fight to Win the Vote*. Penguin, 2019.

Yung, Judy. *Unbound Feet: A Social History of Chinese Women in San Francisco*. University of California Press, 1995.

CHAPTER 12

Women Between the Wars, 1920–1945

In August 1939, nearly all the workers at the Cal San fruit canning factory in Los Angeles walked off the job. It was the height of the peach season. The strike was planned to hit the company at its most financially important time. The Cal San strikers were overwhelmingly women, mostly Mexican Americans with a sizeable group of Russian Jewish immigrant women as well. The work conditions for women in the factory were dangerous, with wet floors and constantly sped-up assembly lines making it easy for workers to slip or cut themselves. And unlike the male workers in the warehouse and shipping departments who were paid an hourly wage, the women working on the assembly lines to prepare the fruit were paid based on their production. As Carmen Escobar, one of the strike leaders, recalled to historian Vicki Ruiz, the women worked at long tables and "the women in the middle horded the fruit. . .and the women at the end of the line really suffered. Those at the end of the line hardly made nothing."

In 1939, the Cal San factory was a tight-knit workplace, ripe for unionization. Many of the Mexican American women were related to others working in the factory, both men and women – the canning industry was a family affair among Los Angeles Latinas. And while the Jewish women were less likely to have kin in the factory, they lived in the same neighborhoods as their Latina coworkers, in Boyle Heights and other parts of East Los Angeles. Organizing the strike was therefore relatively easy because the workers were already connected in a variety of ways. Before they walked out of the factory, Escobar and other strike leaders had already arranged for neighborhood grocers to donate food and organized strikers to distribute it, as well as coordinated pickets of the factory. After two and a half months, the overwhelmingly female union won a five-cent raise, the firing of many of the most abusive supervisors, and union recognition.

The story of Carmen Escobar and her coworkers in the California fruit packing industry highlights many of the key themes of the period from 1920 to 1945. Women, especially married women in their 30s and older, entered the paid labor force in increasing numbers in these years. Their presence in factories, offices, and stores was one aspect of large-scale changes regarding marriage and family life that occurred in the decade after World War I. Women of color, a higher percentage of whom had always worked for wages, found some new opportunities in the 1920s

American Women's History: A New Narrative History, First Edition. Melissa E. Blair, Vanessa M. Holden, and Maeve Kane.
© 2024 John Wiley & Sons, Inc. Published 2024 by John Wiley & Sons, Inc.

workplace. The Great Depression, however, altered conditions for them. While the percentage of white women in the labor force increased over the course of the 1930s, for women of color the Depression was an even starker catastrophe than for others. World War II changed these trajectories yet again, bringing millions of women into paid work for the first time and opening up well-paid factory jobs for African American women and other women of color. Women joined the U.S. military in large numbers for the first time. And Japanese American women, like Japanese American men, were imprisoned for their ethnicity during the war.

The 27 years between the end of World War I and the end of World War II saw dramatic changes for American women, not only at work but also in politics and private life. Some of these changes were reversed or altered within that same period. Because of the rapid rate of change, this chapter will proceed chronologically, touching base with the issues of work, politics, sexuality, and family life repeatedly to trace the shifts from the "Roaring" 1920s, to the Great Depression, to World War II.

Work, Family, and Sexuality in the 1920s

For working-class families like Carmen Escobar's, one of the biggest changes in the 1920s was shifting demographics of who went into the paid labor force. The number of public junior highs and high schools exploded in the 1920s, and many working-class families shifted their work patterns to enable their children to take advantage of the education that was newly available to them. This was particularly true for daughters. Earning a high school diploma opened up a wide range of safer, cleaner jobs for working-class young women, especially as secretaries or other kinds of clerical workers. Those jobs also sometimes paid slightly more than factory work. Working-class families wanted their daughters to be able to earn more in safer conditions. And while wages rose for factory workers during the 1920s, most working-class families still could not make ends meet on a single salary. In response to these trends, families swapped the paid labor of teenage daughters for the paid labor of wives. Teenage daughters were able to further their education, and the labor force participation of working-class married women with children increased sharply.

For other working-class families, it was not only who was doing the work that shifted, but what the work was. From the piedmont of North Carolina across the Appalachian Mountains into east Tennessee, textile factories continued to open in large numbers, keeping up a trend that began around 1890. Rural white families moved to mill towns like Concord, NC and Elizabethton, TN, where the women of the family, and some of the men, worked making fabric. Factory work created huge shifts in the gender dynamics within these families. Daughters had not previously made cash contributions to these families. They had worked – in fields, preserving food, making and mending clothes – but they had not brought in cash. Earning a salary gave the young women more freedom from their families, freedom that the young women of Elizabethton used to go on strike in the spring of 1929. The strikers sought higher wages and a promise by factory owners not to discriminate against union members. Although owners initially agreed, they never paid the higher wages, and the strike failed to secure anything other than a guarantee that union members could go back to work. Even that fell through, however, and many women were blackballed in the industry.

Women of color had fewer new opportunities open to them. While some Latinas in the West worked in canning factories, most worked as domestic workers, as did African American women throughout the country. For those Black women who had moved North during the Great Migration, the reconversion to a peacetime economy at the end of World War I proved a shock. They were pushed out of the industrial jobs they had moved North to fill, and forced back into domestic work, the same dead-end occupational category they had likely occupied in the South. Middle-class Black women nationwide found work as teachers and librarians in the nation's segregated schools, but they were paid less for that work than white teachers were. Because women of all races were paid less than men regardless of field of employment, women of color were doubly disadvantaged.

The workplace was not the only, or the most visible, location of change in the 1920s. A flapper, a young woman with short hair, a loose knee-length dress, and a cloche hat, is one of the most enduring images of the 1920s. This image emerged from magazine and newspaper articles about female college students. Women's rate of college attendance, while still low, accelerated in the 1920s, with a much higher percentage of women choosing co-ed, public universities like the Universities of Iowa and Kentucky, as opposed to the private women's colleges earlier generations had favored. In this co-ed environment, young women experimented with a new phenomenon called dating. Dating mimicked the structure of treating that working-class young people had developed at the turn of the century – the young man would pay for dinner or a movie with the expectation of some kind of physical repayment at the end of the date. Magazines ran articles about "petting parties," where co-eds engaged in a much higher level of sexual play than earlier generations were assumed to have done. However, one thing that did not change were the rules around intercourse. While it was suddenly seen as acceptable, at least among peers, for young women to engaging in necking and petting, intercourse was still forbidden among "nice girls" until they became engaged. Statistics suggest that young people followed these rules. In an era with very limited birth control options and abortion illegal, premarital pregnancy rates did not go up.

For many, the biggest changes that the shifting sexual norms of the 1920s brought were within marriage, rather than outside of it. Marriage was still seen as the end goal for most young people. But those marriages were supposed to be marked by a new emphasis on the friendship and compatibility of the married couple. Unlike nineteenth-century prescriptive literature which spoke of men and women's separate spheres, the 1920s marriage ideal emphasized deep companionship between husband and wife. Marriage was supposed to fulfill the woman completely because she was such good friends with and had so much fun with her husband. Journalists, academics, and activists from both ends of the political spectrum pushed this idea. Feminists such as Doris Stevens, a National Women's Party member who had been jailed alongside Alice Paul in 1917, described marriage as a "vast laboratory" in which feminists could bring about more egalitarian gender norms through their own personal relationships. Many conservative leaders both male and female supported this vision of marriage as women's main fulfillment as a means of checking their political activism. The 1910s had been a time of extraordinary public visibility for women in politics, and many men (and women) were eager to get back to a time when women focused their energies on the home.

Not all marriages were given this kind of value, however. The 1920s was also a peak of anti-miscegenation laws across the country. These laws prohibited people of different races from marrying. They were all state laws, and which kind of interracial marriage was prohibited varied from state to state. Many of these laws – whether forbidding white and Black intermarriage in the Southeast or white and Asian intermarriage in the West – began to be passed in the 1880s. By 1927, 30 states had anti-miscegenation laws in force, and attempts were made to pass such laws in eight more states that year. With the exceptions of Washington and New Mexico, all of the 18 states that did not have these laws were in the Midwest and Northeast. Regardless of where the laws were passed and which racial groups were targeted, the intention was the same: to keep the financial and other material benefits that flowed from marriage, through things like inheritance, largely in the hands of white people.

Eugenics influenced these laws, and it also continued to shape discussions around birth control. In the 1920s, Margaret Sanger pivoted her advocacy in a less feminist direction. She began to argue that birth control should be legal because the government should not interfere with a doctor's ability to treat his patient. Since a diaphragm, the most reliable contraceptive of the time, required fitting by a doctor, this approach gained traction in the decade. In 1921, Sanger organized the American Birth Control League, with several doctors on the original board of directors. Many states eliminated their laws against birth control in the 1920s, while retaining laws that made abortion illegal. Sanger and other birth control advocates also increasingly made eugenic arguments in favor of birth control, arguing that liberalizing its availability would enable what they deemed "unfit" people – the poor, people of color, and those considered "feebleminded" – to have fewer babies. These eugenic ideas were very similar to the arguments in favor of prohibiting marriages between people of different races. Southern state governments opened publicly funded birth control clinics throughout the late 1920s and 1930s with eugenic goals in mind, and the Supreme Court approved state-mandated sterilization programs for "feebleminded" women in the 1923 case *Buck v. Bell*. In spite of activists' eugenic rationale, many people of all races and classes embraced birth control in the 1920s, understanding that having fewer children helped their families economically and improved women's and children's health. Economic historian Michael Haines has found that the average number of births per woman fell from just over three children in 1920 to just under 2.5 in 1930 for white women and from just over 3.5 in 1920 to just under three for Black women. For both groups, the only larger 10-year drop was between 1970 and 1980.

The falling birth rates among African American women is one indicator of the shifts that were happening for many Black women. Those who remained in the rural South, especially the cotton belt, lived lives strikingly similar to their mothers and grandmothers, continuing to work in agriculture or domestic service and finding almost no educational opportunities for their children. Women who had moved North or to Southern cities in the 1910s, however, saw more changes. Many of these were cultural, as blues music and the literature and visual arts of the Harlem Renaissance provided Black female artists the opportunity to make a living as artists for the first time. As historians Daina Ramey Berry and Kali Nicole Gross have stated, women ranging from author Zora Neale Hurston to sculptor Augusta Savage to blues singer Ma Rainey had the opportunity to "redefine how the world viewed them and amplify how they saw the world."

An increasingly urban American also provided more opportunities for same-sex loving women to find partners and communities. 1920s and '30s New York and other very large cities provided spaces for the formation of queer communities of men and women, largely but not completely segregated by race. In New York, for example, most Black lesbians socialized at house parties in Harlem, while the white working-class lesbian scene was focused on bars and restaurants in Greenwich

Village. The gay bar scene came into its own in the 1920s. With the passage of Prohibition in 1918, all bars became illegal. This, paradoxically, meant that gay bars were suddenly viewed no more or less suspiciously by police than any other kind of bar. Prohibition also normalized the presence of women in bars. Because they were (allegedly) not serving alcohol, women's presence in bars was less taboo. Many middle-class white lesbians, however, still preferred socializing in private, hosting dinner parties and organizing weekend trips. Prohibition and the country's rapidly growing cities, along with a general increase in openness to sexual experimentation and difference, all combined in the 1920s to facilitate flourishing lesbian communities.

After Suffrage: Women's Politics in the 1920s

Following the passage of the Nineteenth Amendment, members of NAWSA found new ways to continue their political activism. NAWSA leaders voted to rename the organization the League of Women Voters (LWV). While the LWV's membership than much smaller than NAWSA's had been at its peak, it was still an important organization. The LWV's initial focus was on teaching women how to register and vote and encouraging them to use their new right. The LWV also joined with many other national women's organizations, such as the YWCA and the General Federation of Women's Clubs, to form a national umbrella organization called the Women's Joint Congressional Committee (WJCC). More than 20 organizations belonged to the WJCC, and in the first half of the 1920s, the group had a great deal of success lobbying Congress to pass bills it believed were important to women.

The two biggest successes of the WJCC were the Sheppard-Towner Act and the Cable Act. The Sheppard-Towner Act passed in 1921. This program was designed by the Children's Bureau, a federal agency staffed by women that had been established by Progressive women activists in the 1910s. The intention of Sheppard-Towner was to address the high infant mortality rates in many parts of the country. The bill created a fund which paid visiting nurses to go into poor communities, doing prenatal checks on expectant mothers and teaching them the most up-to-date methods of caring for infants. The bill was important for two reasons. It was the first time that women had organized and lobbied for a particular piece of legislation since the passage of the Nineteenth Amendment, and it showed the strength of women as a lobbying block in the early 1920s. It also represented a new direction in the federal government's involvement in individual citizens' lives. Prior to Sheppard-Towner, the only way in which the federal government interacted with individuals, aside from delivering the mail or drafting men into the military, was through the payment of veterans' pensions. Sheppard-Towner was therefore a first step toward the federal government assuming some level of responsibility for civilian citizens' lives, an approach that became increasingly common during the Great Depression.

The Cable Act, passed one year later in 1922, eliminated a law that had caused American women to lose their citizenship when they married men who were not citizens. Eliminating this provision continued a process which the Nineteenth Amendment had begun, making women's citizenship their own and not something that was attached to or flowed through a husband. It was a critical step toward women's full citizenship. However, the blindness to racial difference (if not outright racism) that had marred NAWSA also affected this bill. Women who married Chinese American or Japanese American men, who were ineligible for American citizenship due to their ethnicity, still lost their citizenship under the Cable Act.

In the second half of the 1920s, the lobbying efforts of the WJCC and other women's groups were much less successful. Partially this was due to politicians' realization that women did not vote as a single block, but rather voted in much the same way men did: they supported the politicians who most closely aligned with their own beliefs on a variety of issues. However, conservative women's groups also organized to discredit the work of the WJCC. Groups such as the Daughters of the American Revolution (DAR) distributed a graphic known as the Spider Web Chart, which alleged that women's organizations and leading activists were not working to improve the lives of working-class people and women, as they claimed, but were in fact trying to advance the goals of "international socialism." This document, and the ideas behind it, were part of the First Red Scare. The Russian Revolution, which overthrew the Russian monarchy and installed a Communist government, occurred in 1917. This event led to a rising panic about Communism throughout Europe and the United States. DAR members and other conservative women were convinced that the goals of Progressive women and, especially, the vibrant pacifist movement that many women were involved with, were actually trying to weaken the United States in order to facilitate a Communist takeover of the country. Pacifist women such as former NAWSA president Carrie Chapman Catt repeatedly denied this accusation, and only a minority of Americans believed the claims on the chart. But the groups that opposed women's pacifism and Progressive activism – which included many former anti-suffragists – had powerful allies in Washington, especially in the War Department. Their influence, along with politicians' beliefs that they had little to gain politically by supporting policies promoted by the WJCC, led to sharp loss in influence for that group in the second half of the 1920s. Most notably, when the Sheppard-Towner Act came up for renewal at the end of the decade, it was not renewed.

The National Women's Party was not part of the WJCC and focused on different issues in the years immediately following suffrage. In 1923 Alice Paul and other NWP leaders introduced an Equal Rights Amendment (ERA), which would eliminate any differential treatment on the basis of sex under the law. Women affiliated with the WJCC were deeply opposed to the ERA in the 1920s, arguing that it would invalidate the protective labor legislation they had worked for decades to pass and, therefore, make the lives of working-class women worse. Paul and her allies disagreed, arguing that protective labor legislation discriminated against women workers. When Paul and other NWP leaders spoke on this issue, they focused on the fairly small but growing number of professional women in fields like law and medicine. A few states such as Wisconsin passed state ERAs but created exceptions for protective labor legislation. This was a compromise that satisfied none of the activists. WJCC-allied women realized that such a law made passing new protective labor laws difficult. And since invalidating the protective labor laws was one of the NWP's main goals, they were furious with those laws' special treatment.

African American women's politics largely focused on different issues than white women. For African American women living in the South, voting remained almost impossible, in spite of the Nineteenth Amendment. Scores of Black women arrived at polling places throughout the South during the 1920 presidential election, much to the surprise of the registrars. Whether or not they were allowed to vote varied, but some Southern Black women did cast a ballot in that presidential election. However, Southern legislatures quickly made it clear that African American women were subject to the same Jim Crow disfranchisement laws as were Black men, including poll taxes and literacy tests. African American activists tried repeatedly in the 1920s to get the National Women's Party to help them fight these restrictions. But Alice Paul and other NWP leaders believed that, because the women were being disfranchised because of their race rather than their sex, the issue was not a "women's problem" that the NWP should address. This refusal by the NWP is a good example of the lack of intersectional understanding by most white feminists and other white activists of the era.

Beyond accessing the ballot, Black women worked on a huge range of political issues in the 1920s. In Washington, D.C., many leading African American women, including NACW leader Mary Church Terrell, affiliated with the newly formed Colored Women's Republican League. They worked to advance the party which had the most African American support in the era, stemming from the Republican Party's role in the Civil War and the abolition of slavery. Black women also worked through both women's clubs and civil rights organizations on anti-lynching activism, a major issue in the decade. The NACW had a Department for the Suppression of Lynching and Mob Violence. The NAACP worked in support of the Dyer Anti-Lynching Bill, a piece of legislation that would have made lynching a federal crime. The NAACP had spent years working with Congressional sponsors of the bill and drumming up support to get it passed. After it passed the House of Representatives in January 1922, the group organized a silent parade in support of the legislation. NAACP leaders tasked Theresa Lee Connelly, an African American teacher in Washington D.C., with establishing a Citizens' Protest Parade Committee. A group of one hundred prominent Black women assisted her in organizing the event, and in June 1922, more than five thousand African American residents of the nation's capital staged a silent march past the Capitol, Congressional office buildings, and the White House in support of the anti-lynching legislation.

Some women were drawn to more radical approaches to solving Black people's problems and operated outside of electoral politics. Numerous women were deeply involved in the Universal Negro Improvement Association (UNIA), founded by Afro-Jamaican Marcus Garvey in 1914 and brought to the United States when Garvey moved to New York City in 1918. The UNIA was a Black nationalist organization, supporting, in the words of historian Keisha Blain, "racial unity, black political self-determination, and economic self-sufficiency." The UNIA was part of a burgeoning Pan-African movement that had grown after World War I and sought to connect peoples of African descent around the globe. Pan-Africanism advocated for an end of European colonization of Africa and improved treatment of Black people globally. Women were leaders in the UNIA from the beginning, including Garvey's first wife, Amy Ashwood, and his second wife, Amy Jacques Garvey. After Marcus Garvey was deported in 1927, Amy Jacques Garvey kept the UNIA afloat in the United States, and many women were leaders in local chapters in cities such as Chicago, New Orleans, and Hampton Roads, Virginia. Black nationalist women also founded their own organizations, especially in the 1930s. Almost all the women in leadership of these groups were working-class or poor. They all advocated for Black economic self-sufficiency and promoted Black capitalism, supported Pan-Africanism and critiqued U.S. foreign policy, and criticized the misogyny of many male Black leaders, including Marcus Garvey. They used the term "black nationalist" to describe themselves. In the 1930s, women such as Mattie Maud Lena Gordon of Chicago were leaders of these organizations, articulating the ways in which the treatment of African Americans was, for example, related to the Italian occupation of Ethiopia and how all people of African descent needed to work together to improve each others' lives.

The Great Depression

When the economy collapsed in the fall of 1929, it changed every American's life in ways large or small. Working-class urban families faced unemployment, hunger, and the prospect of eviction from their homes. Rural families, who had been struggling throughout the 1920s with low prices for staple crops, saw their ability to make a living from the land decline even further. For those that lived in the southern Great Plains, from Kansas through north Texas, the ecological disaster of the Dust Bowl in the mid-1930s made these problems even worse. Middle-class families who owned shops, restaurants, or other services also fell on hard times as their clients' disposable income vanished. The ripple effects touched every corner of society.

The experience of the Great Depression was gendered in several ways. The number of women in the paid labor force actually *increased* over the course of the 1930s. This increase was caused by middle-class women who had not worked outside the home before, especially white women, entering the labor market to help support their families. Many of these women found work as teachers, nurses, or in other traditionally female fields that were somewhat less affected by the crisis.

For working-class women who were in the paid labor force before 1929, however, the Great Depression was a disaster. African American women in the east and Latina and Asian-American women in the west, the majority of whom had worked in domestic service in the 1920s because of racist job discrimination, lost their jobs. As middle- and upper-class families' incomes constricted, cutting back on the amount of domestic labor they paid for was often a first step. Women who did domestic labor in commercial settings like hotels also were either fired or had their hours severely cut back, as hotels sat largely empty. Women of color who had hung onto factory work were often among the first fired during the downturn. In big cities, African American women would stand on street corners, attempting to find daily domestic work in private homes. White women would come by offering as little as 10 cents an hour for hard, physical work. And sometimes they would refuse to pay when the work was completed.

In the face of these difficulties, many working-class women organized. In the mid-1930s Dora Jones, an African American resident of Queens, created a union of New York City domestic workers, urging women to not accept less than the union-supported rate of 50 cents per hour for day work and a written contract from employers. Women participated in strikes in the canning factories of California, as recounted in the chapter's opening vignette. In Texas in 1938, Emma Tenayuca, a woman of Mexican and Comanche ancestry whose family roots in Texas predated the area's inclusion in the United States, led a mixed-sex group of pecan shellers in a massive strike in San Antonio. Women were also deeply involved in the push to organize new unions in industries such as autos and meatpacking under the umbrella of the new Congress of Industrial Organizations (CIO). All CIO unions made equal pay regardless of sex or race one of their key tenants. This policy was particularly necessary for industries like meatpacking that employed many women. In other industries with fewer female employees, such as autos, women were still crucial to the organizing efforts. During the famous 1937 sit-down strike in Flint, MI, women brought ie strikers through broken factory windows, spoke in favor of the strike, and generally provided support to the CIO's efforts. In the Appalachian Mountains of eastern Kentucky, the support of the women of Harlan, who provided food and medical care to striking coal miners, was pivotal in the labor battle that raged between coal companies and miners for nearly the entire decade, earning the town the nickname "Bloody Harlan."

Women also organized around problems arising from the Depression outside of the workplace. Throughout the country, housewives found a variety of ways to feed their families and protest when they believed grocers were charging exorbitant prices. In Seattle, a cooperative system emerged which enabled families to barter for their food, as well as wood for fuel, taking advantage of the huge array of crops and goods that were available locally. In Detroit and New York City, housewives organized boycotts of grocers. Butchers were particularly common targets. In Brooklyn, Clara Lemlich Shavelson, one of the leaders of the Uprising of the 20,000 in 1909, organized other Jewish mothers in her neighborhood to boycott the kosher butchers who had a monopoly on meat for Shavelson and her neighbors. In Detroit, a woman named Mary Zuk led protests that culminated in a group of women setting fire to a meat warehouse to demonstrate their disbelief of butchers' claim that shortages drove up the cost. The actions of the Detroit group were reported nationwide, and similar protests occurred in Chicago, a number of towns in Pennsylvania, Miami, Indianapolis, and other cities throughout the country. The next year, Zuk ran for a seat on the Hamtramck City Council in her Detroit suburb and won, becoming the first woman to ever serve on the council.

At home, the Great Depression also led to changes. The marriage rate dropped sharply, and the birth rate continued to decline, as men and women felt they were not financially able to begin families during the economic crisis. In Chicago and other cities, increasing numbers of doctors performed what they deemed "therapeutic" (and therefore legal) abortions, terminating the pregnancies mostly of married women. They asserted that the psychological strain placed on a woman having a child she did not believe she could provide for made the termination medically necessary for her health, which was the threshold for a therapeutic abortion. However, the law was vague on what was or was not a "therapeutic" abortion, and so physicians who provided the service were still somewhat cautious about advertising their services. Abortion law did not change. But the Great Depression raised awareness of the economic difficulties of raising children at a time of high unemployment, and social acceptance of abortion rose somewhat.

For Native American women, the pressures to make their family structures match those of white Protestants decreased with the passage of the Indian Reorganization Act of 1934. This bill was less focused on assimilation than previous bills and tried to return some autonomy to Native Americans living on reservations. However, many of the Anglo doctors of the Indian Health Service remained at reservation hospitals, and many of them held eugenic beliefs about the "fitness" of Native American mothers. Women who gave birth on reservation hospitals, therefore, likely did not experience any difference in treatment than they had in the 1900s, in spite of the new federal law.

The Indian Reorganization Act was far from the only way in which New Deal policies affected women. The New Deal was the wide-ranging attempt by President Franklin Roosevelt and his administration to solve the economic crisis, beginning as soon as he was sworn in as President in March 1933. Many women were involved in shaping the New Deal agenda and implementing its policies. FDR's Secretary of

Labor, Frances Perkins, was the first woman to hold a Cabinet post. She, and most of the other women who worked for the government, had been active in Progressive reform efforts in the preceding decades. Many, including Perkins, were friends with First Lady Eleanor Roosevelt. Eleanor Roosevelt was a strong influence on her husband, turning his attention to issues affecting women and African Americans throughout his presidency and urging him to appoint the first Black woman to lead a federal agency when he named Mary McLeod Bethune head of the National Youth Administration in 1938.

Virtually all New Deal programs that focused on helping working-class and poor people were based on widespread assumptions about families. The programs prioritized shoring up male breadwinners, making it easier for men to support their families, rather than creating programs where any member of a family could earn money. Many of the public works projects designed by the Works Progress Administration (WPA), for example, were construction jobs building bridges, post offices, and other manual labor projects which did not hire women. The Civilian Conservation Corps, the largest program employing young men in their teens and early twenties, only hired men. There were a few WPA programs for women – canning kitchens and sewing projects and other jobs that were deemed appropriate – but women could not get those jobs if their husband had a WPA job. And women who lived in female-headed households, whether they were lesbians, single heterosexual women, or widows, did not benefit from the New Deal in the same numbers as men because there were so few New Deal programs that hired women. The sex segregation of the labor market, which allowed some women to enter the paid labor force for the first time during the Depression, kept other women from benefitting from the employment programs of the New Deal.

For rural women, the impact of the major New Deal project targeting their families, the 1933 Agricultural Adjustment Act (AAA), varied greatly depending on race and class. The program paid farmers not to plant their fields in an attempt to raise the prices for staple crops by constricting supply. For landowning families – mostly white but including some Black, Latino, and Asian-American families – this policy worked. But most women of color in farming families, especially African American women in the South and Latinas in the west, did not own their land. They worked instead as either tenant or migrant farmers on land owned by others. And while the program instructed landowners to distribute the funds equitably among their tenants, few did so. In the South, white landowners simply told African American tenants their land would not be planted, and often evicted the families if they could not pay their rent. In California and elsewhere in the west, Mexican immigrant migrant farm workers were deported or unable to find work and chose to return home.

Many women workers were also left out of legislation regulating the terms of work. Domestic workers and agricultural workers were ineligible for the work provisions of the 1935 Social Security Act. The bill included not only what we now call Social Security but also federal unemployment insurance. Agricultural workers, domestic workers, and jobs like beauticians and waitresses, who in the 1930s almost exclusively worked in local (as opposed to national) businesses, were also excluded from the 1938 Fair Labor Standards Act which established minimum wages and maximum hours as federal rules for the first time but only applied to "interstate commerce."

There were several reasons for these exclusions. In the case of the Fair Labor Standards Act, Congress believed it did not have the power to regulate businesses which did not cross state lines, a position supported by Supreme Court decisions that had declared earlier pieces of New Deal legislation unconstitutional. White Southern Democrats (who were the heads of many Congressional committees) were deeply opposed to anything that would jeopardize white supremacy in the South. They insisted on leaving domestic work and agriculture, the fields that employed the majority of Black Southerners, out of both the Social Security and Fair Labor Standards laws. But white women reformers, who led the way in writing much of this legislation, also did not push for domestic workers to be included. To do so would have implied that those women's own homes were workplaces no different from the worst sweatshop because it would have made their homes just as subject to regulation by the government. The combination of these forces led to the creation of a New Deal that, through all of these programs, directly benefited less than 10% of African American women.

Their desire to exclude their own domestic workers from labor legislation was not the only place where white women who helped write this legislation made their own biases apparent. Almost all of them agreed with the vision of supporting families by supporting male breadwinners. This can be seen particularly clearly in the portion of the 1935 Social Security Act that created a program called Aid to Dependent Children (ADC), what we today call welfare. Only single mothers were eligible for ADC payments, and those payments were never enough for a woman to fully support her family. ADC payments differed from most other New Deal programs because they were not tied to a job as WPA payments were, but rather were direct payments to women. The women who wrote this legislation had empathy for the children of poor single mothers. But they did not want the government to enable those women to remain single forever, replacing the financial support of a husband with a welfare payment. Nor did they think the government should help a husband support his family through direct payments. ADC, therefore, was deliberately designed to not provide a family sufficient income, a facet of the program that remained part of welfare policy for decades.

World War II

Almost two years before the U.S. military entered World War II, that conflict began changing the lives of American women. In December 1940, President Roosevelt announced the Lend-Lease Program, pledging that the United States would become the "arsenal of democracy" for the world. Factories that had been operating on short hours because of the Depression's impact on consumer demand began running overtime to produce everything from tinned meat to naval ships. Roughly 20% of Americans moved during the first half of the 1940s to take a defense job. Many who moved were women. For working-class women who had always been in the paid labor force, the opening of defense work brought them far more money than they had earned before. African American women who had previously worked in domestic service were particularly drawn to the defense factories, which offered not only dramatically higher wages but also camaraderie on the job and better hours. The percentage of working Black women who made their living through domestic work fell from 60% in 1940 to 44% in 1944.

The shifting careers of African American women were not the only demographic change at work. As the popular Rosie the Riveter image suggests, many women – roughly six million – entered the labor force for the first time during the war. Some of these women went into the defense factories alongside working-class women. But others filled new jobs in traditional female fields, like secretarial work or telephone operators, that the war also generated. The shifts in the age of women workers that had begun in the 1920s also continued during the war. By 1945, 25% of all married women were in the paid labor force, up from 15% in 1939. For women of color, those percentages were much higher. In spite of all these women joining the labor force, however, the majority of women still did not work outside their own homes. In 1944, at the peak of wartime employment, only slightly more than one-third of American women were in the paid labor force.

Those women who worked for the war effort were told repeatedly that their time in the workplace was temporary. Newsreel footage before movies, magazine ads, and statements by businessmen and politicians all emphasized this point. The work of Rosie and her peers in defense factories was cast as an emergency measure, not a permanent shift in American culture. And there was also tremendous pressure from many sources for women to maintain their femininity. Propaganda, especially targeting white women, emphasized over and over that maintaining traditional beauty standards, such as using make-up and wearing high heels, were just as important to the war as factory work, because they allegedly kept the morale of male soldiers high.

Men were not the only soldiers during World War II, however. Every branch of the military created a women's auxiliary, ranging from the Women's Army Corps (WACs) to the WASPs of the Army Air Force. Women in these auxiliary units were not sent to the front lines, but rather were used in military bases throughout the country. They did the work necessary to house, feed, and track trainees in American bases, support them overseas, and provide office support to stateside leaders. Women's work was designed to enable more male soldiers to go to Europe or the Pacific to fight. Because of that, it was also seen as temporary, and the same messages of heightened femininity that all American women received were even more pointed when it came to women in the military. Oveta Culp Hobby, the head of the WAC (by far the largest women's auxiliary), was particularly concerned about the perceptions of the soldiers under her command with regard to femininity and sexuality. She was aware of widespread suspicion of women who chose to join the military, whispers that they were there for sexually immoral reasons – either to gain access to men or because they were lesbians seeking to find other same-sex loving women.

Hobby countered these fears and rumors in several ways. She oversaw the design of the WAC uniform and insisted on a fitted jacket and knee-length skirt, a style that was appropriately feminine but still conservative. The soldiers under her supervision did not receive the same kind of frank sex education talks male soldiers did, nor did their rations include condoms, as they did for male soldiers. For lesbians, Hobby's worries over negative reporting about sexuality and the WAC was actually a benefit. Hobby instructed officers not to target women they believed were lesbians for any kind of harassment, nor were they to bring women up for charges of lesbianism unless the women were engaging in public displays of affection. Fifty years before the "Don't Ask, Don't Tell" policy was officially adopted by the military, Hobby effectively established it as the rule for the WAC. This enabled many lesbians to find lovers and, in some cases, lifelong partners through the military.

The WAC was not such a welcoming space for all women. African American WACs, of whom there were more than 6500 over the course of the war, worked for a military that was segregated by both sex and race and did not really have a plan for incorporating them. As historian Sandra Bolzenius has written, "the War Department reviewed its racial policies with black soldiers in mind and negotiated gender policies with white WACs in mind." WAC officers, therefore, found themselves struggling to assign the Black soldiers under their direction to work assignments that could be segregated by race. Many Black WACs wound up doing janitorial work as "order-lies" on army bases, replicating the same occupational dead-end that Black women confronted as civilians. Disgusted by the discriminatory treatment, in March 1945, 54 Black WAC orderlies went on strike at Fort Devens in Massachusetts. Four of the women – Anna Morrison, Mary Green, Alice Young, and Johnnie Murphy – were eventually court martialed for their refusal to follow orders to clean the base. They were found guilty, but the majority of the public supported the WACs. The public support was far more consistent for the female WACs than for Black male soldiers who attempted similar actions during the war. The NAACP and other civil rights groups highlighted the Fort Devens case frequently as they pushed for the integration of the military after World War II.

Japanese immigrant and Japanese American women faced the starkest discrimi-nation in the wartime U.S. In February 1942, two months after the attack on Pearl Harbor, President Roosevelt authorized military officials on the West Coast to round up residents of Japanese ancestry, regardless of their citizenship status, and deport them to camps away from the Pacific coastline. Military leaders in the area claimed Japanese Americans were security risks to Pacific military bases and shipyards because of their ancestry. Japanese American were required to leave their homes and be interned in a series of camps built between the Sierrra Nevada and Ozark Mountains. Of the over 100,000 people interned, more than 70% were American citizens who had been born in the U.S. Families were given only a few days to arrange for storage of their belongings and care of their property. Many families' homes and farms were auctioned off after they were interned, leaving them virtually penniless when the war ended.

The camp experience was a complex one for Japanese American women. The camps were mostly located in deserts and were therefore dusty and hot. Keeping clothing and sleeping areas clean was a constant challenge. But some young women were also employed in the camps, earning salaries to work as secretaries for military officials or as cooks. These salaries gave the young women some independence, and some young women asserted themselves more in family decision-making than was typical in Japanese American families before the war. As policies allowing Japanese American to leave the camps, so long as they did not return to the west coast, emerged in 1943, many young women left to attend college or work. These women were grateful for the opportunity but found the experience challenging and isolating. They entered communities where few if any people of Japanese ancestry lived and were therefore looked on as exemplars of the race and its loyalty. Many found the constant scrutiny exhausting.

For most American women, wartime changes were smaller but still profound. Combined, less than 40% of American women worked, served in the military, or were interned during the war. However, even for American women who stayed at home, the war brought substantial changes. World War II was a total war, touching every American's life every day. There were shortages of some essential goods, espe-cially gasoline and rubber. These items, along with cloth and foodstuffs like coffee, beef, butter, and sugar, were rationed throughout the war. Women and children were encouraged to plant victory gardens and grow their own vegetables so that canned vegetables could be used by the military. Scrap metal and rubber drives were con-ducted regularly, enabling families to directly contribute to the war effort by recycling these materials into war materiel. And of course, millions of families dealt with the stress of having loved ones fighting overseas for the duration of the war.

Women's contributions to World War II were essential and varied. When the war ended with an American victory, they looked out at a world that had been dramatically remade. Every other major industrial country had had its industrial capacity decimated by bombing during the war. Every other major combatant nation had suffered higher losses of soldiers and vastly higher losses of civilian lives. Having been spared both high numbers of civilian casualties and any destruction to farms or factories, the United States entered the postwar period as the most powerful country in the world for the first time.

Bibliography

Benson, Susan Porter. *Household Accounts: Working-Class Family Economics in the Interwar United States*. Cornell University Press, 2015.

Berry, Daina Ramey, and Kali Nicole Gross. *A Black Women's History of the United States*. Beacon Press, 2020.

Blain, Keisha N. *Set the World on Fire: Black Nationalist Women and the Global Struggle for Freedom*. University of Pennsylvania Press, 2017.

Bolzenius, Sandra M. *Glory in Their Spirit: How Four Black Women Took on the Army During World War II*. University of Illinois Press, 2018.

Cott, Nancy F. *The Grounding of Modern Feminism*. Yale University Press, 1987.

Delegard, Kirsten Marie. *Battling Miss Bolsheviki: The Origins of Female Conservatism in the United States*. University of Pennsylvania Press, 2012.

Field, Connie, director. The Life and Times of Rosie the Riveter.

Gordon, Linda. *The Moral Property of Women: A History of Birth Control Politics in America*. University of Illinois Press, 2007.

Gray, Lorraine, director. With Babies and Banners.

Haines, Michael. "Fertility and Mortality in the United States." **http://EH.net and https://eh.net/encyclopedia/fertility-and-mortality-in-the-united-states**

Hall, Jacqueline Dowd. "Disorderly Women: Gender and Labor Militancy in the Appalachian South." Journal of American History 73, no. 2 (1986): 354–382.

Hall, Jacqueline Dowd, James Leloudis, Robert Korstad, et al. *Like a Family: The Making of a Southern Cotton Mill World*. University of North Carolina Press, 1987.

Hegarty, Marilyn E. *Victory Girls, Khaki Wackies, and Patriotutes: The Regulation of Female Sexuality During World War II*. New York University Press, 2008.

Hicks, Cheryl D. *Talk with You Like a Woman: African-American Women, Justice, and Reform in New York, 1890–1935*. University of North Carolina Press, 2010.

Kennedy, Elizabeth Laposky, and Madeline D Davis. *Boots of Leather, Slippers of Gold: The History of a Lesbian Community*. Routledge, 1993.

Kessler-Harris, Alice. *In Pursuit of Equity: Women, Men, and the Quest for Economic Citizenship in Twentieth Century America*. University of Illinois Press, 2004.

Matsumoto, Valerie J. *City Girls: The Nisei Social World in Los Angeles, 1920–1950*. Oxford University Press, 2014.

May, Vanessa H. *Unprotected Labor: Household Workers, Politics, and Middle-Class Reform in New York, 1870–1940*. University of North Carolina Press, 2011.

McEuen, Melissa A. *Making War, Making Women: Femininity and Duty on the American Home Front*. University of Georgia Press, 2011.

Murphy, Mary-Elizabeth B. *Jim Crow Capital: Women and Black Freedom Struggles in Washington, D.C., 1920–1945*. University of North Carolina Press, 2018.

Orleck, Annelise. "We Are That Mythical Thing Called the Public: Militant Housewives in the Great Depression." Feminist Studies 19, no. 1 (1993): 147–172.

Pascoe, Peggy. *What Comes Naturally: Miscegenation Law and the Making of Race in America.* Oxford University Press, 2009.

Portelli, Alessandro. *They Say in Harlan County: An Oral History.* Oxford University Press, 2011.

Reagan, Leslie J. *When Abortion Was a Crime: Women, Medicine, and the Law in the United States, 1867–1973.* University of California Press, 1997.

Ruiz, Vicki L. *Cannery Women, Cannery Lives: Mexican Women, Unionization, and the California Food Processing Industry, 1930–1950.* University of New Mexico Press, 1987.

Ryan, Hugh. *When Brooklyn Was Queer: A History.* St. Martin's Press, 2020.

Trigg, Mary K. *Feminism as Life's Work: Four Modern American Women through Two World Wars.* Rutgers University Press, 2014.

CHAPTER 13

The Long Fifties, 1945–65

Two African American women, Annelle Ponder and Fannie Lou Hamer, addressed the credentials committee of the Democratic National Convention on August 22, 1964. Ponder, an Atlanta native, was 32 years old and worked as the secretary of the Southern Christian Leadership Conference (SCLC) chapter in Greenwood, MS. Hamer was 47 years old and had spent her entire life as a sharecropping farmer in Mississippi. She had become a well-known civil rights activist in Delta part of the state over the previous two years. The women were attempting to persuade the credentials committee to recognize the Mississippi Freedom Democratic Party, a predominantly African American group of Mississippians, as the official Democratic delegation from the state, rather than the all-white, segregationist "regular" delegation. To do so, Ponder, Hamer, and others testified about the ways in which white Mississippians oppressed Black residents of the state, often under the cover of the law and the Democratic Party. Hamer and Ponder recounted their arrest and violent beating at the hands of local police a year earlier. The two women were part of a group returning by bus from a civil rights training. During a stop in Winona, MS, Ponder and several others attempted to buy lunch at the bus station restaurant. They were refused service, and police arrested them when they left the building. Hamer had stayed on the bus, but when she saw the others being led into police cars, she exited the bus and was arrested also.

When they arrived at the local jail, they were denied their phone call, herded into a single cell, and then called out one by one to be brutally beaten by multiple police officers. Ponder estimated that her beating last 10 minutes. Hamer's was even longer. The assault did nothing to dampen the women's commitment to the cause of civil rights. Both were back at work registering voters and, in Ponder's case, running one of the main civil rights offices in the Mississippi Delta, as soon as they were physically able. As Hamer stated in her DNC testimony, "They just keep on saying wait and we been waiting all of our lives and still getting killed, still getting hung, still getting beat to death, now we're tired of waiting." Ponder and Hamer's testimony shocked white television audiences throughout the country. Hamer and Ponder, however, were just two of the most visible of the hundreds of women who were assaulted or held in unsanitary, cramped conditions in Southern jails over the course of the Civil Rights Movement.

American Women's History: A New Narrative History, First Edition. Melissa E. Blair, Vanessa M. Holden, and Maeve Kane.
© 2024 John Wiley & Sons, Inc. Published 2024 by John Wiley & Sons, Inc.

The Long Fifties, stretching from the mid-1940s to the mid-1960s, was a complex moment for American women. In the workplace and in popular culture, they were being told that their options were very limited. They could find work in low-paying, traditionally female fields, if they worked outside the home at all. And working outside the home was discouraged by a national culture that emphasized domesticity and a traditional division of labor between husbands and wives. The stay-at-home wife and mother were praised as the solution to all sorts of problems, from allegedly rising rates of juvenile delinquency to the Cold War. But reality broke with this ideal in many ways. Working-class women used their unions to gain greater benefits at work. Black women were central actors in the Civil Rights Movement, with Hamer just among the most famous of thousands. Other women of color also banded together to improve their communities, lobbying their cities for improved municipal services and amenities like streetlights and parks and registering their neighbors to vote. Lesbians formed the first organization dedicated to improving their treatment in American society. And even middle-class white women, who dominated the cultural landscape as apolitical wives and mothers, were active in a huge range of political efforts from building the nascent conservative movement to protesting nuclear civil defense drills. These 20 years are often remembered as a period of domesticity for women. But beneath that surface, women of color were at the forefront of movements for racial justice. And for other women, the foundations were being laid for the explosion of their activism that would come just a few years later.

The Civil Rights Movement

Historians generally date the beginning of the modern Civil Rights Movement to World War II, and women were deeply involved in the movement from the beginning. In the 1940s, women around the country were engaged in numerous efforts to eliminate Jim Crow's legal structure and work toward equality for African Americans. In Washington, D.C., Pauli Murray and her fellow Howard University students led sit-ins and other protests against segregated restaurants during the war. In the late 1940s, a 14-year-old named Marguerite Carr and her father filed a lawsuit against segregated schools in the nation's capital, arguing that Marguerite should not have to walk past a new and underutilized white junior high in order to attend a Black junior high that was so crowded students attend in two half-day shifts.

Throughout this period, Black girls like Marguerite Carr were often at the forefront of school desegregation cases. Linda Brown was eight years old when her parents filed the lawsuit that became the Supreme Court's landmark 1954 decision *Brown v. Board of Education*. Ruby Bridges was just six years old when she was chosen to implement that decision in New Orleans public schools six years later. Sometimes mixed-sex groups of Black young people would integrate a single school, as happened famously in Little Rock with the nine students who integrated Central High School in 1957. But even if a group of students went in, being a "first" was still a difficult and often isolating experience for Black youths. Sandra Lewis was one of the Black children who integrated Venable Elementary School in Charlottesville, VA in 1959. Even though a total of nine Black children entered the school together, Lewis was the only one in the fourth grade. She recalled 60 years later that as "the only person of color in the whole fourth grade, at that age, you want to blend in. At that age, you want to go to school and have friends," but that was not her initial experience at Venable. Historian Rachel Devlin has argued that, for many girls, "school desegregation was *their* call to arms, a mission they felt to be their own." Some were raised in families that emphasized the importance of working to help the Black community, doing what earlier generations would have called "race work." For others, such as Doris Jennings Brewer, who tried to integrate a rural Texas high school with her twin sister in 1947, "it was just the natural thing to do and it had to be done. Like mopping the floor."

There were networks of adults who supported these young women and their male peers, and women were often central there too. In Little Rock, the selection of the Little Rock Nine and the coordination of their first day in the school was organized by Daisy Bates, the president of the Arkansas NAACP. Thousands of Black women worked as teachers, educating children not only in the basics of reading, writing, and arithmetic but also inspiring them to be leaders in school integration and other civil rights causes. South Carolina educator Septima Clark took her work as a teacher one step further and developed a Citizenship School curriculum that she taught to hundreds of civil rights volunteers. Clark's Citizenship Schools taught African Americans in the South how to pass the citizenship tests required to register to vote, tests that were deliberately designed for them to fail. Her work in training others was a critical piece of the success of groups like the Mississippi Freedom Democratic Party that Hamer and Ponder testified for. In fact, their group was returning from a training with Clark in 1963 when Ponder and Hamer were arrested and beaten. Throughout the South and throughout this 20-year period, Black women were at the center of civil rights activism.

Rosa Parks is perhaps the most famous woman associated with the Civil Rights Movement, and her activism began well before the Montgomery Bus Boycott of 1955. In the 1940s, she was a field investigator for the Alabama NAACP. One of her primary tasks was gathering evidence in cases of sexual assault of Black women by white men. In September 1944, she began investigating the rape of Mrs. Recy Taylor by a group of six white men in Abbeville, roughly 90 miles from Montgomery. Within two months, Parks had organized the Alabama Committee for Equal Justice for Mrs. Recy Taylor. The group had two goals: to convince local authorities to press charges against Taylor's attackers and to gain national attention for the case. Parks' work succeeded in this second goal – by late October 1944, there were articles in the *Pittsburgh Courier, Chicago Defender,* and other prominent Black newspapers decrying the lack of arrests, let alone charges, against the six men who brutally raped the young mother. Parks' work on behalf of Mrs. Taylor is just one example of moments when the assault of Black women led to widespread community activism. Similar events occurred in 1959 in Tallahassee, for example, when Florida A&M University student Betty Jean Owens was gang raped by four young white men. Local civil rights activists seized on the case, publicizing it widely, just as Parks had done with Mrs. Taylor's case 15 years earlier. In 1959, however, the attackers were not only charged, but they were convicted. The convictions in the Owens case were the first time that anyone in Tallahassee could remember white men being convicted for raping a Black woman.

As her work on the Taylor case died down, Parks continued to be active with the NAACP in Alabama. In 1955, the Montgomery chapter, of which she was the secretary, was searching for a test case to sue the city over its segregated busses. Two other younger women were arrested earlier in the year, and the NAACP had hopes that they might become the face of the lawsuit. But the NAACP continued to be wedded to the politics of respectability, which had shaped the organization from its founding in 1909. One of the earlier women arrested was a teenager, whom they discovered was pregnant and unmarried. The other, Claudette Colvin, had earlier arrests for disorderly conduct on her record. Because of that, the NAACP decided not to use Colvin as the face of their cases. In light of that decision, Parks took action herself and became the test case for the lawsuit.

The NAACP's focus on a lawsuit dovetailed with the efforts of another Montgomery civil rights group, the Women's Political Caucus. In 1955 that organization was led by JoAnn Robinson. Most WPC members were middle-class Black women, many of them K-12 teachers or professors at Alabama State, the historically Black college in town. While the NAACP was focused on a lawsuit against the buses, the WPC had been working for several months to organize a boycott. When they heard of Parks' arrest in early December 1955, they decided to launch the boycott to coincide with her first court appearance, scheduled for Monday, 5 December. The WPC organized the boycott. They printed the fliers, asked ministers to announce it from their pulpits, and arranged carpools for people who needed alternative transportation. The original boycott was entirely their doing, and only after its success on the first day did a group of ministers, who declared themselves the Montgomery Improvement Association, take control of continuing the boycott and name a new minister in town, Dr. Martin Luther King Jr., as their leader.

Not only were women responsible for organizing and executing the original boycott, they were also vital to its success over the full year that the lawsuit wound its way through court and the busses remained empty of Black riders. African American women who worked as domestic workers in white homes traveled long distances for work, longer than most other Black workers. Without the support of those women, the boycott would have collapsed. Women were therefore critical to the success of the Montgomery Bus Boycott at every turn.

As the Civil Rights Movement grew and expanded into the 1960s, similar stories could be told all over the country. Some female leaders of the Civil Rights Movement are well known. Ella Baker was the only woman among the leadership of the Southern Christian Leadership Conference (SCLC), the organization founded and led by King after the Montgomery Bus Boycott ended. She found the experience frustrating; her ideas were rarely taken seriously even though she was the most experienced organizer in the room. Baker believed sexism was at the root of her treatment, and when college students burst to the forefront of the Civil Rights Movement through their sit-ins in 1960, she advised them to create their own organization, rather than affiliate with SCLC. They followed her advice, founding the Student Nonviolent Coordinating Committee (SNCC) in April 1960. Diane Nash, a student at Fisk University, was among the original leaders.

The 1960–1965 phase of the Civil Rights Movement included women at every level. There were women in the highest ranks of leadership for SNCC and CORE. And throughout the South, women were on the front lines of the struggle just as much as men were. They were yelled at, punched, and had food thrown at them during the sit-ins. They were beaten and jailed during the Freedom Rides, the Birmingham movement of 1963, and dozens of other events and places throughout the South. When in jail, Black women faced particular danger of abuse and assault from prison guards. Stories began to circulate throughout the country of dozens of young Black women, in their teens and twenties, packed into single large cells. Often there was not enough room to lay down, and bathroom facilities were insufficient. Sometimes women were not provided with sanitary materials if they were menstruating. And their status as women did not protect them from beatings at the hands of guards, as Ponder and Hamer's stories showed.

Black women were not only on the front lines of the struggle but they were also at the center of networks that supported those front-line activists. As historian Belinda Robnett has documented, Black women throughout the South helped house and feed civil rights activists. They washed activists' clothes after sit-ins, bandaged their wounds after marches, and along with their husbands in many cases, provided the care that front-line activists needed to keep going. The networks that already existed among women through churches, schools, and women's clubs became the networks that channeled civil rights activism. The help and commitment of women who were well established in their communities were particularly important for SNCC activists who were new to town. Anne Moody, a Mississippi native whom SNCC sent to organize in Canton, MS in the summer of 1963, recalled the importance of C.O. and Minnie Lou Chinn, prominent members of the town's Black community. The Chinns were the first locals Moody met in Canton. They housed the SNCC workers, introduced them to other community leaders, and provided a source of comfort and encouragement for the young SNCC volunteers. Women like Minnie Lou Chinn were critical to the civil rights movement in two ways: as activists in their own right, and in the support they provided to the young activists who worked in their communities. And a Black woman from rural southern Virginia, Mildred Loving, was a plaintiff in a critical Supreme Court case. In 1967, the Supreme Court heard the case of Mrs. Loving and her husband Richard, who was white. Their marriage violated Virginia's anti-miscegenation laws. But in the case *Loving v. Virginia* the Supreme Court unanimously declared those laws unconstitutional and stated that "marriage is one of the basic civil rights of man."

Outside of the South women were also involved in other movements to improve the lives of racial and ethnic minorities. In California, the Community Service Organization (CSO) began in 1947 to organize the Mexican American community of Los Angeles and other major cities. Many of the CSO's projects were similar to those of civil rights groups in the South, especially voter registration drives and efforts to stop police harassment of Latino youths. Many activists in the organization came to it from labor organizing in the packing plants and other workplaces of southern California (see Chapter 12). While many of the CSO's projects were mixed sex, some programs focused specifically on the needs of working-class Mexican American women who were not in the paid labor force. Mexican American housewives with young children struggled with access to health care, playgrounds, and other basic public services. The CSO helped them successfully lobby the city council for more money for sidewalks, streetlights, and playgrounds in their East Los Angeles neighborhoods. And the CSO itself began running public health clinics in the neighborhoods after the issue of practically nonexistent access to immunizations and hearing and vision testing for children was raised by the mothers of the community.

Women including Hope Mendoza and Dolores Huerta were early leaders in the group and were also able to move up in the organization. By the mid-1950s, Huerta was working as the CSO's full-time, paid lobbyist in the state capitol in Sacramento. Mendoza, who had entered the paid labor force and become active in her union in the late 1930s, when she was still a teenager, functioned as what one historian described as the "vital link" between the CSO and organized labor that flourished in the early Cold War era. In other cities with large Latino populations – mostly in the Southwest and West, but also in Chicago, New York, and several Florida cities – women engaged in efforts to increase voter registration, fight workplace discrimination, and allow bilingual education in public schools throughout the 1950s and 1960s.

Babies, Suburbs, and Politics: White Middle-Class Lives

Like the Mexican American mothers that worked with the CSO, the majority of American women in these years spent most of their adult lives as homemakers. Only one-third of women worked for pay outside the home in 1950, and that number rose only slightly over the course of the decade. By 1960, 37% of women were in the paid labor force. The image of the 1950s as a time when most women were housewives is not a stereotype, therefore – it reflects most women's lived experiences.

A housewife's life varied greatly depending on class and race. One thing that was universal, however, was the Baby Boom. Women of every racial and ethnic group had more babies in the 1940s and 1950s than had the previous two generations. The average number of children per family climbed from just over two in 1930 to almost four by 1950, and birth rates did not begin to decline until 1957. Families were having more babies, clustering them more closely together, and having them earlier in marriage. Marriage trends also shifted in the postwar period, as couples married younger and women were more likely to marry than in earlier generations. Glen and Lois Dyer were a typical couple. The Dyers married in 1952, when Glen was 24 and Lois 19. Glen was a military veteran, and so was still in college when the couple married. Lois dropped out of college to support him, gave birth to their first child within 18 months of the wedding, and had several more children over the next few years. Everything about this story – the age of the couple, the quick arrival of children into the family, and Lois's time spent in the paid labor force while Glen finished college – were typical of many baby boom parents.

For white families, a move to a new suburban housing development was a central part of raising a Baby Boom family. The Great Depression and World War II meant that very little new housing was built for nearly 15 years. When the war ended, federal government subsidies combined with the demand for single-family homes helped the suburbs explode. The GI Bill, a package of benefits for World War II veterans, offered inexpensive mortgages to returning servicemen. In the 1950s, federal money built the interstate highway system to connect sprawling suburbs with the urban centers where many white-collar workers worked. By the late 1950s, federal money was also flowing to K-12 public education for the first time, helping create a school building boom in the suburbs to educate baby boom children.

While racial, ethnic, and religious minorities participated in the demographic trends that marked the Baby Boom, they were largely excluded from its suburbs. Some suburban developments were off-limits to Jewish families. Black families found it almost impossible to move into the suburbs. Federal home loan guidelines, developed in the 1930s, prohibited lending in predominantly Black neighborhoods. And homeowners' association rules and other forms of restrictive covenants, along with real estate agents who would not show Black families homes in white neighborhoods, kept Black families out as well. So while Black veterans technically had access to the same GI Bill benefits as white veterans did, there were few places for them to actually buy a home. Through this mix of government policies and industry practices, suburbs in the 1950s were almost exclusively white spaces.

The white women in these neighborhoods were heralded throughout this period as a cornerstone of American life. From magazines to television shows to political speeches, the traditional gender roles and affluence of American suburbs were celebrated. American women's roles as homemakers, and the material comforts of their suburban homes, were described as an indication of American superiority in the Cold War. The conflict between the United States and the Soviet Union was often discussed through the lens of family and gender. American magazines frequently mentioned how terrible it was that Soviet women worked as engineers or factory workers while their children went to state-run daycare centers. Soviet media described American life as a horrible one for women, who were stuck in their isolated suburban homes with nothing fulfilling to do.

This connection between women's roles and their relationship to global politics was most clearly stated in a 1959 episode known as the Kitchen Debate. The Soviet Union sponsored a world's fair that year, which included model homes from throughout the world. Vice President Richard Nixon traveled to Moscow to open the American home at the exhibition, and toured it with Soviet leader Nikita Khrushchev, accompanied by many reporters and photographers. As they stood in the kitchen of the model home, Nixon stated that what they could see in front of them – a washing machine, TV dinners, a dishwasher – were the things that made American life the best in the world. American women, Nixon stated, had the most comfortable lives of any women in the world. The nation's ability to support women at home, raising children while surrounded by advanced technology, meant that the United States was superior.

Nixon's analysis of women who did nothing but care for their home and raise their children excluded as many American women as it included. Only middle-class and affluent white women lived in the suburbs with all that new technology. And many of those women were involved in politics or worked part-time jobs outside the home to help pay for all those new products. But the image that Nixon promoted has been the lasting one of 1950s America, perpetuated by the TV shows like *Leave it to Beaver* that depicted that suburban world for generations of Americans through reruns.

For some white women who lived this praised life, the suburbs encouraged political involvement. In the 1950s, both major political parties saw women as critical swing voters and Republicans in particular developed programs to turn housewives into the foot soldiers of partisan agendas. The Women's Division of the Republican National Committee, led by Bertha Adkins, sent postcards and fliers to women in huge quantities. With titles like "Let's Talk About It," the postcards gave women talking points on various policies of the Eisenhower administration on topics like taxes and foreign policy. Women were encouraged to bring these topics into conversation with their neighbors over coffee or at the playground. These efforts, when considered alongside episodes like the Kitchen Debate, demonstrate how thoroughly Republican politicians saw the home as a political space, rather than a space free from politics.

Regardless of their partisan affiliation, many suburban women used their status as mothers to engage in politics. In the booming suburbs of Long Island, they used baby carriages to block the streets in protest over a lack of traffic lights and crosswalks, which made it dangerous for their children to walk to school. Other New York mothers began, in the mid-1950s, to take their young children into downtown Manhattan to protest the civil defense drills that the federal government required in major cities. Instead of going onto the subway platforms when the air raid sirens sounded, as required by law, the women and their children stayed on the street. They claimed that the civil defense drills did not actually protect anyone from a nuclear attack, but only gave the impression that they did. They argued that the federal government should instead be pursuing policies that actually made nuclear war less likely. These protests grew over the course of the late 1950s and early 1960s. The presence of children gave the women's protests an added weight – they were positioning themselves as part of a long tradition in American politics in which women acted not on their own behalf, but as mothers defending their children. This maternalist approach to nuclear policy eventually led, in 1961, to the creation of a nationwide group, Women Strike for Peace. WSP was an influential organization and is credited with convincing President John F. Kennedy to sign the Atmospheric Test Ban Treaty in 1963.

Other women mobilized their status as wives and mothers to pursue very different political goals. Throughout the Sunbelt, stretching from southern California to the Carolinas, a new conservative movement developed in which white women positioned themselves as defenders of "traditional" American structures. Women in southern California were among the innovators in creating new right-wing organizations that sought to defend the United States from the creeping threat of Communism or, as they often called it, "collectivism." Anything that could be seen as "collective," from the United Nations to sex education in schools, was deemed a threat to family autonomy and therefore, in their telling, to the United States. Women throughout the country challenged school board programs that introduced new pedagogy, they wrote letters in opposition to the United Nations to local newspapers and their Congressmen, and they even testified before Congress in opposition to federal funding for a mental health facility in Alaska. Many of these women tapped into organizations and structures that were first developed in the 1920s during the First Red Scare to connect right-wing women throughout the country (see Chapter 12).

These affluent white women used their status as wives and mothers as a justification for, rather than an obstacle to, their political activism. They argued that, as women who did not work outside the home and whose children were in school or grown, they had the time to research the "facts" about government programs at every level. They gathered in groups with names like the Tuesday Morning Study Club in large suburban houses and talked about, for example, how sex education in public schools was a first step to Communism because it replaced parents with teachers. Many of these women described their work as patriotic, arguing that they were the ones most able to see the threats to the country and most able to stand up to them.

For some of these women, the most pressing concern was the maintenance of white supremacy, especially in schools. As historian Elizabeth McRae has argued, white women were at the center of the "household production of white supremacy," teaching their children the racial rules of the era and, in the South, ensuring that their children's schools remained segregated in the face of the *Brown v Board* decision. In just one example, North Carolinian Mrs. Hugh Bell began circulating a petition within months of the *Brown* decision, arguing that integrating public schools would lead to "the decline of the family, the schools, the state, and the nation." This language would have been familiar to grassroots right-wing women in southern California; right-wing women throughout the nation corresponded with each other, sharing talking points and alerting peers about problems in other parts of the country. Bell's petition had over 5000 signatures by August 1954, more than 18 months before Southern male politicians in Washington signed the famous "Southern Manifesto" announcing their intention to disobey the *Brown* ruling.

Even when they were not fighting to maintain legally mandated school segregation, right-wing women throughout the country still worked to keep ideas of racial equality out of schools. In Los Angeles, Florence Fowler Lyons led a 1952 campaign to eliminate the use of UNESCO-created materials in public school after that branch of the United Nations published statements opposing racially discriminatory laws and arguing that race was socially constructed. Lyons and her colleagues in Los Angeles corresponded with women all over the country, and articles in newspapers from Buffalo to Houston supported their position. Senator Joe McCarthy, at the height of his power, also singled out Lyons' work on preventing the use of UNESCO materials in school, calling it "of tremendous importance."

These connections only grew throughout the 1960s, and in 1964 the network of right-wing women was essential to Arizona Senator Barry Goldwater's unexpected success in securing the Republican nomination for president. Conservative women in California were essential to securing his victory in the primary in that state. To even appear on the primary ballot there, candidates had to secure signatures in support of their candidacy. In just one day of neighborhood coffees and door-to-door solicitation, women in Orange County, CA secured nearly three times the number of required signatures to place Goldwater on the ballot. Similar organizations took place throughout the country, and once Goldwater was the nominee, the campaign officially used "Goldwater Girls" to campaign for the candidate. Although Goldwater was defeated by one of the biggest margins in history, his campaign was critical for continuing to build the networks of grassroots conservative women throughout the country who would become more visible in the 1970s.

Sexuality and the Cold War

The conservative white women who worked for Goldwater saw themselves as defenders of the American dream life, the suburban, heterosexual lifestyle depicted in magazines and on TV. In the pages of women's magazines, a good sex life was often discussed as a critical piece of these happy suburban homes. As historian Elaine Tyler May has argued, couples entered Cold War marriages with "heightened expectations for sexual fulfillment." May suggests that the increasing discussion of the importance of sexuality in one's life – a topic that had first been broached widely in the 1920s, when Freud's works became widely available in the United States – was one of the forces pushing the age of first marriage down. People married younger, in other words, so they could start having sex. There was also growing acceptance of birth control within marriage; except among Catholics, the number of married couples using diaphragms (the most common form of birth control in the 1950s) increased steadily.

In 1960, the number of women using birth control skyrocketed with the advent of the birth control pill, known simply as the Pill. Within a few years, millions of women were on the Pill. Doctors prescribing the Pill to married women was not controversial, but the question of what to do about unmarried women seeking birth control was a subject of much debate. In the college town of Lawrence, KS, for example, a debate raged between the campus health center and the county public health office about who should supply KU students with the Pill. The public health office was willing, but undergraduates quickly overwhelmed the facility. The campus clinic, however, refused to prescribe the Pill to single students for reasons of "morality" – they did not want the university to be seen as encouraging sex outside of marriage. In some states the stakes were higher – more than 25 states made it illegal for single women to use or be prescribed birth control, and in some states the prohibition extended to married women as well. In 1960, the Supreme Court heard a challenge to these laws, brought by Connecticut's Planned Parenthood organization on behalf of a married couple who were legally banned from using birth control. However, the Supreme Court decided in *Poe v. Ullman* that, because the law was not enforced, Planned Parenthood did not have legal standing to overturn it. Laws prohibiting birth control for single women remained on the books in more than half the states throughout the first half of the 1960s and, as the next chapter will detail, were not completely abolished until the 1970s.

The fact that the desire to have sex drove early marriages and that single women could not be prescribed birth control indicates the strength of taboos against sex outside of wedlock, even though discussions of sex were everywhere. Sex was increasingly used in advertising, again continuing trends that had started to emerge in the 1920s but been checked somewhat by 15 years of Depression and war. But for girls and young women in their teens and twenties, the pressure to be a "nice" girl who did not have sex before she was engaged was intense. Mass media was full of stories of teenage pregnancy. Magazines like *Reader's Digest* and *Life* published articles with titles like "If Only They Had Waited" and "How to Tell Your Daughter Why She Must Keep Her Self-Respect," emphasizing the dangers of pregnancy and the role of girls in ensuring that it did not happen. Many white teens who became pregnant when they were unmarried in the 1950s found themselves sent to maternity homes in different towns, ordered to have their babies, give them up for adoption, and return home with their "reputation" intact. Theoretically, she would find a husband in a few years and he would never know about her "mistake." Girls who did not want to give up their babies at these institutions were treated for mental health problems and stripped of their children. The accepted estimate is that one and a half million young women had their babies taken from them in this way during the 1950s and 1960s.

One thing that helped this system thrive was the tremendous demand for babies for adoption from couples who could not conceive children on their own. The pressure to fit the Baby Boom mold of a suburban home filled with children was intense. These familial roles were one of the main things that politicians and the media highlighted to distinguish the United States from its Soviet opponents. Anyone who did not fit into that mold, for whatever reason, was seen as somewhat suspicious. And so many families who struggled with infertility were desperate for children. This was equally true for Black couples who could not have their own children, but they had far less opportunity to adopt. Racist beliefs led social workers and others to argue that children born out of wedlock were more accepted within Black communities, and that young Black women therefore did not need to have their reputations "saved" the way white girls did. Social workers also told Black teenagers that there were not adoptive families for their children, even though this was not true. These actions are another example of institutional racism that limited African Americans' ability to participate in postwar abundance. White teenagers who gave up their babies were able to finish high school, perhaps go to college, and get married. Because high schools banned girls who were pregnant from attending, the lack of options for Black teens made a life of poverty more likely for them because they could not finish their educations, at least initially.

For those women who wanted to terminate unwanted pregnancies, abortions were much harder to secure during the Cold War than they had been during the Great Depression. Doctors and hospitals tightened the criteria for "therapeutic" abortions in the postwar era. If a woman wanted a legal abortion, she had to go before a three-doctor panel at her local hospital and plead her case. Doctors on these panels routinely asserted that what the woman needed was not to terminate the pregnancy, but to have psychiatric treatment in order to adjust to the idea of becoming a mother.

This logic was the inverse of that faced by teenagers at maternity homes, where wanting to keep your baby was a sign of mental illness. If the woman seeking an abortion was young enough, the doctor panels would refer her to a maternity home so she could give up her baby for adoption after delivery. Doctors asserted that modern medicine had advanced to the point where abortions were rarely needed to protect the life of the pregnant woman. One 1944 article in a medical journal asserted that therapeutic abortions should be approved only in cases where "the pregnancy threatened the life of the mother *imminently.*" Such cases were quite rare.

In the face of these restrictions, a network of illegal abortion providers emerged. As Leslie Reagan, a leading historian of the topic, has argued "It was not until the postwar period, quite late in the history of illegal abortion, that women's descriptions of illegal abortions include meeting intermediaries, being blindfolded, and being driven to a secret and unknown place where a secret and unknown person performed the abortion." In other words, only in the late 1940s and 1950s did the iconic image of dangerous, "back-alley" abortions reflect the reality of the situation for most women who terminated pregnancies. The lack of access to birth control and legal abortion, the taboos against unmarried motherhood, and the increasing discussion of sex in culture and accompanying pressure toward sex for young people led to increasing danger for women seeking abortions. Making abortions harder to get did not stop women from seeking abortions; it simply made them more dangerous.

If the pressure to conform to sexual norms was intense for unmarried women and girls, it was far more so for gay men, lesbians, and trans individuals. The early Cold War witnessed what historian David Johnson dubbed the "lavender scare," a time when LGBTQ employees of the federal government were targeted for investigation and, usually, the loss of their jobs. The civil service part of the lavender scare was mostly focused on gay men and began from the fact that sodomy was against the law in the late 1940s and 1950s. Sexually active gay men, therefore, were breaking the law. Because of that, the logic went, they were easy blackmail targets by Soviet agents, who would force them to turn over government documents in exchange for keeping the sex lives secret. Dozens of federal employees were fired, officially for "suspicion of disloyalty," but in fact because they were gay, from 1947 to 1954. While almost all civil service employees fired were men, in the military there was increased prosecution of lesbians. Many women who had joined the WAC during World War II had chosen to stay in the military, and those who did so and were lesbians found their relationships, both platonic and sexual, under heightened scrutiny in the early 1950s. Many women whose behavior would not have been considered a priority for investigation during World War II found themselves dishonorably discharged during the Cold War for the exact same actions.

The focus on persecuting LGBTQ Americans was driven not only from Cold War paranoia about espionage but also from fears that there were far more queer individuals in the country than many people realized. In 1948, Indiana University zoologist Alfred Kinsey published his landmark study *Sexual Behavior in the Human Male.* The companion volume, *Sexual Behavior in the Human Female,* appeared five years later. In these works, Kinsey claimed that more than one-third of adult men had had at least one same-sex sexual encounter in their lives, and that 11% of men were "equally heterosexual and homosexual." Seven percent of women fell into this same category, according to Kinsey. When heterosexual marriage and a strict, gendered division of labor was seen as one of the nation's major defenses against an enemy that most believed threatened everything about the American way of life, these numbers were startling, and deeply concerning to many.

Many LGBTQ Americans did not passively accept this atmosphere of paranoia and fear. The early 1950s saw the founding of the first two "homophile" societies in the country, the Mattachine Society for gay men (founded 1950) and the Daughters of Bilitis (DOB) for lesbians, founded by partners Del Martin and Phyllis Lyon in San Francisco in 1955. Because of the atmosphere of suspicion and persecution, the majority of lesbians were closeted; only their closest friends and families knew they were gay. One of the main way lesbians interacted with DOB, therefore, was through its magazine *The Ladder,* which began publication in 1956. Del Martin explained the goals of DOB in her "President's Message" in *The Ladder's* first issue:

> *While women may not have so much difficulty [as gay men] with law enforcement, their problems are none the less real – family, sometimes children, employment, social acceptance. . . . What will be the lot of the future Lesbian? Fear? Scorn? This need not be – IF lethargy is supplanted by an energized constructive program.*

From the beginning, DOB focused on helping lesbians in California find work and camaraderie, reconcile their sexuality with their status as mothers, and provide support to one another. *The Ladder* connected lesbians and bisexual women throughout the country. As Lorraine Hansberry, the famed playwright, stated in a letter she submitted in 1957 under her married initial, L.H.N., "I'm glad as heck that you exist. . . . Our problems, our experiences as women are profoundly unique. . .I feel that The Ladder is a fine, elementary step in a rewarding direction."

In one of the many paradoxes of the era, these years also saw an increase in visibility for trans people, and for one trans woman in particular. Christine Jorgensen became a celebrity in the early 1950s as newspapers reported on her successful "sex-conversion" surgery, which had been carried out in Denmark. For months, Jorgensen appeared in celebrity magazine and gossip columns. The coverage was sensational but not hostile. As historian Joanne Meyerowitz has argued, Jorgensen's "conventional beauty made her a prime candidate for female celebrity status," and many reporters cast her story in terms of the triumph of science, or as a version of the all-American "self-made" person striving for upward mobility and a better life. Doctors across the country reported an increase in patients requesting surgery like Jorgensen had received in Denmark. Almost all were turned down, and often they were referred to psychiatrists. But none of the patients were reported to the police or arrested, and Jorgensen stayed a popular figure in the tabloids for several years. Largely because she conformed so closely to the ideals of female beauty, Jorgensen was not cast as a threat in the same way as, for instance, lesbians in the WAC.

Women and Work in an Age of Abundance

Another area where image and reality did not mesh perfectly was in the labor force. Women's paid employment increased over the course of the 1950s, surpassing the wartime peak by mid-decade. Nearly 40% of all women worked for wages by 1960. Many of these women worked in part-time, "pink collar" jobs such as retail sales or secretarial work. Some of these women were the same ones who were home in the suburbs when their children arrived on the school bus in the afternoons; the wages of wives made the move into the middle class possible for many families in this age of abundance. As one New Jersey shopping mall executive stated in 1957, "housewives make up the greatest proportion of the new personnel." But increasing numbers did not mean increasing opportunities for professional advancement. There was a firm glass ceiling on women in retail – they could not work in the departments that sold the highest-priced, commission items, and they never moved beyond sales positions into management positions.

Not all women workers were part-timers trying to supplement the family income. Many women worked full-time, in either middle-class or working-class jobs. Some of these women worked in the professions, including an important group of mathematicians and engineers known as "computers" who worked for the burgeoning space industry in the 1950s. Katherine Johnson and her peers at NASA are just the most famous of a small group of professional women who excelled in the 1950s and 1960s. In all professional fields, however, women encountered a glass ceiling and almost never rose to leadership positions. Also, the number of women in the professions decline in the 1960s, as older women retired, and fewer young women entered these fields. Because of the social pressure to marry young, many young women had dropped out of college before finishing or had married immediately after and not gone into the paid labor force before marriage as earlier generations had. Because of the decline in female professionals, the wage gap between men and women grew in the 1960s. In 1960, women earned about 61 cents for every dollar a man made. By 1970, that had dropped two cents, and it continued to decline for another five years until beginning to improve in 1975.

Blue- and pink-collar workers were just as vulnerable to the wage gap as professional women were. Workplace discrimination, not only in wages but also in hiring, promotion, and other areas, led many female factory and officer workers into unions in the early Cold War era. From the early 1940s to the early 1950s the number of female union members more than tripled; some three million women belonged to unions by the later date. Unions were a key vehicle for improving working-class standards of living in the early Cold War. They had a tremendous amount of clout with their employers and were able to negotiate pay increases and other work improvements regularly. Women workers also worked both within their unions and with their employers to reduce sex discrimination in their workplace. They lobbied for equal pay for comparable work, support from both government and employers for women's caregiving labor at home, and greater job security. Union women wanted to be treated equally at work but did not want to be treated the same as men. Instead, they wanted employers and the government to recognize and support for their roles as mothers, wives, and caregivers. As historian Dorothy Sue Cobble has put it, "they wanted equality *and* special treatment, and they did not think of the two as incompatible." While they did not achieve all of their goals, the success of some unions was remarkable. The United Packinghouse Workers had, by the end of World War II, successfully organized for policies that gave women workers maternity leave and guaranteed that they could return to their same job with their seniority intact after giving birth. By 1961, one tobacco workers' local in North Carolina had created almost complete wage parity for women and men, with only one category of male jobs paid more than the highest-paid women. The work of union women in the early Cold War did not create the kinds of policies that many women sought – most maternity leaves came with only partial pay, for example, and not all tobacco locals achieved wage parity. These women made important gains along the road to a more equitable workplace for women. Many unions outside of the South, especially CIO-founded ones like the packinghouse workers, also served as critical spaces of cooperation among women of different races. In the South, however, unions like the tobacco locals were more likely to uphold racial segregation and discrimination than challenge it.

In spite of the era's reputation, the Long Fifties saw myriad changes for women. Marriage and birth rates increased, but so did employment and political participation. Queer women organized nationally and openly for the first time. And women of color participated in wide-ranging civil rights activism. The Long Fifties laid the foundation for the incredibly changes that would happen in the subsequent 15 years.

Bibliography

Bailey, Beth. *Sex in the Heartland*. Harvard University Press, 1999.

Canaday, Margot. *The Straight State: Sexuality and Citizenship in Twentieth-Century America*. Princeton University Press, 2009.

Charron, Katherine Mellon. *Freedom's Teacher: The Life of Septima Clark*. University of North Carolina Press, 2009.

Cobble, Dorothy Sue. *The Other Women's Movement: Workplace Justice and Social Rights in Modern America*. Princeton University Press, 2004.

Cohen, Lizabeth. *A Consumers' Republic: The Politics of Mass Consumption in Postwar America*. Knopf, 2003.

D'Emilio, John, and Estelle B Freedman. *Intimate Matters: A History of Sexuality in America*. University of Chicago Press, 2012.

Devlin, Rachel. *A Girl Stands at the Door: The Generation of Young Women Who Desegregated America's Schools*. Basic Books, 2018.

Douglas, Susan J. *Where the Girls Are: Growing up Female with the Mass Media*. Three Rivers Press, 1995.

Fessler, Ann. *The Girls Who Went Away: The Hidden History of the Women Who Surrendered Children for Adoption in the Decades before Roe V. Wade*. Penguin, 2006.

Garrsion, Dee. "Our Skirts Gave Them Courage: The Civil Defense Protest Movement in New York City, 1955-1961." In *Not June Cleaver: Women and Gender in Postwar America, 1945–1960*, 201–226, edited by Meyerowtiz. Temple University Press, 1994.

Johnson, David K. *The Lavender Scare: The Cold War Persecution of Gays and Lesbians in the Federal Government*. University of Chicago Press, 2004.

Lee, Chana Kai. *For Freedom's Sake: The Life of Fannie Lou Hamer*. University of Illinois Press, 1999.

Louis, Billy Jean. "60 Years Later: Charlottesville 12 Reflects on City Schools Integration," September 10, 2019, *Charlottesville Tomorrow*. **https://www.cvilletomorrow.org/ articles/60-years-later-charlottesville-twelve-reflects-on-city-schools-integration**

May, Elaine Tyler. *Homeward Bound: American Families in the Cold War Era*. Basic Books, 1988.

May, Elaine Tyler. *America and the Pill: A History of Promise, Peril, and Liberation*. Basic Books, 2010.

McGuire, Danielle L. *At the Dark End of the Street: Black Women, Rape, and Resistance – A New History of the Civil Rights Movement from Rosa Parks to the Rise of Black Power*. Vintage, 2011.

McRae, Elizabeth Gillespie. *Mothers of Massive Resistance: White Women and the Politics of White Supremacy*. Oxford University Press, 2018.

Meyerowtiz, Joanne. *How Sex Changed: A History of Transsexuality in the United States*. Harvard University Press, 2002.

Moody, Anne. *Coming of Age in Mississippi*. Dial Press, 1968.

Murray, Sylvie. *The Progressive Housewife: Community Activism in Suburban Queens, 1945–1964*. University of Pennsylvania Press, 2003.

Nickerson, Michelle M. *Mothers of Conservatism: Women and the Postwar Right.* Princeton University Press, 2012.

Perry, Imani. *Looking for Lorraine: The Radiant and Radical Life of Lorraine Hansberry.* Beacon Press, 2018.

Ransby, Barbara. *Ella Baker and the Black Freedom Movement: A Radical Democratic Vision.* University of North Carolina Press, 2003.

Reagan, Leslie J. *When Abortion Was a Crime: Women, Medicine, and the Law in the United States, 1867-1973.* University of California Press, 1997.

Robnett, Belinda. *How Long? How Long? African-American Women in the Struggle for Civil Rights.* Oxford University Press, 1997.

Rose, Margaret. "Gender and Civic Activism in Mexican American Barrios in California: The Community Service Organization, 1947-1962." In *Not June Cleaver: Women and Gender in Postwar America, 1945–1960*, 177–200, edited by Meyerowtiz. Temple University Press, 1994.

Solinger, Rickie. *Wake Up Little Susie: Single Pregnancy and Race before Roe V. Wade.* Routledge, 2000.

Swedlow, Amy. *Women Strike for Peace: Traditional Motherhood and Radical Politics in the 1960s.* University of Chicago Press, 1993.

Theoharris, Jeanne. *The Rebellious Life of Mrs. Rosa Parks.* Beacon Press, 2013.

Weiss, Jessica. *To Have and to Hold: Marriage, the Baby Boom, and Social Change.* University of Chicago Press, 2000.

CHAPTER 14

Changes Everywhere, 1965–1980

On a warm Labor Day weekend in 1968, two groups of protestors descended on Atlantic City, NJ. One was a contingent of nearly two hundred women, overwhelmingly white, who had taken busses down from New York City. Organized by a brand-new group called New York Radical Women, they were coming to protest the Miss American pageant, which was held at the beachside resort every September. With signs and chants, they asserted that the Miss America pageant, and all beauty pageants, demeaned women. Pageants, they declared, valued women only for their bodies (shaped and dressed in certain ways) and not their intelligence or character. They upheld a uniform and nearly unattainable standard of beauty. Part of the day's demonstration included a "Freedom Trash Can," into which the women threw what they described as tools of women's oppression: high heels, eyelash curlers, issues of *Cosmopolitan* magazine, and bras. The plan had been to set the trash can on fire, to parallel the burning of drafts cards many of their male peers participated in during that deadliest year of the Vietnam War. But after a request from the city fire marshal not to light a fire on the wooden boardwalk, the trash can was not set alight. Nevertheless, a reporter caught wind of the plan, and the myth of feminists burning their bras was born.

Several blocks away, a more well-established organization had planned a different kind of protest. Organized by the National Association for the Advancement of Colored People (NAACP), 1968 also saw the first Miss Black America pageant. While the NAACP shared the young feminists' critique that the main pageant promoted a uniform standard of beauty, the Miss Black America pageant emphasized that it was the whiteness of that beauty standard that troubled NAACP organizers. They did not object to the overall goal of promoting beautiful women, and indeed by organizing their own pageant, they embraced that goal. But an African American organization embracing Black beauty during the Black Power movement had a very different political context. The NAACP was trying to straddle the line of the Black Power movement and its own more moderate politics. The pageant winner, Saundra Williams, wore her hair natural, as did the first runner-up. The second runner-up straightened her hair and wore it in an updo. Black was Beautiful, the pageant declared, across a range of esthetic choices. The pageant celebrated beauty that was

American Women's History: A New Narrative History, First Edition. Melissa E. Blair, Vanessa M. Holden, and Maeve Kane.
© 2024 John Wiley & Sons, Inc. Published 2024 by John Wiley & Sons, Inc.

indebted to both the Black Power movement and older ideals of middle-class Black respectability. These two simultaneous protests hint at the divisions over goals and tactics that would confront Black and white feminists throughout the 1970s.

The years from 1965 through the end of the 1970s saw the fastest changes for American women of any time in U.S. history. Laws were changed, ideas were changed, demographic patterns shifted markedly. This rapid pace and scope of change, brought about by women throughout the country, was truly remarkable. But there was also enormous resistance to it. The conservative movement which, as Chapter 13 showed, had been growing since the early 1950s, came into its own in the 1970s to challenge all the changes feminists and other activists were creating. It was a truly unprecedented period in our nation's history, one that continues to shape ideas about women and gender and the politics around those ideas well into the twenty-first century.

Feminism and Structural Change

Since the late 1950s, there had been slowly increasing public discussion about women's roles in society. Pressure from labor and professional women's organizations, as well as his own personal belief in women's equality, had led President Eisenhower to endorse equal pay for women in 1957. That same year, women's magazines began running stories with titles like "The Plight of the Young Mother" about housewives' dissatisfaction with their daily routines. In the early 1960s, these rumblings became louder among government officials and white middle-class women. Middle-class white women's disillusionment burst out of those women's magazines and into the national consciousness with the 1963 publication of Betty Friedan's book *The Feminine Mystique.* Freidan used the results of a survey she conducted with her Smith College classmates in their fifteenth reunion year to argue that educated white women who were spending their time as homemakers were unhappy. They described what Friedan dubbed the "problem that has no name," a sense that their lives were missing something. They wrote that they felt unfulfilled by housework and childcare, in spite of social messages that they should be happy with a life made up of those tasks. *The Feminine Mystique* was a huge bestseller and made Friedan a household name.

The Feminine Mystique was published the same year as the first extensive federal report about women's legal stats. In 1961, President Kennedy organized the President's Commission on the Status of Women (PCSW). A group of several dozen female lawyers and government officials was tasked with examining federal law and policies and documenting all the ways they discriminated against women. The Commission's report, titled simply *American Women,* was published in October 1963 and outlined dozens of places where federal law and policies discriminated against women, such as civil service hiring, lack of pay equity, and lack of maternity leave.

A year later, many of the Commission's concerns were addressed when "sex" was added to Title VII of the 1964 Civil Rights Act. Sections of the act banned discrimination in public accommodations (such as restaurants and hotels) and education on the basis of race, nationality, and religion, but not sex. Title VII, however, dealt with employment. Congresswoman Martha Griffiths (D-MI) and other women in Congress had been talking about including sex in Title VII or pushing another anti-discrimination bill focused on employment. When Congressman Howard Smith introduced an amendment that would include women in Title VII (his reasons for doing so are still debated, but many claim he was trying to kill the entire bill), Griffiths and other women's rights advocates in Congress quickly joined in supporting the amendment, which passed narrowly. Sex discrimination in hiring and pay came under the purview of the newly created Equal Employment Opportunity Commission (EEOC), the group created to enforce Title VII. When added to the Equal Pay Act of 1963, which made it illegal to pay men and women differently for the same job, it seemed that equality in the workplace was on the way for women.

However, the EEOC initially refused to take women's complaints about sex discrimination seriously. Aileen Hernandez, the only woman and one of two African Americans among the five original EEOC commissioners, recalled that attempts to raise sex discrimination claims were met with either "boredom" or "virulent hostility" by her male colleagues. The first EEOC director told reporters that the inclusion of sex in Title VII was "a fluke" and that he would not enforce the law.

In 1966, Friedan and Hernandez were among the several hundred women who met in Washington, D·C at the third annual meeting of the state commissions on the status of women. While the federal commission had not required states to undertake similar surveys of their laws, most did so. When representatives of those groups gathered, one topic that came up repeatedly was the lack of EEOC action on sex discrimination claims. Friedan, Hernandez, labor activist Dorothy Haener, African American feminist lawyer Pauli Murray, and others met to design a group that could pressure the EEOC. As Friedan put it, they needed something like the NAACP for women. The name they chose was the National Organization for Women, or NOW. In October, when they met to write a founding statement and officially create the organization, more than three hundred people attended the meeting.

Over the rest of the 1960s, NOW chapters spread slowly but steadily throughout the country. The organization pushed for changes in all kinds of laws – not only employment, but also education, credit, and custody and divorce laws. In the late 1960s, married women had difficulty getting credit in their own names, which meant they had no credit history if they divorced or were widowed. And single women often had to have a male relative co-sign large loans such as car loans or mortgages. Quotas for women's admission to medical and law schools, discrimination in the rates of student loan access, and a host of other policies that had made it harder for women to receive a higher education. NOW members believed that eliminating sex discrimination in these and other laws and policies represented a critical step toward women's equality within American society.

By 1968, other groups of feminists were organizing, less formally than NOW and with far more radical goals. The Miss American protest discussed earlier was one of their first publicly visible actions. These radical feminists, as they were known, tended to be younger than NOW members, and most of them had a history of activism on the political left. They had been involved in the civil rights movement, for example, or in protesting the Vietnam War. They had encountered deep-seated sexism within those movements, especially the antiwar movement, and in 1967 and 1968 decided to leave those groups. They were inspired by Black Power activists, who had been arguing for several years that any oppressed group had to be the source of its own liberation; no other group of people would do it for them or even work effectively with them. And so feminists left the Left in order to work toward eliminating sexism.

Their goals and methods were very different from NOW. Instead of forming a national organization with officers and a founding statement, radical feminists built their activism around a tactic known as consciousness raising. Small groups of women, usually 10–15, would gather and talk about their lives and their problems. In doing so, they discovered that the problems they believed were personal faults – sexual harassment in the workplace, for example, or an inability to get male partners to help with the housework – were shared by virtually all the women present. What they had thought were personal problems were, in fact, society wide. Because they were experienced by all of society, feminists believed they could be fixed through politics, at least partially. This process of consciousness-raising and the politics it led to was summed up in one of feminism's most famous slogans, "the personal is political."

Radical feminists did not believe that changing laws that explicitly discriminated against women was enough to eliminate society's treatment of women as second-class citizens, however. Their goal, as they phrased it, was women's liberation, something that required a far deeper rethinking and reworking of American society. They wanted to change how men and women interacted in every part of society, what marriage looked like, how Americans thought about sex (including sex between women). The sort of reform NOW advocated was helpful, they believed, but it did not go far enough. In New York, Chicago, and other large cities where feminists were active in the 1960s, these differences led to splits both between NOW and radical feminists and among radical feminists themselves. Different groups of radical feminists prioritized different issues. Some staged "zap" actions at bridal fairs, decrying an industry that made getting married seem like a woman's most important goal. Others organized the Miss America protest. Still others began to focus on reproductive rights. These differences did not always lead to tensions or divisions, but sometimes they did.

The most contentious issue for many feminists in these early years was lesbianism. At one end of the spectrum were lesbian separatists. These women argued that, because they lived without men in their personal lives, they were uniquely positioned to establish new, more authentic models for women's lives. In order to do that, however, they advocated for separating not only from men but also from heterosexual feminists, at least temporarily. Their issues were different than "straight" feminists, they argued, and they believed in the value of having lesbian-only spaces in which to work through the specific problems they faced in society. They also argued that attending to lesbians' problems was crucial for all women since, as one early group called Radicalesbians explained in their manifesto "The Woman-Identified Woman," the term lesbian had been used to demean and check assertive women for decades. Addressing lesbians' discrimination, therefore, would benefit all women.

At the other end of the spectrum, in 1969 NOW president Betty Friedan famously described lesbians as a "lavender menace." She believed that focusing on, or even openly discussing, issues faced specifically by lesbians would undermine the entire feminist movement. She did not believe that lesbians should be excluded from organizing, but she felt that the legislative and legal changes NOW was pushing for would benefit them, as they would benefit all women, and that there was no need for special attention to issues confronted only by lesbians. Many lesbian feminists heard this statement as a directive to stay in the closet, to not publicly discuss their sexuality while working for feminist change. And most were unwilling to do that. Issues of lesbianism, as well as a desire for more control of the agenda by local chapters, led to a bitter leadership fight within NOW in the early 1970s, with the faction favoring more local control and a more welcoming attitude toward lesbians winning the presidency in 1972.

Lesbians in the 1970s often felt caught in a bind between two social justice movements, neither of which prioritized their issues. While feminist groups like NOW were problematic, so was the gay liberation movement. In spite of the leadership of trans women like Marsha P. Johnson in the Stonewall uprising in New York in 1969, the gay liberation movement of the late 1960s and 1970s was overwhelmingly male-oriented. Lesbians who were fighting for custody of their children, for example, gained little support from most gay liberation groups. Neither were national feminist groups like NOW publicly supportive. Many lesbians, therefore, had no choice but to form their own organizations to fight custody battles and other distinct causes, regardless of whether they espoused separatism as a political goal or not.

Feminist action exploded nationwide in 1970. All three television networks and most major news magazines did extensive reporting on the movement for the first time that year. Hundreds of thousands of women joined marches for women's rights organized by NOW on the fiftieth anniversary of the Nineteenth Amendment, in August 1970. And in cities large and small, in every part of the country, NOW chapters sprang up and other women's organizations such as the League of Women Voters and the YWCA began discussing feminism and working for feminist change.

At the local level, the splits between radical and liberal feminists were far less prevalent than among national leaders. In Indianapolis, for example, women from a local women's liberation group, the local NOW chapter, the League of Women Voters, and Churchwomen United (an ecumenical Protestant group) all worked together to staff a rape crisis hotline established by the city government, lobby state legislators in favor of the Equal Rights Amendment, and investigate local compliance with the Equal Credit Opportunity Act after that bill was passed by Congress in 1974. In Dayton, Ohio, radical feminists who ran the rape crisis hotline and passed out feminist literature to every woman they encountered there began working to change the qualifications to be a police officer in Dayton, a thoroughly "liberal feminist" project, when they realized that the height and weight requirements kept most women out of the job. And in Durham, North Carolina the YWCA's Women's Center was home to a rape crisis hotline, an abortion referral and women's health clinic, and a monthly lesbian coffeehouse night as well as regular classes and workshops on feminism.

Not only did the 1970s see enormous growth in grassroots feminism, Congress passed a number of feminist bills, and the Supreme Court sided with feminists in many cases. The Equal Credit Opportunity Act of 1974 ensured that all women had access to credit regardless of marital status. Congress included Title IX in the 1972 Educational Amendments to the 1964 Civil Rights Act. The brainchild of feminist Congresswomen Patsy Takemoto Mink (D-HI) and Edith Green (D-OR), Title IX banned sex discrimination in any educational entity that received federal funding. While most often associated with requiring equity in athletics funding and opportunities, Title IX was in fact a wide-ranging bill that eliminated many of the obstacles women faced in higher education. Also in 1972, Congress passed the Equal Rights Amendment, which stated that "equality of rights under the law shall not be denied or abridged on account of sex." As a constitutional amendment, the ERA had to be ratified by three-quarters of all state legislatures and as will be discussed below, led to an organized backlash against feminism that eventually stopped the amendment from becoming law. One thing that paved the way for the ERA's passage was that the old opposition to the amendment by women's groups and labor unions had largely dissipated. Protective labor legislation was now seen by most people as something that harmed, rather than helped, women's position in the paid labor force.

Numerous feminist cases also worked their way through the court system. The list is long and varied: *Weeks v. Southern Bell*, a 1969 case which held that physical requirements (in this case, an amount of weight one had to lift) that were not directly related to the job were discriminatory; *Reed v Reed* in 1971, which held that women could not be shut out as executors of estates; *Frontiero v. Richardson* in 1973, which allowed husbands of female military personal access to the same amount of spousal support as wives received. Many of these cases were argued by the ACLU's Feminist

Law Project and its lead attorney, Ruth Bader Ginsburg. Taken together, the lawsuits created the precedent that discrimination on the basis of sex should receive extra scrutiny from the courts and require persuasive justification and explanation in order to be found constitutional.

The list of feminist accomplishments is virtually endless. National media discussions of feminist actions in major cities, and of legislative change, spurred conversations on the local level throughout the country. Those conversations then led local groups of women to pursue action on a huge range of topics. Feminist change in this era, therefore, was not top down, but rather the result of steadily growing networks of grassroots interest and support. For example, grassroots feminists drew on national leaders' analyses to create the first rape crisis hotlines and battered women's shelters, neither of which existed before the 1970s. These issues were both ones where the "personal is political" framework was vital. Rather than seeing rape as an issue of thwarted sexual desire and domestic violence as a private, family matter, feminist recast both as manifestations of patriarchy and power. Both were ways in which men used violence to subjugate women, feminists argued, and society needed to do more to prevent them. That call spurred local projects like the one in Indianapolis described above.

Similarly, feminists changed ideas of home and marriage. They argued that married men should be involved in their homes, in terms of helping with housework and childcare, declaring that casting this labor as belonging only to women stopped women from reaching their full potential. They contributed to the sexual revolution that had begun in the 1960s, asserting that women should have just as much right to find sexual pleasure in a variety of contexts and ways as men, and not only in marriage. In these arenas, there was no grassroots structure to point to like a rape crisis hotline, but changes in marital expectations show the influence of feminist ideas. Feminists nationally and locally pushed for equal access to birth control and abortion, leading to a pair of Supreme Court victories: *Eisenstadt v. Baird* in 1972, which stated that the government could not ban birth control, and *Roe v. Wade* in 1973, which declared that the government could not ban abortion in the first trimester of pregnancy, and could only restrict it (but not ban it) in the second trimester. Those two cases built on a framework established in *Griswold v. Connecticut,* a 1966 Supreme Court case brought by Planned Parenthood of Connecticut in the wake of their defeat in *Poe v. Ullman* (see Chapter 13). In that case, a divided Supreme Court held that the government cannot prohibit married couples from using birth control because married couples have a right to privacy. The seven justices who agreed with the decision declared that, while there is not an explicit right to privacy in the Constitution, several of the Bill of Rights amendments articulate a right to privacy in particular circumstances, and so that right can be expanded to cover married couples' sex lives. This articulation of a right to privacy provided the foundation not only for *Eisenstadt* and *Roe* but also for *Loving v. Virginia* (see Chapter 13).

Roe was the culmination of nearly a decade of work to liberalize that nation's abortion laws. Beginning the early 1960s and growing out a crisis surrounding a morning-sickness drug called thalidomide that had led to serious birth defects for many babies, activists in California began pushing for a change in that state's abortion laws. They argued that women and their doctors should be able to terminate a pregnancy not only to protect a women's life but also in cases of rape, incest, or severe birth defects. In 1967, the California legislature passed a law, which was signed by Governor Ronald Reagan, making it legal early in pregnancy so long as the procedure was performed in a hospital by a qualified doctor in order to prevent "mental or physical damage to the woman." The law did not spell out the specific cases in which that "mental or physical damage" could occur, allowing doctors to retain the power to determine who could obtain a safe, legal abortion. Colorado passed a very similar law a few months later, and by 1972 a total of 13 states had laws of this kind of the books. Several other states, including deep-South Alabama and Mississippi and heavily Catholic Massachusetts, had amended their laws before *Roe* to make abortion legal to protect a woman's health or in cases of rape or incest. Altogether, 20 states had liberalized their abortion laws in some way before January 1973, when *Roe* was decided. This state-by-state patchwork was a fact advocates of a nationally consistent abortion law focused on, claiming that it was discriminatory on class grounds. An amicus brief filed by a number of progressive religious organizations, including women's religious groups like the YWCA, argued that the state-by-state approach meant that wealthy women had easy access to safe abortions because they could get on a plane, while less affluent women were stuck with whatever their state's rules happened to be.

In the early 1970s, feminists also began advocating for a change in abortion laws from a different angle. They argued that, until a woman had complete control over her body, she could not be treated as an equal in society. Feminists, therefore, wanted to move beyond the liberalized laws that some states had adopted in the late 1960s and adopt abortion on demand, or the legalization of abortion early in pregnancy without a woman having to give any specific reason or fit any special criteria. This was the position that the Supreme Court endorsed in 1973 in the *Roe* decision, at least during the first trimester of pregnancy.

Sexuality, bodily autonomy, and safety continued to be central elements of white feminist activism throughout the 1970s. At the end of the decade (and into the early 1980s), debates around the issues of pornography led to what many scholars see as the final act of "second-wave" feminism. In the late 1970s, a group of feminists led by legal scholar Catherine MacKinnon and activist Andrea Dworkin began working to ban pornography. They argued that all porn was a form of violence against women, that women who participated could not possibly do so willingly, and that those who said they did were suffering from false consciousness. They articulated a link between pornography and rape, arguing that because porn objectified women's bodies for men's sexual pleasure, it cemented the idea that that was all women's bodies were for. By the early 1980s, Dworkin and MacKinnon were working with conservative religious leaders like Jerry Falwell to write local ordinances banning pornography on the grounds that it violated women's civil rights.

A huge, diverse, group of feminists organized in opposition to Dworkin and MacKinnon's work. Lesbian feminists highlighted their utter absence in the pair's analysis and argued that lesbian porn invalidated their claims. Other feminists were appalled by the censorship endorsed by Dworkin and MacKinnon and their willingness to work with openly anti-feminist figures such as Falwell. This fight, dubbed the "sex wars" by the media, contributed to the impression that feminism ended in the early 1980s.

Black Feminism, Chicana Feminism, and Race-Based Organizing

Many of these feminist organizations – from NOW's national office to consciousness-raising group – were overwhelmingly white. But women of color were present in many of these organizations and pushed them to engage with the difference race made in feminist work. Among existing women's organizations, the YWCA proved particularly adept at incorporating women of color, in part because their local chapters had been ordered to integrate by the national office in the late 1940s. In the early 1970s, the YWCA committed to a pair of overarching goals: eliminating racism and enacting feminist change.

The YWCA was particularly important in providing space for what was known at the time as Chicana feminism. Mexican American women organized the first national Latina feminist conference at the Houston YWCA in 1971. Roughly six hundred women attended from throughout the country. Other western Y chapters in cities such as Los Angeles and Denver sponsored members' travel to Houston and provided other funds. After the Houston conference, many local Chicana feminist groups were organized, including the Hijas de Cuauhtemoc in Los Angeles. The goal of the Hijas and other groups like them was to create, in the words of historian Maylei Blackwell, "an autonomous space for women's political participation" where they could engage with the race-based liberation movement they were part of while also challenging the sexism within that movement. Latinas who joined race-based feminist groups did so for just that reason. They were committed to working for racial progress, but they also wanted to ensure the Chicano movement paid attention to the needs and problems of women.

For African American women, working within predominantly white women's groups was often more difficult. Some nationally prominent Black feminists remained active in white feminist circles. Shirley Chisholm, Dorothy Height, Florynce "Flo" Kennedy, and Eleanor Holmes Norton, all well-known Black feminists, were founders of the National Women's Political Caucus, alongside Gloria Steinem, Bella Abzug, and other white women. Kennedy frequently collaborated with Steinem, especially on the issue of abortion rights, and Abzug and Chisholm worked together often in the U.S. House of Representatives, where they both represented New York state. But the feminist movement remained a fraught place for many Black women. Writing in 1971, author Toni Morrison claimed that relationships between men and women, lesbianism, and other topics of sexuality were a "family struggle," rather than appropriate targets of activism. She praised, however, the work of Chisholm in particular and the National Women's Political Caucus more generally as pursuing something "real" as they worked for legal changes in women's status.

Morrison's article spoke to the difficulties many Black women had with white feminist groups and leaders. They were frustrated by white feminists' inability to consider issues from other perspectives, to do anything more than add Black women into the frameworks they had already established. These differences were particularly obvious on reproductive rights and rape. For many feminists of color – not only Black women but also Native American women – reproductive rights were about more than the right to have an abortion. As communities that had long faced forced sterilization by government officials and endemic poverty in many communities, they saw the right to have and raise children as one that was equally under threat, and equally important to protect. But they had difficulty getting white feminists to work with them to address the issue from that perspective. Native American women founded Women of All Red Nations, or WARN, in 1978 to address this wide range of reproductive rights issues. Black feminists also critiqued white feminists' analysis of rape, arguing in the second half of the 1970s that the increasing focus on law enforcement as a solution to the rape problem was not really a solution at all. Black feminists, sometimes in alliance with incarcerated women, pointed out the many abuses that the criminal justice system perpetuated on people of color, as well as the ways in which rape allegations had been a way of punishing Black men since the era of lynching. As with reproductive justice, many white feminists struggled to see the alternative point of view feminists of color articulated on solving the problem of rape. Although the term would not be coined until the late 1980s, it is clear in hindsight that feminists of color were operating from an intersectional perspective in the 1970s, one which considered sex, race, and class as linked and inseparable, while most white feminists were only working through a lens of sex.

Black feminists, therefore, formed their own organizations. Flo Kennedy and Barbara Sloan, among others, founded the National Black Feminist Organization in 1973. Many of the NBFO founders had been active in SNCC during its later, Black Power years and took that Black Power analysis into their feminist work. The NBFO focused not only on issues of sexism but also tried to address poverty and racism in its short life. The NBFO dissolved in 1975, but two years later another group, the Combahee River Collective, was formed in Boston, with Barbara Sloan again a founding member. The Combahee founders were Black socialist lesbian feminists, and their mission statement articulated a bold intersectional vision that declared the impossibility of ignoring any of those identities as they worked to build a more just world.

Another organization made up primarily of Black women was founded around the same time as NOW. Although not started as an organization for Black women, they were always the majority of the members of the National Welfare Rights Organization. The NWRO was dedicated to improving the lives of women who received public assistance, focusing on increasing not only the financial means of their lives but the dignity with which they were treated. In the mid-1960s, only single women were eligible for welfare benefits, and social workers conducted "midnight raids" to ensure that no beneficiaries had men living in their homes. Even an overnight stay by a brother or cousin could cost a woman her benefits if the social worker happened to come by that night. The amount of money allocated to each family was also far below what was essential to feed, house, and clothe more than one person. But the women knew that, without assistance to pay for childcare, the jobs that they could get would earn them even less than welfare did once they paid someone to watch their children while they were at work. They argued, therefore, that even though they were poor they had the right to stay home and be mothers just like affluent white women were supposed to do. By the late 1960s, the organization was led by an African American women named Johnnie Tillmon. Tillmon tried to create more connections between the NWRO and feminist groups, writing an article in the first issue of *Ms* magazine titled "Welfare is a Woman's Issue." But after Congress failed in 1972 to pass a bill called the Family Assistance Plan, which would have created a guaranteed minimum income for families in exchange for high work requirements without sufficient child-care allowances, the NWRO fell apart.

Beyond explicitly feminist or women's groups, the late 1960s and 1970s also found women activists in a host of other movements. Many Black women remained within civil rights organizations or joined newly formed Black Power groups such as the Black Panthers. In the second half of the 1960s, many of these organizations were influenced by the Moynihan Report, a federal report published in 1965 that blamed African American women for many of the problems the Black community was facing. Written by the white, male Assistant Secretary of Labor, the report described Black women as "matriarchal" and Black families as a "tangle of pathology" due to the prevalence of female-headed households among African American families. Many male civil rights leaders accepted much of this analysis and made solving the problems facing Black men, especially problems of unemployment and police harassment, a focus of their activism. This emphasis can be seen clearly, for example, in the Black Panther Party's original uniforms, which projected a hyper-masculine, almost military image through their berets and open carrying of guns.

In spite of this programmatic sexism, many women remained within Black Power organizations. They did so because they believed in the goals of the movement. They believed in teaching Black children African and African American history, art, and culture. They believed in changing beauty norms to celebrate African features and hairstyles. They believed that racism was the most pressing problem confronting African Americans and that working to end racism would improve Black women's lives. They also believe that they could work from within to change the chauvinism of many Black Power leaders. And by the early 1970s, they had done so in many cases. Women like Kathleen Cleaver and Elaine Brown, for example, pushed Black Panther Party leaders to change their position on women's contributions to the movement. In 1970, Panther founder Huey Newton endorsed female Panthers' right to "speak about their own oppression" and further stated, "we recognize women's right to be free." Women also made up many of the grassroots activists of the Black Panther movement, staffing its famous free breakfast programs and contributing writing and art to its nationally distributed newspaper.

African American women were not the only ones who participated in race-based movements in this era. Latinas and Native American women were also deeply involved in the Chicano and American Indian (AIM) movements. From Texas to Colorado to California, as well as in big eastern cities like Chicago and New York, Latinas were part of a movement that advocated for bilingual education in public schools, for an end to school discrimination against Latino students, and for the development of Chicano Studies programs in universities in California and elsewhere. Many of the women who attended the 1971 Mexican American feminist conference at the Houston YWCA remained active in Chicano organizations as well. But some of them paired that work with explicitly feminist organizing within the movement, as discussed above.

Similarly for Native American women, work within AIM and in explicitly feminist groups like WARN often went hand in hand. In 1976, one year before WARN was founded, a meeting of AIM leaders had included "control of reproduction" as one of the five essential elements of sovereignty for Native Americans. This inclusion was part of the inspiration for the founding of WARN, and the women of that group worked tirelessly to draw attention to the problems of reproductive justice that many Native American women faced. Indian Health Service doctors frequently sterilized women without their informed consent. WARN activists spoke with women who asked how to reverse surgical sterilization procedures that they did not know were permanent. WARN activists also pushed for a return of midwifery and other traditional birth practices, both to improve the health of delivering mothers and as a way of reinstating Native American culture. WARN members believed that reproductive justice, racial justice, and cultural preservation were all deeply connected to the overall goal of the AIM movement, which was the preservation of Native American lives and Native American culture. In fact, these arenas of activism were so closely linked in the minds and action of many Native American feminists that the distinctions between them can be difficult to discern.

In short, one did not have to join an explicitly feminist group to be pushing for feminist change and improvements in women's lives. For many women of color, remaining within race-based organizations and pushing those organizations to consider issues of gender within their anti-racist work was an equally if not more successful path to making women's lives better.

Demographics of Women's Lives in the 1970s: Family Change and Economic Collapse

As the feminist movement was peaking, the American economy was collapsing. A wide range of factors, from growing international competition to the strain of the Vietnam War to a lack of industrial innovation, contributed to the problems. Throughout the 1970s, unemployment and inflation both remained high, making it difficult for many American families to support themselves.

In spite of feminist work to desegregate want ads and increase women's employment in traditionally male fields, the labor market was still quite sex-segregated in the 1970s. And traditional women's jobs – clerical work, teaching, retail, and others – weathered the economic storms of the 1970s better than many male fields, especially manufacturing, just as had happened during the Great Depression. The result was an increasing number of women in the paid labor force as women who had not previously held jobs joined their working-class peers. Roughly 37% of adult women worked for wages in 1960; by 1980 that percentage was 52%. The weak economy was only one factor that contributed to this increase. Feminist encouragement for women to work outside the home was also a factor, as was the increasing number of fields that feminist activism opened up to women. As female baby boomers graduated from high school and college in the 1970s, they had a much wider range of options than previous generations of women had had.

Another factor that led more women into the paid labor force was the rising divorce rate. Beginning in California in 1970, most states overhauled their divorce laws, implementing "no fault" divorces. Previously, to obtain a divorce one party had to be "at fault." What qualified as divorce-worthy "faults" varied widely from state to state, from something as vague as "cruelty" to evidence of adultery. Attorneys had been pushing since the early 1950s to eliminate these requirements, as they believed that most divorce petitioners lied in order to get a divorce, thereby committing perjury. Feminists also challenged the idea that divorce was a disaster, or a failure by women. A group of white feminists staged a sit-in at the offices of the *Ladies Home Journal* in 1970, criticizing the magazine as "one of the most demeaning" toward women. Among other complaints, they focused on the magazine's "Can This Marriage Be Saved?" column, which had counseled women for more than two decades that it was their duty to work on improving unhappy marriages rather than leave them. Feminists argued that, instead, women should feel free to leave unhappy marriages and they proposed a "Bill of Rights for Divorced Women." Legal changes like the Equal Credit Act also made divorce seem more financially feasible. As a result of all these changes, the divorce rate doubled over the course of the 1970s. By 1980, more than five out of every one thousand adults got divorced every year.

Many of these divorces were among couples who had been married for a number of years. Gay men and lesbians, who had felt the need for a heterosexual marriage in the context of the early Cold War, left their marriages to live openly as queer people. Women who had been abused or unhappy for years also found more acceptance of divorce in the 1970s. And the image of a man leaving his wife for a younger woman, while a stereotype, also became more acceptable in this decade. The understanding of marriage as a lifelong bond regardless of the circumstances had fundamentally shifted.

Alongside the rising divorce rate, birth rates also fell back to typical levels in the aftermath of the baby boom. The average number of births per woman was still over 3.5 in 1960; by 1980 it was less than two. Many factors drove this "baby bust," including a smaller cohort of women of childbearing age, as well as greatly expanding access to birth control. But even in the late 1970s and early 1980s, as baby boom women moved into their peak childbearing years, the numbers were similar to those of the 1920s, rather than the 1950s. The "baby bust" is another indication of just how abnormal the baby boom was – in subsequent generations, the birth rate settled back into the level it had been for the first several decades of the twentieth century and where it has remained ever since, between 1.5 and 2 children per woman on average.

Women and the Rise of the New Right

While millions of women entered the labor force for the first time, and hundreds of thousands across the country engaged in feminist activism, there was also tremendous growth in conservative women's organizing and activism in the late 1960s and 1970s. Building on the foundations established by grassroots conservative women in the 1950s (see Chapter 13), numerous white women throughout the country continued to grow the conservative movement or, as it was often called, the New Right.

In the late 1960s, a national leader emerged within this movement. Phyllis Schlafly was a wife and mother from the St. Louis suburbs in Illinois, who had gone to law school at night while her children were young. A lifelong activist in Republican politics and a devout Catholic, the mid-1960s were a turning point for Schlafly's activism. She was an early, vocal supporter of Senator Barry Goldwater's 1964 presidential campaign, writing the popular book *A Choice, not An Echo* in support of his candidacy. When Goldwater suffered a historically large defeat to incumbent president Lyndon B. Johnson, Schlafly focused her efforts on growing conservatism within the Republican Party. The tensions within the party were enormous in the mid-1960s, as moderate Republicans sought to limit the rising power of conservatives. The tensions between conservatives, who would become some of feminism's strongest opponents, and moderates, which counted many Republican feminists in their ranks (including 1970s First Lady Betty Ford), remained strong until the late 1970s, when conservatives decisively gained the upper hand. Schlafly was at the center of an early stage of this fight when she announced her candidacy for the presidency of the National Federation of Republican Women's Clubs in 1966. The party regulars in charge of the federation took several steps, including delaying the election by a year, to try and prevent Schlafly and her fellow conservatives from winning. When the election was held in April 1967, Schlafly was defeated. She stewed on this defeat both privately and in print, writing that not only was she shut out of leadership because of her politics but also because the men in charge of the Republican party wanted the federation led by women who would not challenge them or create a genuine, distinct voice for women in the party. Within months of her defeat, Schlafly began sending a monthly newsletter, the *Phyllis Schlafly Report,* to some 3000 conservative women in the national federation.

Between 1967 and 1972, the *Phyllis Schlafly Report*'s subscriber list grew steadily. And Schlafly grew increasingly dismayed at the success of the feminist movement. A fervent Cold Warrior, Schlafly believed that distinct gender roles, with women centering their lives on the home, was one of the factors that made American society superior to Communist societies. The feminist movement seemed to be challenging that belief and also challenging what many people, including Schlafly, believed to be

Biblically ordained roles for women in society. In February 1972, Schlafly devoted her entire newsletter to the Equal Rights Amendment, calling the issue "What's So Wrong with 'Equal Rights' for Women?" In this issue she argued that the ERA was a direct assault on families, on "the most important and precious right of all – the right [of a woman] to keep her own baby and be supported and protected in the enjoyment of watching her baby grow and develop." Motherhood, Schlafly argued, was women's highest calling, ordained by God. Feminists had been challenging this framing of motherhood for years; in the ERA Schlafly saw an effort the put the weight of the federal government behind a feminist analysis that, in her understanding, said that women should strive to be anything except a mother.

Within months, Schlafly had organized a national anti-ERA group called STOP ERA (STOP was actually an acronym for "stop taking our privileges"). Women around the country, especially white women who were middle-aged or older and who lacked a college education, flocked to the movement. They protested at almost every state legislature where the amendment was up for debate. They leaned into the traditional gender roles they were supporting. In North Carolina and Georgia, STOP ERA activists sent legislators loaves of bread with tags that read "From the Bread Bakers to the Bread Winners." Women protested that the ERA would eliminate sex-segregated bathrooms, would deny women custody of their children or alimony if they divorced, and would require women to be drafted into the military. Feminists were able to easily argue away the first two, but the draft issue proved particularly difficult. Feminists declared that, while women would be required to register for the draft if the ERA passed, the military could still assign them to non-combat duties. This argument was disingenuous; if the ERA passed and a woman sued to gain access to a combat role in the military, she would almost certainly have won her case. But the ERA was being debated in the immediate aftermath of the Vietnam War, which ended in January 1973. The draft, therefore, was a very difficult subject for feminists to work around. While there were tens of thousands of women who actively worked to prevent ERA ratification, the media focus on the debate between women benefitted the overwhelmingly male politicians who voted against the amendment by keeping them out of the spotlight. The ERA eventually failed, ratified by 35 states when 38 were necessary for the amendment to become law.

In addition to STOP ERA, several other anti-feminist organizations emerged that worked alongside Schlafly's group. One was called the Women Who Want to be Women, or WWWW. Their name gives a clear sense of what anti-feminists believed they were fighting against. They felt that feminists were trying to eliminate all distinctions between men and women. Another group, founded in New York state, was Right-to-Life. This organization, made up overwhelmingly of Catholics, especially women, was the first organization to work against the *Roe v Wade* decision and the expansion of abortion rights. Protestant groups that eventually engaged in anti-abortion politics, such as the Southern Baptist Convention, did not begin to unequivocally oppose abortion until the very end of the 1970s. Catholic women on Long Island and elsewhere, however, were opposed and organizing from the start, with support from their parish priests and others in the Catholic hierarchy. To these women it was abortion rights, and not the ERA, that threatened their status as mothers and the respect and protection they believed society gave them because of their motherhood. They organized and began a political party, National Right-to-Life, that exerted significant influence at the state level in New York and ran a presidential candidate in several states in 1976.

The tensions between feminist and anti-feminist, and the ways in which those tensions reshaped American politics, came to a head in 1977. In that year, the Democratic-controlled federal government provided funding for a feminist conference to celebrate International Women's Year, which had been declared by the United Nations two years earlier. Feminists working in Washington, led by Congresswoman Bella Abzug, had lobbied hard for the conference for several years. They developed an ambitious structure – each state organized a meeting to elect delegates to the national convention and ratify the slate of feminist goals prepared by the IWY Commission in Washington. Each state's elected delegation was required to mirror the state's population in terms of racial and ethnic diversity, which meant that large numbers of African American, Native American, and Latina women were incorporated into this federally sponsored feminist event. In mid-November, all the state delegates would gather at the convention center in Houston, officially adopt the platform, and formally dedicate the federal government to implementing feminist change. Women who attended remembered the event as a remarkable weekend, filled with joy and sisterhood and made especially meaningful due to the diverse group of women who attended. Gloria Steinem, in a 1978 book, stated that the conference held out the promise of a "new openness and inclusiveness in national politics."

But across town, Schlafly led a counter-conference. Held at the Houston Astrodome, the Pro-Family Conference provided a space for anti-feminists to voice their objections to feminism and, especially, to feminism being funded by the federal government. The fate that Schlafly had warned of in 1972 – that the federal government would be brought fully onto the side of a movement that, in her telling, would stop women from being the wives and mothers God had made them to be – seemed to be coming true. The Pro-Family conference was the first major event where STOP ERA and anti-abortion activists came together. The new anti-gay-rights movement also had representative in the crowd, and the convention heard a message of support from Anita Bryant, one of that movement's leaders. Schlafly later described Houston that weekend as the "Battle of Midway," a reference to a decisive World War II naval battle. Houston was the moment when the two movements came together in the same city and articulated their vastly different visions for American women's lives at the same time, with the eyes of the nation firmly upon them. Which side would be victorious? As the United States moved into the 1980s, it became clear that while Schlafly did not score a decisive blow in her "Battle of Midway," she gained the upper hand.

Bibliography

Barasko, Maryann. *Governing NOW: Grassroots Activism in the National Organization for Women*. Cornell University Press, 2004.

Blackwell, Maylei. *Chicana Power!: Contested Histories of Feminism in the Chicano Movement*. University of Texas Press, 2011.

Blair, Melissa Estes. *Revolutionizing Expectations: Women's Organizations, Feminism, and American Politics, 1965–1980*. University of Georgia Press, 2014.

Celello, Kristin. *Making Marriage Work: A History of Marriage and Divorce in the Twentieth-Century United States*. University of North Carolina Press, 2012.

Critchlow, Donald T. *Phyllis Schlafly and Grassroots Conservatism: A Woman's Crusade*. Princeton University Press, 2005.

Duggan, Lisa, and Nan T Hunter. *Sex Wars: Sexual Dissent and Political Culture*. Routledge, 2006.

Echols, Alice. *Daring to Be Bad: Radical Feminism in America, 1967–1975*. University of Minnesota Press, 1989.

Evans, Sara M. *Personal Politics: The Roots of Women's Liberation in the Civil Rights Movement and the New Left*. Random House, 1979.

Ezekiel, Judith. *Feminism in the Heartland*. Ohio State University Press, 2002.

Farmer, Ashely D. *Remaking Black Power: How Black Women Transformed and Era*. University of North Carolina Press, 2017.

Harrison, Cynthia E. *On Account of Sex: The Politics of Women's Issues, 1945-1968*. University of California Press, 1988.

Luker, Kristin. *Abortion and the Politics of Motherhood*. University of California Press, 1984.

Mathews, Donald G, and Jane Sharron De Hart. *Sex, Gender, and the Politics of ERA: A State and the Nation*. Oxford University Press, 1990.

Morris, Robin. "Organizing Breadmakers: Kathryn Dunaway and the Georgia STOP ERA Campaign." In *Entering the Fray: Gender, Politics, and Culture in the New South*, 161–183, edited by Wells, and Phipps. University of Missouri Press, 2010.

Nadasen, Premilla. *Welfare Warriors: The Welfare Rights Movement in the United States*. Routledge, 2005.

Randolph, Sherie M. *Florynce "Flo" Kennedy: The Life of a Black Feminist Radical*. University of North Carolina Press, 2015.

Rivers, Daniel Winunwe. *Radical Relations: Lesbian Mothers, Gay Fathers, and their Children in the United States since World War II*. University of North Carolina Press, 2013.

Roberts, Blain. *Pageants, Parlors, and Pretty Women: Race and Beauty in the Twentieth Century South*. University of North Carolina Press, 2014.

Rosen, Ruth. *The World Split Open: How the Modern Women's Movement Changed America*. Penguin, 2006.

Rymph, Catherin E. *Republican Women: Feminism and Conservatism from Suffrage through the Rise of the New Right*. University of North Carolina Press, 2006.

Springer, Kimberly. *Living for the Revolution: Black Feminist Organizations 1968–1980*. Duke University Press, 2005.

Spruill, Marjorie J. *Divided We Stand: The Battle over Women's Rights and Family Values that Polarized American Politics*. Bloomsbury, 2017.

Taranto, Stacie. *Kitchen Table Politics: Conservative Women and Family Values in New York*. University of Pennsylvania Press, 2017.

Taylor, Keeanga-Yamatta. *How We Get Free: Black Feminism and the Combahee River Collective*. Haymarket Books, 2017.

Theobald, Brianna. *Reproduction on the Reservation: Pregnancy, Childbirth, and Colonialism in the Long Twentieth Century*. University of North Carolina Press, 2019.

Thuma, Emily J. *All Our Trials: Prisons, Policing, and the Feminist Fight to End Violence*. University of Illinois Press, 2019.

CHAPTER 15

Women in Contemporary America, 1980–2020

In 2010, a small group of Black feminists, mostly academics, began a blog called the Crunk Feminist Collective (CFC). Over the next five years, the blog became a space to articulate what CFC founders Brittney C. Cooper, Susana M. Morris, and Robin M. Boylorn call "hip-hop generation feminism." As their founding manifesto described it, "we identify with hip hop because the music, the culture, the fashion and the figures provide the soundtrack to our girlhood and young womanhood." All of the writers came of age in the 1990s, a peak time for women in hip hop, with artists like Queen Latifah, Lauryn Hill, and Erykah Badu topping the charts. At the same time, a more misogynistic vein of hip hop was also emerging. The CFC members began their collective and began publishing their writings in order to make an explicitly feminist voice of younger Black women who identified with hip-hop music and culture publicly visible. In the manifesto, they made their feminist politics explicit, writing "we claim the right to resist the forces of racist, sexist, heterosexist domination by any means necessary."

In articulating an intersectional feminism that named racism, sexism, and heteronormativity as forces that all harmed Black women, the Crunk Feminist Collective was part of a long tradition of Black feminist thought. By tying their work explicitly to hip hop, they were connecting to a major cultural force of the late twentieth and early twenty-first centuries. From 1980 into the twenty-first century, as organized feminist activism faded from mainstream view, popular culture became a major site of feminist discourse and debate. Also, by publishing a blog, the Crunk Feminism Collective was similar to other feminist organizers of these years that used the internet (and, earlier, zine publication) to spread feminist ideas through media outlets that were often hidden from those who did not participate in them. While the national news media repeatedly declared feminism dead in these years, it is more accurate to describe it as underground, organizing through zines, listservs, and blogs. And ironically, the news media declared feminism dead while documenting the many

American Women's History: A New Narrative History, First Edition. Melissa E. Blair, Vanessa M. Holden, and Maeve Kane.
© 2024 John Wiley & Sons, Inc. Published 2024 by John Wiley & Sons, Inc.

public ongoing feminist battles – over reproductive justice, equity in the workplace, and LGBTQ rights among others. At the same time, conservative women's activism also continued to flourish. While these decades are sometimes called "post-feminist," feminism and debates about women's roles in society were constant in these years. But they existed in spaces and formats that differed from earlier generations of activism.

The Fights Continue: Gay Rights and Abortion Rights

One arena that was very much in the public view in these years was the gay rights movement. Beginning in the late 1970s, some cities and counties passed ordinances that forbade discrimination on the basis of sexual orientation, only to find those ordinances frequently challenged by local conservative activists and overturned by the courts. Anita Bryant, a former Miss America from Florida, became one of the leaders of the anti-gay rights movement after she successfully spearheaded a campaign to overturn Miami-Dade County's nondiscrimination ordinance in 1977. Bryant was one of many prominent women leaders in anti-gay rights and anti-choice activism in these years. Others included Dr. Mildred Jefferson, an African-American physician who was the president of National Right to Life in the late 1970s, and Elaine Donnelly, a close associate of Phyllis Schlafly who worked in the Department of Defense and opposed efforts to allow gay men and women to serve openly in the military in the 1980s and 1990s. Schlafly also remained a leading figure in these and other anti-feminist and conservative arenas until her death in 2020.

Until the mid-1990s, the Supreme Court sided with Bryant, Donnelly, and other opponents of equal rights for LGBTQ people. In the 1986 cases, *Bowers v. Hardwick* the Supreme Court upheld laws banning sodomy, arguing that sex between people of the same gender was "a crime not fit to be named" and forbidden in the "ancient roots" of the law. As legal discrimination continued throughout the 1980s, the AIDS crisis also emerged. Although gay men were never the only victims of AIDS, they were the majority of casualties in an epidemic that, in its first decade, killed more Americans than were killed in combat during the Vietnam War. Lesbian women worked alongside gay men at the forefront of building community support structures to care for AIDS victims. ACT UP, the most prominent organization fighting against homophobia and AIDS stigma and for improved funding for AIDS research, was founded in New York City at the Lesbian and Gay Community Services Center in Greenwich Village in 1987. Over the next several years, ACT UP organized many public actions to protests the stigma around AIDS and the lack of funding for AIDS research, including a "die-in" in front of St. Patrick's Cathedral in Manhattan and a protest march to the White House in 1991.

New York City was not the only place where lesbians and gay men worked together on AIDS and other health issues in the 1980s. In 1983, a group of gay men and lesbians in Durham, North Carolina organized the North Carolina Lesbian and Gay Health Project. Other centers were founded in Boston, Los Angeles, Philadelphia, and other major cities. By the mid-1980s, the National Gay Task Force listed a total of more than four hundred clinics, counseling services, and community health organizations that specifically worked with lesbians and gay men. While many of these organizations focused the bulk of their resources on the AIDS crisis, they also argued repeatedly that the heterosexist and patriarchal assumptions by medical practitioners caused lesbians and gay men to frequently receive substandard or even harmful medical care. For trans individuals, these problems were both more acute and more hidden. Because, in the 1980s and 1990s, homosexuality was no longer labeled a mental illness by the psychiatric profession but trans identity was, there was a fissure between the two communities when it came to health care. Trans people were still fighting for even basic levels of acknowledgment within the medical profession, a fight that continued into the twenty-first century.

In addition to health care and the AIDS crisis, another major avenue of gay rights activism, especially among lesbians, was child custody. Beginning in the mid-1970s, a number of lesbians (and smaller numbers of gay men) who had previously been in heterosexual relationships fought public court battles to retain custody of their children. Virtually all of these efforts were unsuccessful until the mid-1980s. But in that decade the number of lesbian and gay parents increased rapidly, due to the development of *in vitro* fertilization and more openness to gay parents adopting children. The rights of these parents were fiercely contested in some parts of the country and accepted and supported in others. But nationwide, the increasing numbers of gay parents turned activists' attention to the problem of legal rights for their families. Building on arguments first made in custody cases in the 1970s, lesbian and gay parents in the 1980s and 1990s fought for legal parenthood for both partners, equal access to adoption, and domestic partnership and marriage rights for gay couples. In 1995, the Supreme Court ruled in *Romer v. Evans* that states could not restrict the rights of LGBT individuals if their only motivation for doing so was "animus," or prejudice. One year later, Congress passed the Defense of Marriage Act (DOMA), which prohibited same-sex couples from accessing any of the federal rights given to married heterosexual couples, such as tax breaks and Social Security benefits for widows and widowers.

In the twenty-first century, a series of lawsuits overturned DOMA and other laws that discriminated against gay men and women. In 2003, the Supreme Court overturned its *Bowers* decision in *Lawrence v. Texas*, which declared anti-sodomy laws unconstitutional and explicitly extended the right to privacy to cover same-sex sexual acts. A decade later, the Supreme Court considered the case of Edie Windsor. Windsor and her partner, Thea Spryer, had been married in New York State, where same-sex marriage was legal. However, because of DOMA, when Spryer died Windsor was ineligible for the widow's benefits that heterosexual people received from Social Security. Windsor sued the federal government, and in the 2013 case *U.S. v. Windsor,* the Supreme Court declared DOMA unconstitutional. Two years later, in *Obergefell v. Hodges,* the Court declared same-sex marriage legal nationwide. Building on its previous cases about marriage and privacy, including *Loving v. Virginia* (see Chapter 13) and *Eisenstadt v. Baird* (see Chapter 14), the Court declared that "the fundamental liberties protected by the Fourteenth Amendment's Due Process Clause extend to certain personal choices central to individual dignity and autonomy," and no government could take away those liberties.

In addition to these legal battles, lesbian activists were also at the forefront of the some of the most innovative grassroots feminist organizations of the 1990s. One of those was Southerners on New Ground, or SONG, a lesbian feminist collective organized by a group of black and white lesbian Southerners who were frustrated by the lack of intersectional thinking they saw at national gay rights' groups like GLAAD and the National Gay & Lesbian Task Force. SONG drew on its founders' history not only with gay rights groups but also antiwar and civil rights work to create an organization that worked in the South to address gay rights, race-based civil rights, and to improve economic opportunities for minorities. In the 2010s, as the founders stepped away and a new generation of leaders took the reins at SONG, their website described the group as "a home for LGBTQ liberation across all lines of race, class, abilities, age, culture, gender, and sexuality in the South."

The 1980s and 1990s also saw retrenchment in reproductive rights. There was some overlap between those working to protect the rights enshrined in the *Roe* decision and those focused on the AIDS crisis and lesbian health. As historian Tamar Carroll has written, "the legacy of feminism" was apparent in ACT UP and other groups that adopted the "skepticism of biomedical authority" born out of the feminist health movement of the 1970s. In ACT UP's case specifically, many lesbian activists were the ones responsible for "the technical stuff" of both how to critique big structures and how to organize to challenge them, according to one male ACT UP leader. And many of those same lesbian feminist were also involved in the founding of the Women's Health Action and Mobilization group in New York, known as WHAM!, which fought to protect abortion access. In 1991, WHAM! burst onto the national scene when its members hung a large banner declaring "Abortion is health care. Health care is A RIGHT" across the base of the Statue of Liberty.

Activists in WHAM!, the National Abortion Rights Action League (NARAL), and other abortion access groups were facing uphill battles. The number of anti-abortion activists had grown rapidly since the late 1970s, and clinics were frequently surrounded by protestors who created gauntlets of verbal abuse targeting women seeking abortions. In 1986, a violent anti-abortion group known as Operation Rescue was organized in Kansas City and quickly spread throughout the country. Operation Rescue members used violence to shut down abortion clinics, including acid attacks on clinic buildings and staff, bombing of clinics, and attempted and successful assassinations of abortion providers. In 1989, a legal challenge by Kansas City abortion opponents made its way to the Supreme Court in the case *Webster v. Reproductive Health Services*. In that case, the Supreme Court declared that states could prohibit the use of public funds for any aspect of abortion care, from counseling to performing the procedure, as the federal government had been doing with Medicaid dollars since the late 1970s under the Hyde Amendment. A portion of the court also stated that abortions could be limited at any time, even during the first trimester. But the Court was split on what the *Webster* decision meant in terms of *Roe*'s protections.

In 1992, the Court heard another case which pro-choice activists feared would invalidate *Roe* altogether. In *Planned Parenthood of Pennsylvania v. Casey*, the Court considered three restrictions that Pennsylvania had placed on abortion access: parental consent for minors seeking abortions, a mandatory 24-hour waiting period between when a woman first spoke with the abortion provider and when the pregnancy was terminated, and spousal consent for married women seeking abortions. Defenders of *Roe* focused on the final provision, arguing that it was absurd to require a woman in an abusive marriage, for example, to get the permission of her abuser to not bring a child into that home. In its decision, the Supreme Court upheld the first two provisions but struck down the spousal consent rule, stating that such a provision placed an "undue burden" on women. The Court further stated that they supported the "essential holding" of *Roe* that women had the right to terminate a pregnancy prior to the viability of the fetus and that the state could not unduly restrict that right. The "undue burden" language in *Casey* became the primary standard against which abortion restrictions were judged until 2022. Laws that placed an "undue burden" on women's access to their federally guaranteed right to abortion were routinely struck down by federal district and appeals courts.

These legal setbacks did not stop many states' continued efforts to restrict abortion access, often through laws that required clinics to meet the same physical space standards as hospitals and doctors at those clinics to have "admitting privileges" at hospitals within a certain distance. The goal of these bills was to make it impossible to establish or maintain abortion clinics in the states that passed such laws, mostly in the South and Midwest. In 2016, the Supreme Court struck down those laws in the case *Whole Women's Health v. Hellerstedt.* The Court found that the rules did nothing to improve women's health and safety, their alleged purpose, but did place an undue burden on women who had to travel hundreds of miles to secure an abortion if the rules had been adopted. The language from *Casey,* therefore, remained the standard for any restriction of abortion rights.

In 2022, that standard was overturned in the case *Dobbs v. Jackson Women's Health.* Of the five Supreme Court justices who had issued the majority opinion in *Whole Women's Health* case just six years earlier, only three were still on the bench. That transition of justices led to a radically different finding. Based on a selective reading of history, Justice Samuel Alito wrote in the majority opinion that since the right to abortion was not "deeply rooted in the Nation's history and tradition," there was no Constitutional grounds to support a right to abortion. Justice Alito's version of history disregarded the quickening doctrine that had been in place at the time of the Constitution, a doctrine which made abortion legal in roughly the first trimester of the pregnancy, as *Roe* had done (see Chapter 5). After the *Dobbs* decision was issued in the summer of 2022, more than a dozen states rushed to pass laws that banned abortion entirely, or had previously passed "trigger laws" that made abortion in their state illegal if and when *Roe* was overturned. Some of these state laws did not include exceptions to protect women's lives, thereby creating more draconian abortion laws than had ever existed in the nation's history. While these laws went into effect, however, new state constitutional amendments to ban abortion that went before voters as ballot referendums in Kansas and Kentucky failed in the six months after the *Dobbs* decision.

Daily Life at the Turn of the Century: Work, Immigration, and Family

Abortion and gay rights were just two of the arenas where changes begun in the 1970s continued throughout the rest of the century and into the 2000s. Women's employment rate kept climbing throughout the 1980s and 1990s. By the mid-1990s, three-quarters of women were in the paid labor force. Since that time, however, women's rate of labor force participation has declined somewhat. In 2016, the Bureau of Labor Statistics reported that women's labor force participation – which counts all employed women, whether full-time or part-time, plus those looking for work – had fallen since a peak around 2000. The decline occurred in all race and ethnic groups and was sharpest among women without college degrees and among Asian-American women. Women with a high school degree, for example, saw their labor force participation fall by almost 8% between 2000 and 2015. Women with a bachelor's degree or higher, by contrast, dropped their labor force participation by less than 1%. The declines were similar between Black and white women but were larger among Asian-American women (whose labor force participation fell by 3.5%) and smaller among Latinas, whose labor force participation generally is lower than the other three racial & ethnic groups the statistics trace. Even after the declines of the early twenty-first century, however, the increase in women's labor force participation since the mid-1970s is remarkable. For example, fewer than half of all mothers of children under 18 worked outside the home in 1975. In 2015, nearly 70% did so.

As women entered the workforce in growing numbers, they found a job market still largely segregated by sex and, in spite of the 1963 Equal Pay Act, still paying women less than men. These two phenomena were related – because so many jobs remained overwhelmingly male or overwhelmingly female, they did not fall under the Equal Pay Act's provisions, which only required equal pay for identical work performed "under the same circumstance." Starting in the late 1970s feminist attorneys and, especially, women active in labor unions tried to find a way around this problem by creating the framework of "comparable work." The comparable work idea, developed in most detail by the government employee union AFSCME, assigned points to a wide range of job attributes, including required education, skill, difficulty, and danger, and reimagined how those traits might be measured. For instance, it pushed back against assumptions that jobs that did not require physical labor were less difficult, arguing that dealing with unhappy customers at a DMV office every day might be more difficult than driving a garbage truck. AFSCME deployed this methodology in Washington State, beginning in the late 1970s. In 1983, a judge found that refusal to pay women equally for comparable work violated Title VII of the 1964 Civil Rights Act and ordered the state to pay thousands of women back wages. The judge's decision came two years after AFSCME organizers in San Jose, California negotiated comparable work provision into their contracts with that city. The movement seemed to be picking up steam, but in 1985 both a federal appeals court and the EEOC came out against comparable work as a solution to pay inequity, invalidating the Washington state victory. The Equal Pay Act therefore remains the only method women workers have to combat pay inequity. In 2009, Congress passed the Lilly Ledbetter Fair Pay Act, strengthening the law by clarifying that employees facing wage discrimination can sue over that discrimination whenever they become aware of it and can sue for back pay at previous jobs, not just over discrimination in current jobs.

These efforts to improve women's wages were particularly important in the context of the 1980s and 1990s, when economic policy shifts by the federal government led to major changes in the social safety net and in cost of living. One historian has described the economic picture of the 1980s as an "hourglass society," one in which economic policy changes caused both the top and bottom of the economic scale to grow while the middle class shrank. Far more people saw their economic standing decline than saw it improve, and low-income women bore the brunt of these changes. Housing costs increased rapidly while wages stagnated. Welfare benefits shrank and, following the passage of a bill signed by Democratic president Bill Clinton in 1996, lifetime access to those benefits was eliminated, replaced with a strict cap of no more than seven years' worth of benefits over a person's lifetime. Many states set even shorter windows of eligibility. Poor women, especially single mothers, also faced the same challenges that NWRO activists had outlined in previous decades regarding the mismatch between wages at the bottom of the economic ladder and the high cost of childcare (see Chapter 14). For many women, then, efforts to improve wages through unionization or new interpretations of the Equal Pay Act were vital attempts to keep their families housed, fed, and clothed.

While never the majority, the number of women workers represented by unions grew throughout this period. Beginning in the late 1990s, labor organizers turned their attention to efforts to organize domestic workers. The number of women working as domestic workers increased in the 1990s and has continued to slowly climb or hold steady ever since. This increase was driven mostly by two factors: an aging population that required more help around the house, both in terms of cleaning and personal care, and the continued increase in women working outside the home. Middle- and upper-class women who worked outside the home often hired other women to clean their houses. The increase in demand for domestic workers also coincided with an increase in immigration to the United States that began in the 1980s. Changes to immigration law in the 1960s and 1980s enabled more legal immigration, and global economic forces and policy changes, similar to those affecting people in the United States, made it more difficult for people to support their families in many places around the world. The result was a huge increase in the number of immigrants to the United States compared to the middle decades of the twentieth century. Women and men have come from all over the globe to live and work in the United States; 13% of the US population, roughly 40 million people, were foreign-born in 2010, compared to less than 10% in 1960. Women and men have migrated in roughly equal numbers, with slightly more women than men coming to the United States in these years. In 2020, one-third of immigrant women worked in service jobs of some kind, and those doing domestic work in private homes (as opposed to working in hotels or restaurants) were the worst paid and, often, the most exploited.

In 2000, a group called Domestic Workers United emerged in New York City to help domestic workers become aware of their rights to a minimum wage and to organize for improved treatment. Domestic workers were finally added to federal minimum wage laws in the mid-1970s, a triumph of the previous generation of organizing. But many domestic workers at the turn of the century were immigrants who were often not aware of these rights. In 2007, Domestic Workers United joined with a dozen other local domestic workers groups to form the National Domestic Workers Alliance (NDWA). The NDWA's leadership reflects the largely immigrant make-up of this workforce in the twenty-first century. The group's president, Ai-Jen Poo, is the daughter of Taiwanese immigrants. Most other board members represent affiliate groups of South Asian, Filipina, and Latina workers. In 2011, the NDWA sent representatives to a convention in Switzerland that sought to establish global rights of domestic workers, including the right to written contracts, freedom from harassment on the job, and decent working & living conditions. However, while one-third of employed immigrant women work in the service sector, more than one-third are employed in management, business, sciences, or the arts. As with all women, therefore, immigrant women's work experiences vary widely based on ethnicity, class, and education level.

Regardless of their place of birth, workplace, or salary, one topic that affected a large number of women workers in these years was sexual harassment. In 1980, the Equal Employment Opportunity Commission (EEOC) defined sexual harassment as a form of gender discrimination in the workplace that violated Title VII of the 1964 Civil Rights Act. The EEOC identified two different kinds of harassment that broke the law: quid pro quo (a requirement that a woman engage in some kind of sexual activity with a male at work or face consequences such as firing or lack of promotion) or the creation of a "hostile work environment" based on unwelcome sexual advances, discussion, or imagery in the workplace. In 1986, the Supreme Court heard a challenge to this rule when it considered a lawsuit brought by Mechelle Vinson, an African American teller at the Meritor Savings Bank in Washington, D.C. Vinson testified that she had been repeatedly harassed and coerced into sexual activity by her supervisor in the five years she worked at the bank, a job she began when she was just 19 years old. In a unanimous decision, the Supreme Court declared in *Meritor Savings Bank v. Vinson* that sexual harassment did constitute employment discrimination and was therefore illegal under Title VII.

While the law on sexual harassment was settled by the mid-1980s, the issue did not become widely discussed until 1991. In that year, another Black woman, Anita Hill, spoke before the entirely white and male Senate Judiciary Committee to oppose the appointment of Clarence Thomas to the Supreme Court. Thomas had been Hill's supervisor in the Oklahoma City office of the EEOC in the late 1970s and early 1980s. In front of Senators and television cameras, Hill told a chilling story of repeated sexual harassment by Thomas. Thomas quickly decried Hill's testimony as a "high tech lynching" orchestrated by white feminists who opposed his nomination because of his hostility to reproductive rights and his generally conservative politics. Thomas was confirmed, but Hill's testimony spurred widespread discussion of workplace culture and the harassment that women still routinely faced a decade after the EEOC declared such treatment illegal.

In 2017, sexual harassment and sexual violence at work again became a major topic in the media with the rise of the hashtag #metoo. The Me Too organization was actually begun more than a decade earlier by African-American activist Tarana Burke. Burke was living and working in Selma, Alabama in the late 1990s when she encountered a 13-year-old girl who had been sexually assaulted and did not know whom to tell or what to do. Burke realized that resources for young Black women in this impoverished, rural area were few, and so she began an organization to help those girls. Herself a survivor of sexual violence, Burke began using the phrase "me too" in her organizing, and in 2006 started the Me Too organization. The goal of the phrase and organization was to bring women and girls together around their shared experiences of sexual harassment and sexual violence. The organization provides resources for supporting survivors, training workshops to encourage survivors to become leaders in combating sexual violence, and other services. In 2017, actress Alyssa Milano added the hashtag #metoo to a social media post about sexual harassment by leading producers in Hollywood and the harassment and exploitation that the actress faced. The term took off, and Burke's organization moved to the forefront of newly visible feminist organizing in the 2010s.

There were also substantial changes in patterns of marriage and child-rearing in the 20 years on either side of the millennium. Marriage rates have declined throughout the era. In 1980, 2.5 million Americans got married. Between 1980 and 2010, the rate fluctuated year to year, but the overall trend was down, with just over two million Americans marrying in 2010. The divorce rate has also dropped. Fewer people are marrying, but more people who do so are staying married. While the statistics are not disaggregated, the rise in same-sex marriage in these years mean that heterosexual marriage rates have dropped more than the numbers indicate.

Birth rates have followed slightly different patterns from marriage rates. The number of births per woman remained fairly stable in the 1980s and 1990s, after falling from the baby boom peak. But around 2005, the birth rate began dropping again and continued to slowly decline throughout the 2010s. While commentators from all points of the political spectrum have decried this decline, the data present a positive picture. Almost all of the decline in overall birthrates has been caused by falling birth rates among women ages 15–24. According to the Guttmacher Institute, in 1990 nearly 60 out of every one thousand women aged 15–19 gave birth. By 2017, that number had fallen sharply, with 20 women out of every one thousand in that age group giving birth. Birthrates among women aged 20–24 years have also declined, although more modestly. For women aged 25–34 years, birth rates have been stable, and they have increased among women 35–45. What the data show, therefore, is that rather than signaling a crisis, the falling birth rate means that more women are finishing their education, or beginning their careers, before having children. These trends lead to fewer babies being born every year, but they mean that those babies are more likely to be born to women who have the educational and career experience necessary to keep their families out of poverty. This is certainly not universally true, as 20 out of every one thousand teenage girls giving birth annually still represents a major challenge to those young women and their children. But rather than being a problem, the overall trends suggest healthier outcomes for American women and children in the long run.

Another major change in the area of marriage and family life in these decades was the elimination of marital rape laws. Until the 1970s, it was legally impossible for a husband to rape his wife; sexual access to one's wife had been a key part of coverture that had remained in American law ever since the colonial era. But between 1978 and 1993, every state removed the marital rape exemption from its books. This achievement took painstaking work by feminists at the state level, who worked hard to persuade overwhelmingly male state legislatures that this was not just a symbolic step but something that materially improved women's lives.

Partisan Politics and Grassroots Activism

The late twentieth and early twenty-first centuries were also times of impressive gains for women in electoral politics. Beginning in the early 1980s, the Republican Party became concerned about the "gender gap," in which female voters favored Democrats. Because of these concerns, some Republican Party activists were dedicated to recruiting more women to run for office on the GOP ticket. They found many willing women, some of whom had long political careers, including Kay Bailey Hutchinson, a Texas Republican who held elected positions in the state government off and on for 20 years before she was won a special 1993 election to the US Senate. Hutchinson was part of a large wave of women legislators who came to Washington in the early 1990s. 1992 was dubbed the "Year of the Woman" by the media, as it saw over one hundred women running for US House or Senate seats. Fifty-four of those women won their elections, including Carol Mosely Braun, an Illinois Democrat who became the first African-American woman Senator that year, and Nancy Pelosi, who won her fourth term in the US House of Representatives. Pelosi still serves in the House as of 2022 and became the first female Speaker of the House in 2007. The number of women in Congress has risen since the early 1990s; half of all the women who have ever served in Congress have been elected since 1998. The 2018 midterm election saw another big jump in women members of Congress, with over one hundred women winning seats that year, including a record high number of women of color.

As historian Emily Suzanne Johnson has argued, the media and many in politics continue to assume there is one way that "women" vote and that they always vote for women, multiple contradictory elections notwithstanding. This habit was perhaps most apparent in the 2008 presidential election season. During the primary, both Hillary Clinton and Barak Obama sought the Democratic Party's nomination. Many prominent older feminists, including Gloria Steinem and former vice-presidential candidate Geraldine Ferraro wrote editorials arguing that all women had to vote for Clinton, and that supporting Obama was a rejection of feminism. On the other side of the political aisle, Republican nominee John McCain chose Alaska governor Sarah Palin as his running mate partially on the belief that she would attract women's support. Some supporters of Palin's choice even claimed women disappointed that Clinton did not secure the Democratic nomination would vote Republican to support her. Both candidates drew on well-established networks of grassroots women to support their efforts – NOW and other feminist groups for Clinton and Concerned Women of America (CWA) and other conservative women's groups for the Republicans. Palin's selection was particularly important for McCain to secure the support of CWA and other conservative women's groups, as his own politics were more moderate than those of many organized Republican women.

CWA's prominence in pushing for Palin's nomination and supporting the McCain-Palin ticket highlights another continuity in gender and politics in the twenty-first century. As they had since at least the late 1860s, white women continued to make up a large number of grassroots conservative activists. These women, who like their predecessors were likely to identify as religious and to promote traditional gender roles of women as wives and mothers, continue to support conservative politicians and seek office as conservatives. The media's consistent conflation of "women" and "feminist" when discussing politics has continually obscured the vibrancy and size of conservative women's grassroots activism. This tendency led to astonished headlines in 2016 when Donald Trump secured a larger percentage of white women's votes than Hillary Clinton did, even though Trump's success with white women voters should not have been treated as a surprise. There has always been a large group of women, especially white women, who favor the policy goals of conservative politicians, whether on issues of abortion and sexuality or fiscal and foreign policy.

Electoral politics was not the only arena where women were active politically. In the twenty-first century, many grassroots lobbying groups emerged which feature the kinds of maternalist arguments that have marked women's activism throughout American history. In 2004, Moms for America was organized in Dayton, Ohio. On its website, the group describes its mission as focused on mothers in the home who are "raising a new generation of patriots [who will] heal our nation from the inside out." This and other conservative women's grassroots groups function in ways similar to conservative women's groups in the 1950s (see Chapter 13). They see American democracy as under threat from forces such as feminism, gay rights, and atheism, and identify women and the home as the first and most important line of defense in protecting their vision of the United States. But in the twenty-first century maternalist arguments have not been used only by conservatives. In 2012, following a mass shooting at Sandy Hook Elementary School in Connecticut in which two dozen children lost their lives, gun control advocates organized Moms Demand Action for Gun Sense in America, often referred to as Moms Demand. The group began actively lobbying state legislatures to pass background checks and waiting periods for gun purchasers and close loopholes in national databases that tracked those who were not allowed to own firearms due to domestic violence arrests or other reasons. In arguments that echoed those made by civil defense activists in the early 1960s,

Moms Demand argued that the lockdown drills schoolchildren were subjected to did not keep them safe and, in fact, may cause psychological harm. Moms Demand argued that, instead of teaching children how to behave if an armed person enters their school, the government should be doing more to actually protect children from gun violence.

Feminist activism also continued to grow and evolve at the local level. In these years, it was not as visible as it had been in the 1960s and 1970s, and many news magazines and other outlets ran stories declaring feminism "dead." Many of the groups that had sustained radical white feminism in the 1970s fizzled out by the mid-1980s. But far from dying, feminism instead reinvented itself and maintained itself outside of the mainstream media's view. Feminist activists were among the earliest users of Internet chat boards in the 1990s. Barbara Ann O'Leary was a leader in this movement. In early 1992, she was hired by Bella Abzug, the former Congresswoman and prominent 1970s feminist activist, to help organize Abzug's new group, the Women's Environmental and Development Organization (WEDO). O'Leary partnered with another new organization, the Association for Progressive Communication, to begin providing email services to feminist groups. These efforts matured around the massive U.N.-sponsored Fourth World Conference on Women, held in Beijing in 1995. O'Leary established a listserv, Beijing95-L, to connect women throughout the United States who would be participating in the conference or who wanted to contribute ideas to the delegates. In the mid-1990s personal email, listservs, and chat boards were just coming into their own, and feminists were able to harness them to build robust national and international networks.

Women of color were at the forefront of feminist organizing around the turn of the century. Not only SONG, discussed above, but also SisterSong: A Women of Color Reproductive Justice Collective and INCITE! Women of Color Against Violence were part of a network of feminist organizations formed by and focused on women of color. SisterSong was organized in 1997, using a grant from the Ford Foundation to coordinate the work of 16 organizations – four each representing African American, Native American, Latina, and Asian-American women – to pursue reproductive justice work. Reproductive justice, as opposed to reproductive rights, was a framework named by Black feminists earlier in the 1990s. It sought to encapsulate not only the right to abortion, but the wider range of experiences that women of color struggled with in terms of reproductive autonomy and bodily integrity. Reproductive justice, as the organization defines it, is "the human right to maintain personal bodily autonomy, to have children, not have children, and parent the children we have in safe and sustainable communities." The reproductive justice framework of SisterSong focuses not only on birth control and abortion access but also environmentalism, economic and educational opportunity, safety, and the ways in which all those categories are inflected by race. This framework draws on work by feminist of color since at least the late 1970s. In 1980, for example, the Native American women's organization WARN issued a report declaring that uranium mining on the Pine Ridge reservation in South Dakota was causing miscarriages and threatening women and children's health. Fighting the mining operation was, therefore, an act of reproductive justice. SisterSong's significance was the scale it brought to this kind of work. By bringing groups such as WARN into coalition with other, similar groups of other women of color, SisterSong was and remains able to gain access to more funding and increase the visibility and success of their activism.

A similar coalition of activist of color, focused on violence against women, was formed in 2000. INCITE! Women of Color Against Violence was organized to find alternatives ways to prevent violence against women. Many of INCITE's critiques echoed those first articulated in the late 1970s and early 1980s – that mainstream white feminist's focus on fighting violence against women through the criminal justice system was not a truly feminist solution, as that system was itself rife not only with sexism but racism. INCITE's members believed that jail time and fines did not prevent violence and also had disproportionate negative effects on communities of color. In addition to these critiques, which small groups of feminists of color had been making since the 1970s, INCITE's members also criticized feminists' reliance on nonprofit grant-funding agencies. They argued that these agencies forced groups to focus too narrowly, so that they could show "results" at the end of the short grant-funding cycle. In the 20 years of its existence, INCITE! has continued to put forward an agenda for ending violence that centers on women of color. In the 2010s, the organization began working with the emergent Black Lives Matter and prison abolition movements and broadened its statement of purpose to declare that it was "a network of radical feminists of color organizing to end state violence and violence in our homes and communities."

One area of deep tension within feminist communities in these decades was the role of trans women within the movement. While most feminists were welcoming of all women, a vocal minority began to argue that trans women should not participate in some feminist spaces or events. This tension can be seen most clearly around the Michigan Womyn's Music Festival, an event begun by lesbian separatist feminists in 1975. The festival's policies were often controversial; since its founding, for example, women could not bring male children over the age of four to the festival itself, but instead were required to leave them at an adjacent boys' camp while they attended the festival. Some lesbian mothers actively protested this policy, especially in the first decade or so of the festival's existence. In the early 1990s, a trans woman was asked to leave the festival and festival organizer Lisa Vogel announced a "womyn-born womyn" policy, declaring that trans women could not attend the festival because, according to Vogel, they were not women in the same way as "womyn-born womyn." This policy became increasingly controversial in the 2010s, leading prominent musical groups like the Indigo Girls to stop playing at the festival and contributing to the closure of the festival in 2015. The position outlined by Vogel and others has become known as "trans exclusionary radical feminism," or TERF, and is grounded in a kind of biological determinism that has always been present in some strands of American feminism. But earlier generations did not use those beliefs in an exclusionary way as it is used in the twenty-first century.

Much of the media discussion of feminism's death, therefore, was about the death of a particular kind of feminism, shaped and staffed by straight white middle-class women, and challenges to the policy victories that those feminists had secured, like abortion rights. And that kind of white middle-class feminism did lose numbers and influence in these years. But a vibrant feminist movement was still present, made up of women of color, LGBTQ women, and their straight white allies. And even the media's declaration of (white, straight) feminism's death seemed misplaced: in 1992, an estimated 500,000 women converged on the National Mall in Washington, D.C. for a pro-choice march called "We Won't Go Back: A March for Women's Lives." The estimated crowd for this march was larger even than the 2017 Women's March in D.C. that protested the inauguration of President Donald Trump and his history of sexist and racist behavior.

Popular Culture at the Turn of the Century: Contradictory Images of Women

Another space where feminism flourished outside of the mainstream media's eye was in popular culture. In the early 1990s, the riot grrrl movement emerged out of the punk music scene. Led by Kathleen Hanna, the band Bikini Kill began touring in 1991, one of the only punk bands made up largely of women and singing and speaking directly to the experiences of young women from a feminist perspective. Hanna paired her music with the feminist convictions she had developed while working at a domestic violence shelter in Olympia, Washington as a college student, as well as her own experiences with domestic and sexual violence. Hanna recalled that, after early Bikini Kill shows, young women and girls in the audience would come up to her, tell her their stories of violence, and ask her what to do. As Sara Marcus described in her history of riot grrrl: "how could the girls [Hanna] met on tour possibly fight against what was being done to them if they lost their ability to name it, to analyze it, to see how it was part of a system?" Hanna and Bikini Kill were not the only ones asking these questions. In the early 1990s, riot grrrl zines started being produced all over the country. Zines were homemade magazines that were written by individual girls and groups of girls, photocopied, and mailed around the country. The feminism of riot grrrl was focused largely on issues of sexual violence and personal freedom: one famous image from a zine declared that girls were not there for boys to "laugh at me, make fun of me, harass me, abuse me or rape me anymore." The Sallie Bingham Center at Duke University, which has been archiving zines since the early 2000s, now has a collection of more than three thousand different issues, mostly from the 1990s.

Riot grrrl was part of "third-wave" feminism. A disparate movement of singers, writers, intellectuals, and activists, third wave was made up of women who were too young to participate in the feminist activism of the 1970s. In *To Be Real,* a foundational third-wave anthology edited by Rebecca Walker, she described the problem that many young women had with feminism. Many young women, Walker argued, believed that being a feminist was not "joining a community of women and men working for equality," but rather required them to hate men, not shave their legs, never wear makeup or skirts, or any number of a long list of things that, according to Walker and others, young women believed were required in order to be considered feminist. They, therefore, rejected the label of "feminist" because they did not check every one of these boxes. The goal of *To Be Real* and other third-wave texts was to break down those beliefs and create a "new" way to be feminist. Third-wave activists also called out the previous generation of feminists repeatedly for their lack of intersectional thinking, frequently asserting that because second-wave feminism was made up only of white middle-class women, it had nothing to offer to those who did not fit within that definition.

Third-wave feminists' analysis of the problems with second-wave feminism is a strong indication of how thoroughly the media and some prominent second-wave activists' later writings distorted what had actually happened in the 1970s. The lack of knowledge about the activism of Black feminist both in 1970s and later is particularly striking and, in some ways, strange given that *To Be Real* included pieces by Black feminist who had been active since the 1970s, such as bell hooks. But many young women were drawn to a rejection of the kind of feminism they found described in *Ms.* magazine in the 1990s. In the introduction of her book on riot grrl, Sara Marcus described feeling that the feminism she found in that magazine or in her local NOW chapter did not really speak to her as a teenager. While she and many other riot grrrl activists shared a focus on abortion rights with those older feminists, other issues like equity in the workplace seemed remote to teenagers coming into adulthood in the 1990s, when feminism was allegedly dead. It is not surprising, therefore, that a new generation of activists exaggerated the flaws of their predecessors. Second-wave activists had done much the same in their time.

The message that feminism had done its work and was a relic of the past was particularly prominent in mainstream media in the 1990s and 2000s. As media scholar Susan Douglas has argued, television and other media in those years "c[a]me to over-represent women as having made it – completely – in the professions" and other public arenas. It paired this celebration – what Douglas terms "embedded feminism" that acknowledges the accomplishments of the 1970s – with hyper-sexualized visions of young women. Whether through shows like *Girls Gone Wild,* the overt sexualization of teenage pop stars like Britney Spears and Christina Aguilera, or the "girl power" of the Spice Girls dressed in miniskirts and push-up bras, this sexualization was described as a feminist victory because women were deploying their sexuality themselves.

Such sexualization was also evident in hip-hop culture, where it existed more uneasily alongside the many overtly feminist hip-hop artists of the 1990s. Women like Lauryn Hill and Queen Latifah rapped about their determination to be strong successful women. In the chorus of the title track of the best-selling 1998 album *The Miseducation of Lauryn Hill,* Hill sang "I made up my mind to define my own destiny," a sentiment that was shared by many female hip-hop artists in the era.

But powerful women artists' presence in hip hop waned in the 2000s, and more misogynistic songs increased. As Aisha Dunham wrote on the Crunk Feminist blog in the early 2010s, many female hip-hop fans had developed strategies to "manage misogyny" they heard at clubs or elsewhere. But Dunham argued that a change was necessary, and connected the misogyny of Black men in rap to the policies of the federal government in the era of the Iraq War:

> *Managing misogyny has become an unwanted, collective experience for women and girls of color from the hip hop generation(s). Language that humiliates, demonizes, objectifies, and threatens is a form of violence . . . . We know how language impacts our lives. We are witnessing how the state deploys labels such as terrorists, insurgents, or enemy combatants to dehumanize (and kill without accountability). What about the words echoed by the Black (male) speaker and transmitted by state-regulated media to dehumanize Black women and girls? How does the language of hip hop sustain an environment conducive to our continued sexual and gender exploitation?*

In connecting culture to an intersectional feminist analysis, Dunham was part of the major feminist trends of the turn of the twenty-first century. Far from disappearing, feminism shifted. More women of color assumed leadership roles in the movement, and they often worked in ways that were not reported on by the national news. But the explosion of feminist activism in the 2010s shows that the 30 years which preceded that decade were a time when valuable, foundational feminist work was being done, in spaces and by people that some might not expect to be feminist leaders.

The flourishing of visible feminist action in the second half of the 2010s is also partially attributable to the results of the 2016 presidential election. When Hillary Clinton, the first female candidate to become a major party's nominee for president who was supported by a majority of women, especially women of color and unmarried women, lost to Donald Trump in spite of revelations about Trump's overt and aggressive sexism, many women were devastated. Others, however, were overjoyed, believing that Trump would implement policies that focused on conservative Christian families and their needs and values. Conservative women, therefore, also became more active after 2016 as they worked to build Trump's brand of conservative nationalism into the center of the Republican Party. And the demographic trends seen since the 1980s – increasing labor force participation by women, alongside declining marriage, divorce, and birth rates – all continued apace throughout the 2010s.

Women at the end of twentieth and beginning of the twenty-first centuries had experiences similar to all other generations of American women. They were talked about in popular culture and also used popular culture to articulate their beliefs. They worked, married, and raised families. They disagreed about politics. By telling this long history of American women, we hope that *American Women* will illuminate the debates about women and nuances of women's lives throughout US history and, more importantly, inform women's own actions going forward.

Bibliography

American Immigration Council. "Immigrant Women and Girls in the United States: A Portrait in Demographic Diversity." Accessed March 1, 2021. **https://www.americanimmigrationcouncil.org/research/immigrant-women-and-girls-united-states**.

Burke, Tarana. *Unbound: My Story of Liberation and the Birth of the Me Too Movement.* Flatiron Books, 2021.

Carroll, Tamar. *Mobilizing New York: AIDS, Antipoverty, and Feminist Activism.* University of North Carolina Press, 2015.

Chappell, Marissa. "Reagan's 'Gender Gap' Strategy and the Limits of Free-Market Feminism." Journal of Policy History 24, no. 1 (2012): 115–134.

Cooper, Brittney C, Susana M Morris, and Robin M Boylorn. *The Crunk Feminist Collection.* Feminist Press, 2017.

Douglas, Susan J. *Enlightened Sexism: The Seductive Message that Feminism's Work Is Done.* Henry Holt & Co, 2010.

Hower, Joseph. "'You've Come a Long Way – Maybe': Working Women, Comparable Worth, and the Transformation of the American Labor Movement, 1964-1989." Journal of American History 107, no. 3 (2020): 658–684.

Johnson, Emily Suzanne. "Palin Versus Clinton: Feminism, Womanhood, and the 2008 Presidential Election." In *Suffrage at 100: Women in American Politics Since 1920*, edited by Taranto, and Zarnow. Johns Hopkins University Press, 2020.

Levenstein, Lisa. *They Didn't See Us Coming: A Hidden History of Feminism in the Nineties.* Basic Books, 2020.

Marcus, Sara. *Girls to the Front: The True Story of the Riot Grrrl Revolution.* Harper, 2010.

Martos, Alexander, Patrick A Wilson, and Ilan H Meyer. "Lesbian, Gay, Bisexual, and Transgender (LGBT) Health Services in the United States: Origins, Evolution, and Contemporary Landscape." *PLOS One* 12, no. 7 (2017).

Nadasen, Premilla. *Household Workers Unite: The Untold Story of African-American Women Who Built a Movement.* Beacon Press, 2015.

Rivers, Daniel Winunwe. *Radical Relations: Lesbian Mothers, Gay Fathers, and Their Children in the United States Since World War II.* University of North Carolina Press, 2013.

Taranto, Stacie, and Leandra Zarnow. "A History of Women in American Politics and the Enduring Male Political Citizenship Ideal." In *Suffrage at 100: Women in American Politics Since 1920*, edited by Taranto, and Zarnow. Johns Hopkins University Press, 2020.

Turk, Katherine. *Equality on Trial: Gender and Rights in the Modern American Workplace.* University of Pennsylvania Press, 2016.

Walker, Rebecca. *To Be Real: Telling the Truth and Changing the Face of Feminism.* Anchor Books, 1995.

White, Deborah Gray. *Too Heavy a Load: Black Women in Defense of Ourselves, 1894-1994.* Norton, 1999.

Ziegler, Mary. *Abortion and the Law in America: Roe v. Wade to the Present.* Cambridge University Press, 2020.

Index

American Women's History: A New Narrative History, First Edition. Melissa E. Blair, Vanessa M. Holden, and Maeve Kane.
© 2024 John Wiley & Sons, Inc. Published 2024 by John Wiley & Sons, Inc.